Texas Sportswriters

The Wild and Wacky Years

Bob St. John

Republic of Texas Press
Plano, Texas

Library of Congress Cataloging-in-Publication Data

St. John, Bob.
    Texas sportswriters : the wild and wacky years / Bob St. John.
        p.   cm.
    Includes index.

    1. Sportswriters--Texas--Biography. 2. St. John, Bob. I. Title.

GV742.4 .S82   2001
070.4'49796'0922764--dc21   2001031965
                                                    CIP

Printed in the United States of America

ISBN 978-1-55622-797-4
10 9 8 7 6 5 4 3 2 1
0107

All inquiries for volume purchases of this book should be addressed to
Wordware Publishing, Inc., at 2320 Los Rios Boulevard, Plano, Texas 75074.
Telephone inquiries may be made by calling:
(972) 423-0090

Dedication

For Blackie, who influenced us all...or should have.

Contents

Contents

Foreword

When Bob St. John asked me to do the foreword for this book, I wanted him to take down my thoughts and compose it himself. Then he would show it to me for my approval. I changed my mind when I read the beginning, "Unknown to our fans Bob St. John played a major role in our success. He has always been too modest to take well-deserved credit. Yet he was always there, giving needed advice on running an organization to me, offering Tom Landry and his staff valuable coaching tips, and advising Gil Brandt on drafting players who made us champions." So you can understand why I decided to take a more active hand in writing this foreword.

The sportswriters we had in the 1960s and 1970s were a good group of guys. Among them were some excellent writers and top reporters. There was also a group that you might say had this rampageous, mischievous side. Gary Cartwright spearheaded the original group. His activities when he wasn't on the job were almost as well known as his writing. When Bob St. John first started covering our team in 1967, I saw him as a pleasant individual, perhaps a little shy and reserved. I never dreamed that just below that exterior was this playful rascal, who would scheme with Frank Luksa to create all sorts of havoc. Had I known everything that was going on I would have tried to put them all under house arrest.

Don't get me wrong. I did respect Bob's integrity, fairness, and ability as a writer to the extent that I fully cooperated on the biography he wrote on me, *Tex: The Man*

Who Built the Dallas Cowboys. Even my wife, Marty, said he did a great job of capturing me. I'm not sure whether that's good or bad.

Some of the antics of Bob and Frank that I knew about were indeed humorous. After Bob left sports to become a general columnist, training camp did seem more peaceful in the early morning hours when you were trying to sleep. Even Luksa seemed to calm down and act his age, which must have been terribly painful for him. The generation of sportswriters that followed them was certainly different. They were more businesslike and didn't seem to have any interest in shenanigans. I suspect they aren't having as much fun.

Maybe it was the old sportswriter in me, but I suppose I must admit that I wasn't always a bystander. I did indeed play a part in the Distinguished Soup Nose Award during a ceremony on the flight back from one of our last regular season road games. I was the presenter, shaking hands and congratulating the winner, a reluctant Verne Lundquist. One of the most astonishing things was that Bob actually never won the DSNA. I understand he did finish second a number of times and one year placed second, third, fourth, and maybe fifth.

Besides the main culprits, you will also read in this book about sportswriters such as Randy Galloway, Dan Cook, Gary Cartwright, Bud Shrake, Tex Maule, and even Blackie Sherrod, who unwittingly became involved in unusual situations. You'll meet old-timers such as George Rayborn and Jinx Tucker. There's also the episode when I was a young sportswriter, which would have likely gotten me at least a vote for the DSNA.

I will always remember the great run we had with the Dallas Cowboys, the twenty straight winning seasons and the excitement and thrill as we went from young upstarts to champions and America's Team. I loved it when the writers would refer to us as having "class."

This book has caused me to remember the other side of those years and some of the fun-loving sportswriters who covered us. This book made me smile and then laugh all over again. I expect you will, too.

—Tex Schramm, former Dallas Cowboys president-general manager and member of the NFL Hall of Fame

Acknowledgments

I want to thank all the characters who, willing or otherwise, are a part of this book. My special appreciation to Frank Luksa, Curt Mosher, and Harless Wade for refreshing or solidifying my memory about various escapades...or being overridden when deemed necessary by the author. And here's a toast to the late Doug Todd for input and participation in some unusual happenings. And my hat is off to Dave Campbell, Dan Cook, Gary Cartwright, and Al Ward for especially taking time to help. Naturally, I am grateful to the guys I worked with on *The Dallas Morning News* sports staff. So here's to Walt Robertson, Sam Blair, Harless Wade, John Anders, Carlton Stowers, Randy Galloway, Mike Jones, Steve Pate, Bill Livingston, Ed Knocke, Temple Pouncey, Gene Wilson and in memory of John Barker, Merle Heryford, Roy Edwards, Henry Stowers, Andy Anderson, and Tom Williams. If I've left out anybody I apologize because forgetfulness is part of the aging process. I HOPE that's what my problem is, anyway.

But there's no way I could forget my wife, Sandy, for her patience and help. She also seemed to have an understanding about what was going on during those wacky days, which might be grounds for getting an honorary vote for the Distinguished Soup Nose Award.

Introduction

When I think back on my days at *The Dallas Morning News* I do so with mixed feelings of guilt and gratitude for the great freedom given us to write and unfortunately at times to be ourselves. Yet I am thankful that we survived those years of fine madness although I am not sure whether we were better or worse for the experience. With time and perspective I certainly appreciate our boss Walter Robertson even more. He overlooked some of our madcap activities and did not know about other adventures or he would not still have a full head of hair.

I suspect Dave Smith, who replaced him, would have had us killed. When asked if this assumption were accurate, he paused for a few seconds and said, "Hmm? Well, maybe not killed but just slapped around a little."

They just don't make sportswriters like they used to do—to the everlasting gratitude of sports editors, wives, and Americans everywhere. Nowadays the sportswriters seem to take themselves more seriously and are more businesslike and well behaved, while living the so-called normal life. Of course there are exceptions, but they are mostly in the shadows of the profession, whereas we were difficult to ignore because we never banged the drum slowly. But those old days are rapidly being buried beneath a more serious, regimented world as are so many things.

As a biased observer I believe they don't have as much fun as we did, certainly lacking the camaraderie we enjoyed. When we weren't out of town on assignments, we actually were required to come into the office to do our columns and stories. You see, our office presence was preferred by powers that were over other available methods of sending in stories from home, such as via carrier pigeons, dictation over the telephone, or delivery by wives or kids. When on the road we used Western Union and eventually telecopiers, which were heavier than portable typewriters and added to the luggage burden. With the advent of the computer age, only the deskmen, editors, and assistants are office regulars. If a columnist shows up, he or she is probably just lonely.

With the size of staffs now I suspect many of them only know each other by name, whereas we were thrown together and bonded. We read and discussed books like crazy, went to the theater, tipped a few vesper cocktails, and sang every song we ever knew, often to a SRO crowd of ourselves. Dave now has over eighty people on his staff, whereas Walt usually had about a dozen, although his staff reached the massive total of sixteen when I left the sports department in January 1978.

After seventeen years as a sportswriter (fourteen with the *News*) I wrote state and metro columns until early retirement in January 2000. After I had written a column on the front of the Metro Page for years, a prominent judge in Dallas told me he always enjoyed my sports writing. I was lapping up the compliment when he asked, "By the way, what are you doing now?"

I'm glad I was a sportswriter during the madcap days and even more happy that I survived those hellion times. This book is personal, my actions and reflections on those wild and wacky times of sportswriting in Texas, which for better or worse won't pass this way again.

Many known and unknown sportswriters of the era are not mentioned, and if they're still around, I'm sure they're very grateful for being excluded. And if you failed to read the warning label, it is repeated here. "Attempting to duplicate the actions of the author and/or other characters in this book can be hazardous to your health."

—Bob St. John

Shenanigans in the Oaks

"Lookit, one of these days you guys are going to get into bad trouble."

–Gil Brandt, VP, head of scouting

Now that the statute of limitations has run out, I can take you behind the scenes at the Dallas Cowboys training camp during those bygone days when sportswriters, well some of us anyway, seemed to be in the grips of the forces of darkness. We weren't just observers on assignments but would insert ourselves onto a playing field of our own making, sometimes dragging our comrades and the very people we wrote about along with us. This was never more evident than in training camp.

I would like to rationalize that the atmosphere of training camp made us do it. You see, the Cowboys training camp, as others of its kind in the NFL, caused a kind of surreal existence in which we lived on college campuses in dormitories. Could this somehow have influenced us to revert to the prankish, mischievous days of our youth? During the eleven-some-odd years I covered the Cowboys, we stayed with the team in training camp, which allowed us to be closer to the action, feel the pulse of the team, and no doubt was also a way for our newspapers to save money on hotels. It was indeed unfortunate for the coaches, scouts, and club officials that for years they were housed in the same dormitory as the sportswriters. That would change, much too late.

The scene was a serene, conservative Christian college, California Lutheran, which was situated in a picturesque setting at the base of sprawling foothills of a mountain range. If the atmosphere at the school did not seem ideal for our shenanigans, the city where the college was located, Thousand Oaks, certainly did.

Now Thousand Oaks is one of those typical Southern California communities composed of endless three- and four-bedroom ranch-style houses with pools and shopping centers that seem to spring up overnight with clothing stores and pizza to go. It is a city where daily soap operas come to life, of late afternoon philosophical martinis, and where a great deal of the population is devoted to hedonistic pursuits. It was a small community, almost an afterthought, of some 15,000 when the Cowboys

first began to train there in 1963. But by the time Jerry Jones had purchased the team and moved camp to Texas in the 1990s, the population had catapulted to over 200,000. Sometimes your imagination would run away with you at the Oaks but it seemed like a large number of residents were divorcees raising 1.3 children and basking in the sun of alimony.

Thousand Oaks is only forty miles north of Los Angeles on the Ventura Freeway, one of those multi-laned concrete and steel structures bordered by short-order places, eucalyptus, and suburban communities. It is also in the Canejo Valley, Spanish for rabbit, which unlike people tends to bounce around with a purpose. It was one part of a vast ranching area where cattle and horses were raised and certainly lent itself to filming Westerns and other movies. Part of *Gone with the Wind* was filmed in the area as were segments of the Lassie series and various TV Westerns, including *The Rifleman.*

Western star Joel McCray had a ranch on the other side of the mountain range by the college,

Virginia Mayo lived in the Oaks, but we never saw her, and Academy Award winner Ben Johnson resided in nearby Westlake. With the proximity of Beverly Hills, Hollywood Hills, etc., stars often showed up at practice. Among them were Burt Reynolds, Glenn Campbell, Joey Heatherton (after she married Lance Rentzel), Kenny Rogers, Chill Wills, Strother Martin, Dub Taylor, and young starlets on their way up or down.

Noted college coaches would also visit training camp. It was a good deal for them. They'd watch practice and visit with Tom Landry and his staff and were treated like royalty by Gil Brandt, director of scouting, and his scouts. Consequently, when the staff would visit campuses or wanted to check on a prospect, the college coaches tended to remember this. One of the visitors was Bill Peterson, who was coaching the University of Houston but would later become head coach of the Houston Oilers. Bill was a good guy and a good coach, but sometimes he would get confused in the emotion of the moment.

Once when he was coaching the Oilers he gave the team a pep talk in training camp. "One word!" he said. "Men, I want you to remember ONE WORD. SUPER BOWL!" Another time when he was angry at an official he yelled, "I'm not going to take this standing up!"

But he was an excellent coach who also had once coached at the University of Florida. Asked how he felt to be inducted into the Florida Hall of Fame, Bill replied, "I'm very appreciative of being indicted."

Gil would usually take the visiting college coaches out to eat. Sometimes he'd bring them into Los Robles, one of our favorite eating and drinking establishments. But mostly he kept them away from the press. That was wise.

To take a break from our hardworking schedules, we'd usually spend time at Malibu or Zuma beaches on weekends. They were only about a 40-minute drive from training camp through Malibu Canyon or if you preferred excitement when you drove, you could go over the narrow, steep, winding road of Decker Canyon. On one such ride through Decker, my old friend Harless Wade was sitting in the backseat as I carefully and skillfully drove us down the canyon. He was sluggish and needed to be livened up a bit. Suddenly, my foot hit the floorboard. AGAIN AND AGAIN! "You crazy SOB, now the brakes are out!" yelled Harless, bracing for the worst as he became more and more creative in calling me names. However, I saved the day. I had not been pushing on the brakes but pounding on the floorboard.

Anyway, it is at the beaches where the eye is quicker than the mind and where the beautiful, bronzed California girls congregate. Perhaps it was because we were away from home, the war and loneliness if you will, but there seemed to be so many of them that you began to think that it must be something in the drinking water. It was one such young woman who captured the fancy of Dick Mansperger and set my faithful companion (win or tie) Frank Luksa Jr. and I on one of our initial escapades.

— ❑ —

Dick Mansperger, a former assistant coach at UCLA, was a nice looking, good-natured bachelor in those days when he was a scout for the Cowboys. Like the rest of us, he would spend a great deal of time in a place called Los Robles. Sheila was a barmaid there. And she wore a torero hat, silk blouse, short skirt, and boots. Before being asked to behave, customers sometimes called to her, "Ahhh, Toro!" Anyway, Mansperger was stricken by her beauty, but unlike others of her gender, Sheila would have nothing to do with him. Night after night he would try to win her favors to no avail. He told her he was crazy about her. He told her she was special, different. For Dick it was not one of those I'll-love-you-forever-until-tomorrow deals. He was mad about her.

I had watched this scene with compassion. So one fateful night while having a late dinner with Luksa, who then worked for the *Fort Worth Star-Telegram*, it occurred to me to try to make a difference in Mansperger's life. So I pleaded with Sheila to come back to the dormitory and surprise Mansperger in his room.

There was nothing sordid about my request. In the quiet darkness of the early morning hours she would be guided to his room, walk in and say something spiffy like "Hello," and leave. Luksa and I, peeking through the door from the shadows of the hall, would hurriedly escort her down the stairs and out to the car before anybody, Mansperger notwithstanding, noticed.

She told me I was crazy and refused. She didn't get off until 2:30 A.M. so the plot had time to thicken. I promised her Dallas Cowboys T-shirts if she would only participate as the star of our plot. She finally agreed when I convinced her falsely that she would be the FIRST woman ever to enter the Dallas Cowboy dormitory after hours.

"You lie," she said. "Are you sure I'd be the first, the very first?"

I told her of course she would, then kicked Luksa under the table. "Does he look like a guy who would lie about something like that?" lied Luksa.

She made us promise never to tell anybody because they might get the wrong impression.

The assignment wouldn't be easy, but I was able to enlist Luksa's reluctant help. It would be the first time I allowed him to join my adventures or vice versa. Once he got into the spirit of such madness, he not only would help but also wanted to direct that and future operations. The intrigue, danger was there that night we snuck Sheila into the dorm. What would we say, for instance, if Tom Landry happened to wake up and caught us? A friend of mine once said he'd rather be caught in misdeeds by his wife than moralistic, infallible Tom Landry. That feeling was prevalent.

We solidified our best-laid plans so there could be no false move. Luksa would enter the dorm as a scout. When he signaled it was clear, I'd rush in with Sheila. We'd hide her in the telephone booth at the foot of the stairs near the entrance. It would serve as a kind of way station to catch our breath. Then we would take her up the stairs, and down the dimly lit hall to Mansperger's room we'd go. Nobody locked doors in the dorms in those days, although years later that would change when a creature known as the Slasher would be on the prowl. But that gruesome, frightening story will be told later.

After a couple of drinks, Sheila was getting into the spirit of things and agreed she would actually KISS the sleeping Mansperger on the forehead then say she'd just dropped in to say, "Hello, big boy." Then before he could collect his thoughts she would add, "But it appears you're asleep so I'll just be on my way." We giggled like kids as we thought what Mansperger's reaction might be when he woke up and saw the woman of his dreams.

About 3 A.M. Luksa signaled from the front door of the dorm that it was okay for us to enter. I grabbed Sheila's hand and rushed her inside the door. She'd just gotten inside the phone booth when Ernie Stautner, the Cowboys defensive line coach, came down the hall from the film room, where he'd been working most of the night. Sheila ducked down, and Luksa and I crowded against the booth like it was about to tumble over. I almost passed out. My voice was high and quivering as I tried to engage him in conversation about the defensive line. Ernie yawned and said he had to get some sleep when Luksa started lecturing him on how to coach defense. He grinned, assuming we'd had too much to drink, and disappeared into his room.

I took Sheila by the arm and we bolted up the stairs. We got to Mansperger's room, and ever so quietly I opened the door. Sheila crept inside as Luksa and I covered our mouths to muffle our snickers of laughter. She stood over the bed, bent over, and planted a kiss on his forehead. He raised up, stared at her momentarily, and said, "Oh, hello, Miss." Then he laid his head on the pillow and went back to sleep.

We froze. Our lives flashed before our eyes. It was not Dick Mansperger she kissed. IT WAS BILL PETERSON! We later found out Mansperger had left camp on assignment that afternoon and his room had been given to Peterson.

Sheila, wide-eyed, started to scream and then put a hand over her face and took off. Luksa and I were on her heels. It had taken approximately twenty minutes to sneak her into the room and seconds for us to get out of there and back to the car and speed off into the night with Sheila taking our names in vain.

The next day I spent a lot of time hanging around Peterson as he watched practice from the sidelines. I casually brought up the subject of dreams and mentioned some weird ones I'd had. I mean, here was this poor guy trying to watch practice and I was trying to be Freudian. Finally I just asked him if he'd had any unusual dreams lately. "No," he said. "Why?"

— ❑ —

Some of the fondest memories I have during my first training camp in 1967 were the sessions held in what we called the Five-Thirty Club, a room in the dormitory set aside for coaches, club officials, and members of the media to unwind following afternoon practice. There was always an ample supply of beverages, ranging from soda pop and lemonade to beer, preferred by most in late afternoon. For purposes of etiquette any whiskey drinking would have to wait until later.

However, there were always those among the media, one in particular, who insisted he was on European time and the bewitching hour for serious cocktails had long passed. Those sessions were great for those of us who covered the team because we'd pick up information and perspective on the team that we might not have otherwise gotten. When the coaches relaxed you'd also hear anecdotes about players or the old days when they played ball.

Once Ermal Allen, the backfield coach who later became a special assistant, was asked about Amos Marsh, a running back during the early years of the team. Amos was big and fast and capable of breaking loose, except he was prone to drop the ball. Ermal was reminded that Amos once misjudged a high punt that came down and hit him right on top of the head. Ermal, pondering the situation, responded, "Oh, that wasn't a big deal. It was just his way of fielding a punt." That reminds me of when an irate reader wrote Bud Shrake, then a columnist for *The Dallas Morning News*. The guy not only berated

Marsh for dropping the ball but also got on Bud's case for being so critical of him. He ended the letter by saying, "And after you read this you can give it to Marsh." Shrake answered, "I tried to hand it to him but he kept dropping it."

My personal favorite topic in those days was defensive end Willie Townes, one of the players I befriended. Willie had a lot of talent, but the coaches were always on him for being overweight. Poor Willie fooled the coaches into thinking he was really trying his best to take off weight by eating very little in the lunchroom, just a little fruit and yogurt. Then they found out he was sneaking out at night, going to the grocery store to stack up food in his room. But Willie had a good sense of humor and laughed when I wrote he had a "recurring fantasy dream he was a grocery store."

> **Amos once misjudged a high punt that came down and hit him right on top of the head. Ermal, pondering the situation, responded, "Oh, that wasn't a big deal. It was just his way of fielding a punt."**

Willie played from 1966 to 1968 before a knee injury and excess weight ended his career. Poor Willie would report to camp eighteen to twenty pounds overweight each year and subsequently be fined. He was fined so much the money went into a "Willie Townes Memorial Fund" which was used for a team party.

One year Willie worked very hard during the off season to keep his weight down and even bragged that he'd be below his prescribed weight when he reported to training camp. So he came in twenty-one pounds overweight. He swore he'd made the weight before leaving Dallas and then figured out what had happened. "Sea level is different here than in Dallas," he proclaimed. "It's lower in Thousand Oaks so consequently my weight goes up when I get here. So I shouldn't be fined."

I argued it seemed logical to me, but the coaches refused to dignify anything that seemed logical to Willie or me.

— ❑ —

Dick Nolan, who later became head coach of the 49ers and Saints, was Landry's secondary coach and defensive coordinator. He'd also played with Landry for the New York Giants during the days when goalposts were situated on the goal line, rather than at the back of the end zone. Nolan weighed about 170-175 and wasn't too anxious for the Giants' next game against the Los Angeles Rams, who had a pair of huge bull-like running backs, Deacon Dan Towler and Tank Younger. They both outweighed him by some forty pounds so he went around telling Landry and the other defenders to hit them and then he'd jump on for the ride. As fate would have it, the Rams drove inside New York's five-yard line. The Giants defenders braced for the charge of either the Deacon or Tank. Quarterback Norm Van Brocklin handed off to Deacon, who ducked his head and charged with all his fury. A huge hole opened up, and he gained even more

momentum as he went toward the end zone line. Only thing is he ran smack into the goalpost.

"When we later looked at the films, you could see the guy hitting the goalpost so hard it actually gave and then sent him catapulting backward," said Nolan. Deacon ended up flat on his back, his helmet twisted on his head and a galaxy of stars flashing through his brain. It was as if he'd been dynamited! So Nolan sashayed over to Deacon, bent over and stuck his finger right into the running back's face, and said, "Yeah, Deac, you come through there again and next time I'll REALLY hit you!"

I loved those stories and sessions in the Five-Thirty Club where things got pretty lively as the assistant coaches would tell stories and kid one another. Nolan, a contemporary of Ernie Stautner, would ask the defensive line coach, "Ernie, how did it feel wearing those leather helmets when you played?"

So I have no idea why I, a mere rookie then, decided to liven up things BEFORE the morning practice with the moral support of Steve Perkins, who drank on arbitrary time. I'm not proud of what happened and would take it back if I could but, as they say in the business, it was just a foolish rookie mistake.

— ❑ —

Now Landry was not a drinker, taking only a very occasional beer while I covered the team, but like his coaches, he did like his lemonade, which was in a large container with disposable paper cups nearby in the Five-Thirty Club. Some of the coaches would stop by and have a cup or so of lemonade on the way to morning practice.

One night I came in late with Perkins. We stopped by the Five-Thirty Club, which was quiet and deserted. We were seized by the moment, the time, place, and imagination of that early morning hour. With Perkins' encouragement I got a bottle of vodka and poured it into the lemonade. Vodka was the beverage of choice because it's difficult to smell and taste when it's mixed with a sweet drink. I stirred it with the empty bottle and we went to our rooms. At that time it seemed funny to see how loose some of

the coaches might be at practice the next morning. In the stark light of day it didn't seem so funny. I snapped awake early the next morning, realized the mistake, and hustled down to the Five-Thirty Club with the intention of emptying the lemonade cooler, but it was too late. Landry was there, sipping a cup on the way to practice. One assistant had three, and a visiting writer from Los Angeles had four then sat down on the couch with a silly grin on his face.

At various times during the morning practice, I thought I denoted a certain uncharacteristic looseness among some of the assistants, one of whom had a very red face. But it could have just been my imagination.

— ❑ —

One of the main topics, outside of football, during one summer of the mid-1970s was the great white shark, or *Carcharodon Carcharias* to those of us who considered themselves experts in residence during training camp. Most of us had read Peter Benchley's book *Jaws* and/or seen the movie, and the great white shark craze had been sweeping the country. Perhaps, as experts tell us, such a craze is only a fad. Nonetheless, the obsession with the big shark was very prevalent around the beaches of Southern California. Three weeks into training camp, two shark attacks had been reported and three great whites had been harpooned along the California coastline.

"There have been two shark attacks reported and three great whites harpooned along the California coastline," I mentioned to Luksa as we treaded water one Sunday afternoon about thirty yards off Zuma Beach, waiting for another Big Wave. He had just belittled me after I'd shown him my combination windmill, nose dive body-surfing technique in which I miss the crest of the wave, somersault toward shore, and am sent crashing to the ocean floor, hitting my face and nose as my feet then breach the surface like a periscope.

The sun peeked out of the smog, reflecting on the water and distorting my vision momentarily. I blinked then saw something move in the distance. It seemed to be coming toward us.

"Look!" I said. "Maybe that's a great white!"

Luksa gazed across the water in the direction I was pointing. The fear that had crossed his face quickly changed to a sarcastic grin as he said, "Fool, that's a boat."

"Yeah," I said, "a boat looking for great whites so they can warn helpless swimmers and surfers or harpoon the creatures before they attack."

Pointing to my nose, which is larger than average and skinned by the ocean floor, he laughed and said, "If it bit off your nose it wouldn't have to eat again for a month."

We caught the Big Wave and it carried us toward shore and then we hurried back out before another one came. Something went past us, just below the surface and I said, "Hey, what's that?"

"Will you shut up!" Luksa answered. "It looked like a paper cup or something."

Neither of us said anything for a while, but I was ten to fifteen feet away from Luksa and could see him not only waiting for the Big Wave but also scanning the horizon for any sign of danger, like a fin for instance. I probably rationalized that he deserved a thrill for what he said about my nose when I made my way around behind him, dove under the water, and started toward him like...like, well a great white closing in on its prey. Then with all the power and force I could muster, I grabbed his lower leg, clamping hard with my fingers and shaking it before quickly coming back to the surface to see if I got a rise out of him.

"AIIIEEEEEEEEE!" he screamed, leaping five or six feet out of the water and flattening out in mid-air as he frantically looked for the foot he thought the shark might have taken.

I laughed hysterically and said, "Ha, bet you thought it was a great white, didn't you?"

His wet hair stood straight up, and he screamed, "I'LL KILL YOU FOR THAT! I'LL KILL YOU!" He swam toward me with a vengeance, and I took off for the beach. "I HOPE A SHARK GETS YOU AND BITES OFF YOUR....!" He wasn't talking about my nose either.

There were four other sightings of great whites that summer, but sometimes people's imaginations run away with them and they see what they don't see. Besides the two shark attacks that were recorded, no others were reported, including the one on Luksa.

— ❏ —

To combat the painful, negative effects of nightlife during training camp, some of us would get carried away during the daytime hours. I, for one, would lift weights and jog up the hill behind the practice field and play pickup basketball games. It wasn't that I was trying to win the conditioning battle but rather just stay even or play for a tie as it were. The most tiring, heated, and dangerous things were our basketball games where you faced the prospect of all sorts of injuries while trying to relive the great mediocre days of a long passed athletic career. But, hey, like the players, we understood that injuries were just part of the game.

I originally thought the worst injury was Dreaded Stomped Foot (DSF) as usually applied by

Cowboys linebacker and assistant coach Jerry Tubbs. Jerry weighed about 225, making him much larger, for instance, than PR guy Curt Mosher, club vice president Al Ward, and myself. Jerry's favorite shot was a driving six-step layup in which he'd clear out the lane. If he didn't knock you down he'd step, or stomp if you will, on your foot. He also had a five-step hook shot in which he'd first step on your foot and then shoot the ball. It hurt a lot playing with or against Jerry.

During the course of our games, I jammed two of my typing fingers and had to learn to write hurt. However, by taping them together, I could continue playing basketball. Then the final day of training camp in 1968, Frank Luksa was up at the crack of noon and I was able to talk him into a little one-on-one basketball, knowing full well that he was easy prey. I should not have been fooled that he might actually make a layup, but I went high into the air to block his shot. Only thing is he didn't leave the ground, he just stood there. So I came down on him, falling to the floor with what

turned out to be a cracked rib. While I was on the floor writhing in pain, Luksa continued trying to make the layup, which he did on the sixth try and declared himself the winner.

Trainers Larry Gardner and Don Cochran had begun to put me on the player's injury list each day before taking it to Tom Landry. They said he read the list studiously and then did a double take when he saw my name. He didn't laugh but did grin.

When Landry would see me he'd shake his head slowly and say, "St. John, I'm glad you're not my responsibility." He would also say things such as "Didn't see you at the scrimmage, St. John. You better start coming out. How else will you know all the players when the season starts?" And once when I got back to camp early one morning after going to an all-night party at the home of a movie director (I can't remember his name) in Hollywood Hills, Landry saw me limp in and commented sarcastically, "I see you're up and at 'em early today, St. John."

— ❏ —

Curt Mosher and I were doing pretty well in two-on-two basketball games so a couple of large visiting college coaches, hearing about our victories, challenged us to a game. Their strategy was obviously to beat us up. Early in the game one of the coaches shoved me into some chairs by the out-of-bounds line, and I messed up my foot and ended up in a cast AFTER the game was over. I always liked to play with Mosher because he was a passer who let me shoot all the time. However, crippled I was useless and darned if Mosher didn't get hot; we beat them then refused a rematch, and they walked away red-faced and angry. I don't blame them, getting beat by a couple of scrubs.

"St. John, I'm glad you're not my responsibility," Landry repeated like a chorus when he saw me the next day in a cast up to my knee.

"St. John," said Willie Townes, "if you didn't have bad luck, you wouldn't have any luck at all."

Lance Rentzel, watching me hobble down the sidelines, remarked, "I believe you're faster this year."

Here I was hobbling around in a cast and couldn't even go to the beach because it would cause my foot to sweat and itch, and I'd get sand in the darn thing and was getting no sympathy from anybody. Everywhere I'd go people would ask, "What happened to you?" I really got tired of explaining I'd been hurt in a silly basketball game. One afternoon I was talking to Tex Schramm on the sidelines when yet another stranger walked over and asked, "Hey, what happened to you?" The guy was persistent so, noting there had been some minor thefts in the dorm, I told him I'd been asleep on the third floor of the dorm during practice and saw a guy sneaking out of a room with stolen goods under his arm. When he tried to escape I'd tripped him, thus breaking my foot.

Right: This picture of Bob St. John appeared in the *Thousand Oaks* newspaper with a cutline telling how he'd injured his foot while tripping a would-be thief in the dorm where the writers stayed at California Lutheran College.

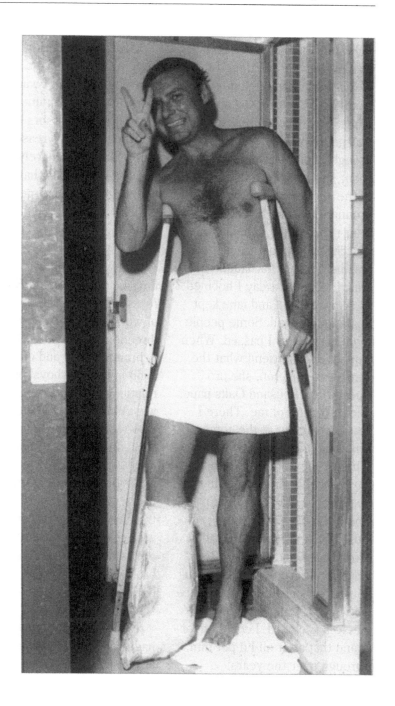

Schramm laughed and said it was indeed a brave thing I did.

We didn't know the guy was from the Thousand Oaks newspaper. I didn't even realize what was going on when Mosher brought a photographer into my room, just as I was stepping out of the shower with a towel around my waist, a cleaning bag over my cast and hobbling on crutches. I thought the picture was being made for laughs. It wasn't. The next day I hobbled to a scrimmage, and fans kept shaking my hand. Some people even clapped as I passed. When I questioned a friend what the devil was going on, she produced the Thousand Oaks paper with a picture of me. There I was coming out of the shower with a stupid look on my face. The cutline told how I'd injured my foot while tripping a thief in the dorm. I wrote a column about the experience, and my boss, Walter Robertson, called from Dallas and said the story couldn't be true and was ridiculous even for me. I sent him the clip from the newspaper. He never apologized. I could understand that after all I'd put him through over the years.

After a week Perkins and I came in late one night, and when I mentioned I wasn't going to wear the cast anymore, he got a huge pair of scissors he kept in his room for some reason or other. Slowly but surely we cut the cast off. I would have sworn he enjoyed it each time I said, "Ouch."

— ❑ —

Andy Anderson was the Cowboys beat man for the *Fort Worth Press* when it folded. He was out of work and had no idea which direction to go. Then Tex Schramm called and offered him a job in the Cowboys' public relations department. So there was Andy helping Doug Todd, who was assistant to public relations director Curt Mosher and later took his place.

Unfortunately for Andy, Doug had returned to Dallas to hype the club's annual Salesmanship preseason game when the biggest story of the 1976 camp broke as Roger Staubach and his backup, Clint Longley, got in a scuffle.

During passing practice Clint had used a racial slur in cussing at Drew Pearson, who had let

Carlton Stowers and Deane Freeman check Doug Todd after a long night in training camp. (Photo by Bob Griffin)

one of his passes get away. Roger, standing next to Clint, took exception to this. One thing led to another, and they fought after practice, but it amounted to little as Roger threw him to the ground and the fight was broken up. Clint was even more upset after newspaper accounts put him in a bad light. So he lay in wait for Roger the next day in the dressing room. When Roger was taking off his shoulder pads, his hands up in the air as he pulled them over his head, Clint slugged him. Roger fell into the weight scale and suffered a gash over his eye. Randy White then literally picked up Clint and held him while D. D. Lewis and Ed Jones held Roger, who later went searching for his attacker. Fortunately, Clint, whose story didn't jibe with other accounts, was nowhere to be found. Alan Stone, then a radio reporter, had found Clint, who asked him to take him to the airport. Alan was puzzled about what to do, but I encouraged him to get Clint out of there before Staubach found him.

So there was Andy being barraged by calls from all over the country as news leaked out about the fracas. Media types were running in and out of his office, asking questions while he was taking call after call. Finally, he got a call from KRLD in Dallas. The caller told Andy, "Wait just a minute."

Andy sat impatiently as he had to listen to a commercial. Nervously, he waited and waited for it to end. Andy had figured it was a taped commercial and finally barked, "I don't have time for this commercial BS! I'm up to my ass in alligators!" There was a pause. People in radio land had heard Andy's definitive remark. There was a pause and the announcer said, "Uh, ha-ha, well Andy, moving right along, uh, could you maybe tell us...."

— ❑ —

I would go back to training camp to work on magazine articles and books, but that last time I spent in Thousand Oaks actually covering the team for *The Dallas Morning News* would prove more eventful than we ever could imagine. It would involve mystery, intrigue, and mistrust. It would be talked about for years. It was the time of...*The Slasher.*

2

Tales of the Slasher

"There were reports of strange noises, animals being hurt...and scribbling on the door across the hall that could be interpreted as, well, threatening."

—Officer in Thousand Oaks

In the early morning hours that fateful summer night the moon went behind the clouds, darkening the hills that touched the edge of California Lutheran College. A sudden breeze rustled the brush in a kind of no-man's land, separating the hills from the dormitories where the Cowboy players, team officials, the media, and visitors fitfully slept. You see there had been rumors and talk about a sick, mysterious being known as *The Slasher*, who was cutting the throats of dogs around the school and leaving them to be dragged off by lurking animals of the night or slowly devoured by vultures. But you know how rumors start then magnify, and fear becomes the worst enemy of a person's imagination. If *The Slasher* was murdering dogs, human beings might be next.

— ⊔ —

There was a shuffling in the brush near the window of the dormitory room shared by recent arrivals to the Dallas Cowboys training camp Tom Turbiville, then a writer for the *Irving News*, and Ken Carter, who was with the Texas State Network. Was the creature known as *The Slasher* about to strike again? They had heard talk about *The Slasher* earlier that evening and like others before and after them had at first begun to laugh as if it all were a camp joke. Their smiles froze like still photographs when experienced veterans such as Frank Luksa and I grimly stared at them through swollen, beady eyes that seemed to show the horror we felt, although it was actually due to lack of sleep. Good grief, men, this is no joking matter!

Now Tom and Ken were good, decent, innocent human beings who had fallen asleep, dreaming the dreams good, decent, innocent human beings dream. Then it happened.

Near their window there was loud, nightmarish howling as if it were the devilish Hound of the Baskervilles, followed by a sad, pathetic yelping cry of a wounded animal, and they came awake, hearts pounding, and turned on the lights and...and. About that time clouds cleared the moon, which brightens the blackest of nights. Bad timing. Hoarse from all the howling and yelping and tired and sleepy from another long night, I quickly retreated from outside their window to the nearby brush, tail raised and squatting low on all fours like a lurking animal, as Turbiville and/or Carter peeked through the blinds. Other lights came on in the dorm. I waited, heart pounding, and when the moon once again went behind the clouds, I made a mad, stumbling dash for the dorm, hurried down the hall, and was about to enter the room I shared with Luksa when several people in various stages of awakening appeared.

Before anybody could say anything, Luksa, standing at our door, remarked, "What was that terrible noise? Did anybody hear what I did?" He paused, looking into their puzzled faces and added, "If some of you are playing sicko games I don't appreciate it. Some of us have to get up and work in the morning."

Regaining my breath if not my composure, I contributed, "You guys can laugh if you want, but I'm not only locking the door but putting a chair against it." Somebody laughed and belittled my fear, but shortly thereafter doors quickly closed and locks snapped into place.

"Did it occur to you that we're both fully dressed and were hardly just awakened," I mentioned back in our room.

"Nobody noticed," answered Luksa. "It wouldn't be the first time we went to bed fully clothed."

But the game had begun. We weren't through yet, never dreaming officers would knock on our door the next morning. It appeared we'd gone too far this time, practically scaring a couple of nice guys sterile. Our careers would be over, our families disgraced, humiliated. And to think, unlike other episodes before and after, it all had begun in such innocence. I've reflected on just how

it all got started and will now come clean and share with you that episode, which was talked about for years, long after I got out of sports and before Luksa became respectable, so to speak, in the senior years of his career.

Perhaps even today when the clock strikes 2 or 3 A.M., the lights are dimmed, the wind is howling, and the moon goes behind the clouds there will be tales of *The Slasher.*

— ❏ —

By the summer of 1976 new dorms had been constructed at Cal Lutheran. Cowboy officials had concluded it would benefit all concerned if members of the media and other selected guests were no longer housed in the same dorm as Cowboy coaches and officials. We called our quarters at the far corner of a cul-de-sac of dormitories the Riff-Raff Hotel and named the recreation area with a bar, munchies, etc., the Starlight Ballroom. Rumor was that I was one of the main causes, or

> "Nobody noticed. It wouldn't be the first time we went to bed fully clothed."

"curses" as Schramm put it, that brought about the separation policy. But that's another story, and I now refer to the circumstances leading up to that fateful night.

Luksa and I had returned to the Riff-Raff Hotel after having dinner at Boccacio's, a fine restaurant overlooking the water at nearby Westlake.

We stopped by the Starlight Ballroom for a nightcap and were confronted by new arrivals Carter and Turbiville. They seemed a little disoriented but were friendly and mentioned it was the first time they'd visited training camp and, for that matter, Southern California.

"Well, the only thing I know about the state is the Charles Manson case," Turbiville said, grinning. "I guess people like that aren't around anymore."

I looked at Luksa, saw his eyes roll back in his head, and knew he smelled blood. After allowing the proper time to elapse, he said, "Oh, it's still a little crazy out here. Frankly, I don't like it anymore...at least since Bob found that dog out there on the trail going up the hill."

Turbiville and Carter became quiet, interested. "It made me sick," I said, shaking my head slowly, then staring at the floor. "There was this smell...and there...there it was, bloody. Anyway, nice to meet you. I'm out of here. Good night."

"What dog? What are you talking about?" asked Turbiville.

"Oh, nothing really," said Luksa. "Just a...well, Bob always jogs from outside the dorm up the hill behind the practice field because he has serious brain damage." He paused. Nobody laughed so he continued, "He came across this dog on the trail. Its throat had been slashed."

"You mean somebody cut a dog's throat?" muttered Turbiville.

"Come on, you guys," said Carter. "Get off it. Who'd cut a dog's throat?"

"Slashed," corrected Luksa. "Slashed."

They laughed, somewhat nervously I thought, waiting for one of us to tell them it was a bad joke, which of course it was. Instead I looked off in the distance at the nearby wall. "Well anyway, goodnight, guys...Oh, by the way, Frank, have you seen that kid today?" Frank said that as a matter of fact he had not. We needed a suspect. The kid was it.

— ❏ —

The name of the kid and his newspaper will not be mentioned because neither Luksa nor I want to become a part of the Witness Protection Program. Actually, he wasn't really a kid but we just thought of him that way so we'll call him the kid. Okay? The kid was out of place, more fitted for covering rock concerts and such. His hair was long and he dressed more like he was part of a rock band, wearing long designer jeans with frayed cuffs and pinkish shirts, rather than our standard sloppy attire of cutoffs, T-shirts, tennis shoes, and gimme caps. He was a quiet guy, very pale because he stayed out of the sun. He would telephone players in their rooms for interviews, rather than meet them face to face. He usually would be seen bringing a hamburger or something back to his room to eat. As he matured that would finally change. He had the room above us in the dorm, and sometimes you had to attack the ceiling with a broom to get him to turn down the loud music.

Luksa did try a couple of times to offer him advice in his unenviable way. Frank would come in late, go to the guy's room, and pound on the door. The guy would meekly open the door, and Luksa would barge in and take a seat. One time when I was witness, Frank got to the point, saying things such as, "Get out! Talk to people! Do something! This isn't healthy! Are you in there? Can you hear me! I want you to get out of this room and into the world!" The frightened kid would nod in agreement. But he needed a push. So we even talked him into going to the beach. He was unaware of suntan lotion, which we didn't notice, and ended up with the whey burned out of him. Along with everything else he had to go around with skin peeling. Another time I took him out to Orlando's, a local spot owned by a nice couple who loved the Cowboys and even us. He got soused on Harvey Wallbangers and wanted to take the Orlandos' daughter home with him. I practically had to bodily drag him away. I thought that was a good sign he was maturing, but Luksa still had no pity.

— ❏ —

The newcomers weren't likely to see the kid so, unbeknownst to him or us, he would become part of our plot. The kid would later change his MO, but it suited our plan at that time because he often would only come out at night. Naturally, Luksa and I had already dropped hints about him because it was better that he be feared than belittled.

And Steve Perkins had once remarked after stopping by the Starlight Ballroom for two to five nightcaps, "That kid's weird. He's different, scary." This comment was quite amusing because Steve was a little different himself. So were we all. Ah, the eyes of the beholder. But of course we jumped right in and told Steve how strange noises came from the kid's room in the early morning hours. I mentioned it sounded like the Bates Motel with voices of a woman talking to a young man

and how once I'd gone to his room to ask him to please turn down his stereo, and the kid answered the door in a gown, which looked like a cape, and was holding a butcher knife.

Naturally, Steve would not have believed this had his mind not been clouded by booze. Perhaps in the deadly perspective of morning light as he would ordinarily view it about noon, he would think how foolish and silly we were. Yet the seed of possibility, no matter how far-fetched, was planted in his mind. The seed would grow. Thereafter, he would avoid the guy or seem a little uneasy around him even though the kid would try to be friendly and say, "Hi there, Steve. How's...how's it goin'?" Perkins would hurry away.

Late at night we'd usually bring up some weird story about the kid, and Steve would sometimes say, "Will you shut the [F-word] up!"

Dr. Joseph Bailey, father of Schramm's top assistant, Joe, and a noted heart specialist, visited camp to aid in giving physicals to the players. One night he overheard us talking to Steve about the kid. You know how those things go. Aware that he was eavesdropping, I supplemented the unusual stories about you know who.

When rumors of the sicko killing dogs began to surface, Dr. Bailey concluded without reserve, "I know who *The Slasher* is. It's that kid!" The poor kid who wouldn't harm a bug, but suddenly we had a prime suspect, a name to occasionally drop in conversations.

— ☐ —

And Luksa was saying to Turbiville and Carter that night of *The Slasher*, "Oh, come on. It couldn't be him. But the other night I happened to pass his room. The door was slightly opened and it looked like...like the sheets on his bed were on the floor sla-slashed to ribbons."

"What?" said Carter. "You mean somebody cut up his sheets?"

"Slashed," corrected Luksa. "Slashed his sheets. Did he, uh, do it or did someone else? Maybe I just imagined what I saw. These are strange times."

About that time one of the Cowboy scouts, John Wooten, passed through the Starlight Ballroom on the way to his room. Some of Gil Brandt's scouts were assigned to our dorm, as a kind of punishment I suppose. John was a huge guy, an All-NFL guard who once ran interference for Jimmy Brown with the Cleveland Browns. He's also extremely clever, very quick, and I consider him one of the best impromptu actors of our time. Quickly sizing up the situation, John jumped right in. "You talking about that poor little puppy dog?"

"I'm afraid so," said Luksa.

"I'd like to get my hands on the SOB that did that!" said John, holding up his hands, big as catcher's mitts. "I'D TEAR HIM APART WITH MY BARE HANDS!" Then his voice softened, he blinked, and tears seemed to appear in the eyes of this mountain of a man as he continued, "I used to have a little dog like that. He was my best...the best friend I ever had."

He closed his eyes, then opened them. "Oh, I don't mean to get carried away, but there's a lot of sickos around these days and LITTLE PUPPY DOGS

CAN'T EVEN DEFEND THEMSELVES!"

Luksa and I were mesmerized by John's performance, and the newcomers were stunned, looking as if they'd been suddenly slapped with a wet towel.

"Hey, come on you guys," said Turbiville, breaking the momentary silence. "I didn't hear or read anything about this."

"Somebody said they found another dog this morning," said Luksa.

John, back in normal voice, added, "Listen, we're trying to keep this quiet. Imagine what a distraction it would be to the team if it got out. We'd appreciate it if you guys would keep it under your hat. Goodnight, fellows." The big man slowly walked down the hall, muttering something about a little puppy dog and then raising his voice, "I'll kill the SOB if I ever catch him!" Honestly, I wanted to applaud, but there was still work to be done.

The newcomers agreed they wouldn't say anything, but it was obvious they'd swallowed it hook, line, and sinker. It was after they'd gone to their room that something came over me. I don't know exactly what it was, just some kind of madness beyond my control. So that was when I took off into the night and became both the howling creature and the poor little dog under attack.

It wasn't over. About 3 A.M. Luksa, who had been lecturing me on some long forgotten subject, determined our prey weren't duly frightened. "Ah, now for the coup de grace." Luksa went into the hall, crept to the newcomers' door, and scribbled with his pen in shaky block letters, "You Are Next!" He then rattled their door and raced in sock feet back to our room. I overcame a momentary temptation to lock him out.

— ⌐ —

The next morning I was awakened by a commotion in the hall. I got up to check and found three members of the cleaning crew for the dorms. They were staring at the words on the door. "Somebody around here's crazy," said one. "It's probably a joke," said another.

"Some joke," said the third.

"Did you hear about the dog that had its throat slashed?" I interrupted.

Turbiville came out, bleary-eyed. He stared at the words on the door as I said, "I don't believe this. This is crazy. Some kind of joke." Carter appeared, also saw the words. Finally, he said, "We did hear some funny noise last night, and there was a pounding on the door. What's that kid's name? Anyway, I was just too tired and sleepy to get up and answer."

"I'm going to talk to Schramm," I told them. "If something crazy is going on around here, I'm moving to a motel."

As I walked back to the room, one of the cleaning people asked Turbiville and Carter if they'd heard about the dog that had its throat slashed.

Luksa and I discussed the grim situation, sometimes laughing, sometimes being serious, and wondered what it all meant. By then I'd begun to worry. The

> So that was when I took off into the night and became both the howling creature and the poor little dog under attack.

story was becoming too big for me, bigger than life. I didn't sleep well that night and heard loud knocking on our door the next morning. Luksa, fortunately as it turned out, answered the door. I heard a man identifying himself as an officer. Luksa acted dumb, a natural state for him.

"We'd like to ask you a few questions about some strange happenings around here, sir," said the officer.

Long pause. "Certainly, feel free to do so," said Luksa.

"There were reports of strange noises, animals being hurt . . . and scribbling on the door across the hall that could be interpreted as, well, threatening. I'm sure it's nothing, but you understand we just have to check these things out. Have you heard any strange noises at night?"

Long pause. Luksa cleared his throat, a strange noise in itself, before answering, "No, I haven't heard anything unusual. However, I'm a sound sleeper. But we'll certainly let you know if we do. Uh, you might question my roommate, Bob St. John. He hasn't mentioned anything about it but he's very forgetful. He is a very light sleeper."

"Is he here now?"

"No, but I'll have him get in touch with you."

"Thank you, sir. We don't mean to frighten you but we have to check these things out. We'll just keep a closer watch out here."

Long pause. Luksa's voice was higher as he answered, "Thank you, officer."

I had listened to the conversation behind the door of my bedroom. My heart was pounding, my knees felt weak. Had I answered the door and been confronted by the officer, I'm afraid I'd probably have fallen on my knees, hugged his legs, and tearfully confessed. Yes, we knew we'd gone too far, but it was too late to turn back. We also knew if we confessed there would be a lot of embarrassment, not to mention the fact that Carter and Turbiville surely would try to maim us. We even tried to play down the story the remainder of training camp, but it was too late.

Mysteriously, *The Slasher* vanished that night. But two weeks later I sat next to Dan Reeves, then a Cowboy assistant, at lunch. "Did you hear something about a dog with its throat cut being found around here?" he asked. I told him I faintly remembered somebody mentioning it.

And one summer five years after I'd left sports, I stopped over in Thousand Oaks on the way to visit friends in Monterey. I went to dinner with some writers in camp, and a new guy on the Cowboys beat asked me if I'd ever heard about dogs they used to find near the dorm with their throats slashed.

3

Different Drummers

"What are you doing here?... You're a freeloader!"

—Jungle Jamey to Tex Schramm

During a visit to the Dallas Cowboys training camp in Wichita Falls a few years ago, one great difference I noticed from the old days was that there weren't any real characters, those madcap hangers-on on the premises. Maybe things are just much more serious now with tighter security, or if they are nearby, the media just chooses to ignore them and stick to chronicling what happens with the team, ignoring such distractions. We, especially me, could never resist them.

When four skydivers appeared over the field at Midwestern State University to participate in opening ceremonies for camp, I had brief hopes that Jungle Jamey, Bow-Wow, or maybe even Bubbles Cash were dropping out of the sky. No such luck. They were just normal skydivers, one bringing the symbolic football to kick things off.

I knew the other aforementioned with the exception of Jungle Jamey, although after extensive research it seemed as if I knew him. I talked to several people acquainted with the guy during training camp. Distracted from my purpose of covering the team, I filed only a brief on what was happening with the Cowboys and wrote a column on J. J. This upset Tex Schramm a bit and no doubt my boss Walter Robertson, but I couldn't help myself. Tex even asked his PR guy, Curt Mosher, to find a subtle way to suggest to me that I write more about the actual team and what was going on in training camp. "Why don't you write more about the actual team and what's going on in training camp?" Curt asked me subtly. Anyway, I spent a lot of time, which might have been determined as wasted, researching J. J.

Gil Brandt and Ben Agajanian both swore that all other camp followers dimmed in comparison with J. J., who seemed as much a happening as a person—a showboat, flimflam guy who stuck to you like a discarded wad of gum on the sole of your shoe or perhaps an aberration. Before he was Jungle Jamey he was Jamey the Beachcomber, and no telling what he called himself when he once walked Broadway with a monkey on his shoulder. He also called himself "The World's Greatest Gate Crasher," and some evidence

attested to that fact. All indications were his real name was John Baccellei or Baccelei or Bacilerri. The spelling varied as did the man.

J. J. had hung around the New York Giants when they won the NFL title in 1956 and had taken a liking to their young defensive coach, Tom Landry. So he showed up in a cloud of dust at the Cowboys' first training camp in Forest Grove, Oregon, in 1960. He arrived in this ancient car with football shoes hanging from the bumper, a leather helmet from the Red Grange era, and bits of uniforms on the roof and baby shoes, doll heads, and various other souvenirs attached to other parts of what had once been an automobile.

But this wasn't the most unusual part. When he climbed out of the contraption, he was wearing an African hunter's hat with a snakeskin band, a shirt looking like it had belonged to a Luftwaffe pilot who had crashed and burned, ragged shorts, and no shoes. He did sometimes wear tennis shoes, which he appeared to have taken off a sleeping street person. His companion was a large white rabbit that he called "Texas Free-loader" and kept on a leash as if it were a neighborhood dog. Tied around J. J.'s neck was a piece of meat, which he'd sometimes take a bite out of.

He presented a birthday cake to a bemused Landry, and he was there to help the Cowboys get off to a good start in their first season in the NFL. Furthermore, he predicted the Cowboys would play the Philadelphia Eagles for the championship.

He spoke in a loud voice with words coming in a kind of cadence. "Da-de-dah-hey-hey-hey." Taking a bite out of the meat, he would say, "Good-bear-meat-yeah-yeah-yeah." In camp he shagged balls, told stories of his experiences with Nehru and Charles de Gaulle, and slept under the piano in the recreation room or in the middle of the practice field so he could "get-some-fresh-air-da-de-dah."

Kids, their curiosity running wild, were attracted to him. So he organized them into the "Jungle Jamey Fan Club." They all got pictures of J. J., and Gil said the kid who brought him the most candy was

automatically named president of the club. J. J. and Tex disliked each other. J. J. questioned why Schramm, neither a player nor coach, was around in the first place. Schramm not only questioned J. J.'s presence but his existence.

Once when the team and officials were having lunch, J. J., there to bum a meal, walked up to Schramm and said, "What-are-you-doing-here-da-de-day. You're-no-player-you're-no-coach. You're-a-freeloader!" Schramm was so shocked he was at a loss for words other than a few profanities here and there. The players and coaches seemed to like J. J. around so Schramm was more tolerant than usual, certainly more than he would have been in later years. But he was known to search for J. J. late at night, failing to find him sleeping under the piano in the recreation room. Bad timing. J. J. also had sleeping quarters on the practice field and was probably there or up in a tree or wherever.

However, Gil Brandt treated J. J. well and invited him to the races. Of course they were stopped when J. J. tried to land his car in the parking lot. Told there was no way he could park that thing there, J. J. responded indignantly, "Listen, cad, I'm one of the builders of this track. Where is Mr. Cline? Bring him here immediately and tell him you have refused to allow me to enter." The poor attendant backed down and let them park, apologizing for not recognizing him.

Brandt recalled another time when J. J. materialized at the College All-Star game and J. J. asked him to go out to eat. "When I got my bill at the hotel there were extra charges for meals," said Gil. "I checked and the manager told me Jamey had come to his office and said he was with Murchison and Bedford Wynn and was allowed to sign my bill. When the guy resisted, J. J. told him they were going to buy this hotel and fire him. So the guy had let him sign my bill."

Over the years J. J. offered his services, whatever they might be, to the Chargers, Rams, 49ers, Raiders, Saints, Oilers, Lions, Eagles, and Giants. He was with the Lions when George Plimpton was

researching his book *Paper Lion.* Plimpton, who actually played quarterback for a few downs during training camp, mentioned J. J. in his book. J. J. carried a copy of the book to show everybody the part where he was mentioned, whether they wanted to see it or not.

In 1958 the Eagles tossed him out of their dressing room during halftime of a particular game because he smelled so bad, so bad you could get a whiff of him over the odor of a bunch of dirty, sweaty players. They thought they'd gotten rid of him until their charter flight was leaving Chicago on the way back home. Suddenly J. J. jumped out of the toilet compartment and shouted, "Did-you-miss-me?"

When he first latched on with the Giants, he almost fooled them into thinking he was one of those soccer kickers trying out for pro football. But they let him hang around, and he attached himself to place-kicker Ben Agajanian. When I was in training camp that summer doing research on J. J., Ben was kicking coach for Landry. He would start talking about J. J. and then his voice would get higher and take on a nervous tone.

But when Ben was with the Giants, he felt sorry for J. J. and would give him money and let him serve as a sort of valet incognito. Ben even took J. J. out to eat at a nice restaurant. They went up to the bar for a drink, and J. J. emptied all the peanut bowls into his pockets. But he flubbed it when he tried to get an apple into his pocket. He dropped the apple and it started rolling on the floor.

"I whispered to him, 'Please let it go. Please let it go.' But he didn't. J. J. was on the floor in a flash going after the apple." Ben called for the check and left a good tip. "Hey-everybody!" said J. J. "See-that-folks. My-friend-is-a-big-tipper. Yeah-yeah-big tipper." Ben said they'd filled up the peanut bowls by that time, and as they left J. J. put more into his pockets.

The story goes that the final blow with the Cowboys came when J. J. showed up in Dallas and talked his way into the Cotton Bowl at halftime during a game. He convinced a guard that he was bringing special shoes for Don Meredith to help him

withstand being trapped. When the team trotted back on the field for the second half, J. J. was with them. That did it for Schramm. It also proved the end of J. J. and the Dallas Cowboys.

But his exploits as a gate crasher continued. He once busted into the Rose Bowl leading two goats. He claimed the goats were mascots of the University of Washington. He got into the Stanley Cup playoffs by convincing a guard he was Gordie Howe's brother.

I practiced what I believed to be J. J.'s cadence and sneaked up behind Ben Agajanian and barked, "Yeah-yeah-yeah-Ben-Agajanian-yeah-yeah." He turned, stared at me, and walked away, obviously failing to be amused.

— ❑ —

I know Bow-Wow was real because I used to talk to him when he'd visit the Cowboys training camp in Thousand Oaks. He'd show up sporting a Hollywood tan, a crewcut, and wearing a tennis outfit with none other than "Bow-Wow" embroidered on a pocket of his knit shirt. His real name was

Wojciechowioz S. Wojtkiewicz, and his business card identified him as president of Trancas Motion Pictures and Television Productions in Beverly Hills. He told one of the Cowboys secretaries that he was a Polish prince and was going to put her in the movies. As far as I know that never panned out, but then again, you can never be sure when it comes to Bow-Wow.

Trancas was as difficult to track down as Bow-Wow unless he wanted you to find him. Once I called the telephone listing on his card and an operator came on the line and asked what number I was dialing. I told her and she began, "Calls for that number are being taken in Paris, France, at the following exchange...." However, friends I had in Los Angeles claimed if you wrote Bow-Wow in care of Beverly Hills that he'd get the letter.

The guy really got around all right, claiming he knew this or that star or starlet and even mentioned that at one time he had been married to noted Hollywood gossip columnist Sheilah Graham. Sheilah had an affair with F. Scott Fitzgerald and wrote about their relationship in her biography, *Beloved Infidel*. They even made a movie out of it starring Gregory Peck and Deborah Kerr. Sure enough when I read her book I noticed she noted once making an awful mistake by marrying a guy named Wojciechowioz S. Wojtkiewicz, commonly known as Bow-Wow.

I liked Bow-Wow, although I was a little scared of him because he loved to play tricks on people, which as you might have gathered was something I didn't, uh, condone. After we met I did get strange calls over the years but wasn't fooled in the least. I had mentioned my schoolboy fascination for Kim Novak so one day I answered the phone in the office and a sexy female voice said, "Bob, this is Kim." Sure. Hmm, now I wonder.

> I know Bow-Wow was real because I used to talk to him when he'd visit the Cowboys training camp in Thousand Oaks.

Maybe you've seen Bow-Wow and didn't know it. He once sat near Coach John Wooden on the UCLA bench during the NCAA championships and was also seen on the sideline by the Los Angeles Rams when Tommy Prothro coached the team. He had somehow befriended the two coaches.

When Tommy and his wife, Shirley, visited camp after he'd left the Rams, he confirmed that I had reason to beware of Bow-Wow. Seems one night before Christmas Tommy was relaxing in his home when the doorbell rang. Sleepily, he got up and slowly moved to the door. He yawned, opened the door, and there before him stood a young woman, wrapped in cellophane and wearing nothing else but a red ribbon around her middle. Tommy stood there for minutes, stunned, gaping. "Well," he reasoned, "what would you do if you opened your door and there was a naked woman wrapped up like a Christmas present and your wife was in another room?" Gape. Finally, Tommy yelled, "Shirley, ohhh Shirley! Come here! Don't walk! Run!"

"We asked her to come in," said Shirley. "It was cold out there. She came in and said she was staying with us for a few weeks. I said to heck you are and then we both knew it was Bow-Wow's doings. We called him to come and get her. She had ... chill bumps all over her."

Another time when the Prothros were out of town, Bow-Wow had a picture of Shirley blown up to life-size and put on a poster that read, "Wife for Sale." Then he nailed up the sign outside their house. "We got a number of calls," said Tommy.

Tommy did explain that people didn't always take Bow-Wow seriously when maybe they should have. "Years ago," said Tommy, "Bow-Wow happened to mention that he was taking Jane Wyman to the Academy Awards and asked if Shirley and I wanted to come along. Well, you know, I knew there was no way he was taking Jane Wyman to the Academy Awards, but I humored him and politely declined, saying we had other plans.

"Then we were watching the Academy Awards on television

and the camera was on Jane Wyman, who had won an Oscar. Standing next to her was her escort, Bow-Wow."

Once Bow-Wow house sat for the Woodens. When they got home all their furniture was gone. The phone rang and a caller said, "If you have any more pieces left, I'd like to buy them, too." John almost fainted. Bow-Wow had sold all their furniture. (Not really. It was hidden in the backyard.)

Former UCLA assistant basketball coach Jerry Norman was a favorite target of Bow-Wow. Bow-Wow was driving a new Cadillac around and asked Jerry to go ahead and try it out. Norman drove off and Bow-Wow ran to the phone, calling the police and telling them somebody had stolen his car. Poor Jerry. They took him in. "This guy says he knows you," a cop told Bow-Wow. "Never seen him in my life," said Bow-Wow.

Bow-Wow didn't drink or smoke and claimed he never had. One of his favorite tricks when he'd go to one of those Hollywood parties was to put liquor on his hand. "Everybody could smell it," he said. "So I started acting drunk. You know, I go around hugging and grabbing all the young starlets." They'd just think he must be somebody famous, that he was just drunk and an okay guy. Besides, knowing him might lead to that big break in the industry.

Well, I don't know what happened to Bow-Wow, but if I could find that old card he gave me, I'd call and get the number in Paris, France. It wouldn't surprise me if he answered.

— ❑ —

Tom Landry got a lot of letters, but one was written by a guy I believed had the makings of a zany camp follower. He wrote:

"Dear Tom,

"I would like to work in building a training machine that would help your team develop better on defense. What I had in mind was a long 'T' on the back of a one-and-a-half ton truck and about 20, 30 feet away from the body. We would mount a training dummy, see. We would build sheet metal guards around the truck to make sure nobody got run over. Sort of a type of cowcatcher in front.

"Tom, anybody can tackle a tackling dummy when it's standing still. But when one is coming at you at 30 or 40 miles per hour it should make good training."

The guy included a self-addressed envelope. I'm sure he was disappointed when Landry politely turned down his suggestion.

— ❑ —

It was in the late 1960s that Dallas stripper Bubbles Cash came on the scene at Cowboy games. She wore a micro-mini-skirt and tight top and sashayed slowly up and down the aisles when the team played at the

Below: Bubbles Cash detracts from action on the field during a Cowboys game in the Cotton Bowl.

Cotton Bowl, claiming she couldn't find her seat and in no way meant to disrupt the game or draw attention to herself. It was difficult to miss Bubbles, 42-23-40, from the press box because she always seemed to be near there. This guy was usually with her, more than eager to give her name to any newspaper types and also let those who were interested know which club they could find her gyrating in what could have been called dancing.

She even appeared at a Cowboys game against the Saints in New Orleans, once again hunting for her seat. Only thing is she tried to get onto the bandbox where Al Hirt entertained at halftime, which most agreed was an odd place to be looking for her game seat. The notoriety wore off and she faded away. I found her for a column years ago. She was running a liquor store, and after we'd talked for a while, said she might run for governor.

Distinguished Soup Nose

4

> "One martini is all right, two is too many, three is not enough."
>
> —James Thurber

Over the years people have falsely claimed to be eyewitnesses to the founding of the Distinguished Soup Nose Award. They have not only circulated twisted, demeaning versions of what actually happened but also spread exaggerated rumors about DSNA alumni. It was, after all, the dedicated performances by these men, often under self-inflicted duress, which earned them the DSNA and everlasting applause and gratitude of their peers who were afraid they might win. The DSNA was something non-winners still hold very dear and the record must be set straight! During my years as a sportswriter, I was fortunate to have witnessed historical events such as the University of Houston's 71-69 upset of UCLA before 52,693 in the Astrodome, Roger Staubach's "Hail Mary Pass," the Cowboys first Super Bowl victory, and yes, YES, the founding of DSNA.

It happened in the fall of 1967 on a rainy night in Philadelphia, that City of Brotherly Love where fans even boo Santa Claus as he circles the field at halftime during the Yuletide season. Members of the Dallas Cowboys entourage had gathered the night before the game with Philly for a quiet dinner in the famous Old Bookbinders. Tom and Alicia Landry were there as were some of the assistant coaches, club officials, and members of the media, including a Certain Photographer (CP). His name will remain anonymous, even to him because as nearly as I can determine he never knew. This will be true in certain other cases in order to protect the guilty.

Now CP had the reputation of nipping a bit too much even among those of us in the media, which was a pretty sad state indeed. Frankly, although admittedly ashamed in later years, we all enjoyed too many vesper cocktails, pre-meal drinks, and after-dinner delights. That historical evening CP warmed up by getting soused on the flight from Dallas to Philly and, we later learned, proposed to a stewardess just before landing. I do believe the gods of fate had a warped sense of humor. Of all the tables reserved for our group, CP staggered to one where the Landrys, the epitome of reserve and class, innocently prepared for a quiet dinner with, perhaps, interesting conversation. Thank goodness assistant coach Ernie Stautner was also at the table.

Cowboys publicity director Curt Mosher and I, each knowing our limit, were finishing our third martinis at an adjoining table as the waiter began serving salads and/or soups. We watched CP in helpless awe. Would he spill a drink on the Landrys or flip over backwards, his feet knocking the table with all the trimmings on them? Would he reach across the table with his fork and stab at Alicia's salad because he couldn't wait to be served or ask her to dance? Or would he ask Tom to dance? No, he sat there with a silly grin on his face, gave a Hook 'Em Horns sign, and mumbled to the waiter, "Gimme another one and have one on the house your ownself."

The waiter politely placed a bowl of French onion soup before him. CP's head hovered precariously close to the soup as if he were trying to read small print without his glasses. Then it happened. Splash! His face

Above: Bob St. John, Steve Perkins, Andy Anderson, Harold Ratliff, Frank Luksa, Curt Mosher, and Ed Fite pause before covering the Dallas-Philadelpia game in the Cotton Bowl in 1967. Perkins, Anderson, and Luksa would one day win Distinguished Soup Nose Awards. (Dallas Cowboys photo)

dropped into the bowl. I later claimed his ENTIRE HEAD was submerged, but Mosher, citing me for unneeded exaggeration and rightly so, insisted that only his nose entered the soup. Ernie, with quickness befitting an NFL hall-of-famer, grabbed CP by the collar and pulled him out of the soup, possibly saving him from a fate worse than inspiring creation of the DSNA. Somewhat revived, CP wiped his face with a napkin (probably belonging to someone else), complained the soup was too hot, and was helped out of the restaurant by Stautner. En route he asked the hatcheck girl to marry him.

Mesmerized and instinctively knowing we had witnessed something rare and historical,

Mosher and I decided an annual award should be given in CP's honor. With this in mind and with great insight into ourselves and other colleagues in the media, we came up with the Soup Nose Award. It would be given annually to a member of the media or Cowboys public relations representative who most undistinguished himself while on a road trip with the team. It would live in infamy. Perhaps subconsciously, and yet in a way showing respect to the Pinocchioan tradition, the name of the award kept getting longer each year. From a humble beginning as simply the Soup Nose Award (SNA), it became the Distinguished Soup Nose Award (DSNA), the Annual Distinguished Soup Nose Award (ADSNA), the Annual Distinguished Soup Nose Award of America (ADSNAA), and reached a crescendo, if you will, as the Annual Distinguished Soup Nose of the Year of America Award (ADSNYAA) before, in a fit of common sense, we settled on DSNA.

Tex Schramm, president and general manager of the Cowboys, was appointed honorary chairman of DSNA because he'd once been a sportswriter and showed integrity, perspective, and modesty that would one day be the cornerstones of the DSNA. Why, even while in Alhambra High School in San Gabriel, Calif., during the 1930s, Schramm not only played fullback but more importantly was sports editor of the school newspaper and annual. Actually, he mostly blocked for star tailback George Leyer, one of the most outstanding players in the area.

Swivel-hipped George ran, twisted, and fought for 352 blood and guts yards on sixty-three carries against defenses set to stop him. Meanwhile, Schramm sneaked through for less than 80 yards on only nine carries because you naturally give the ball to your best back. Those with the most rushing yardage are listed first, but even then Schramm appreciated the value of teamwork and sharing the glory. In the school annual Schramm listed himself as the team's No. 1 rusher with an 8.2 average per carry and workhorse George as No. 2 with a 5.7 average. This would be like listing Daryl Johnston ahead of

Emmitt Smith in rushing statistics. This gesture certainly would have been in the true spirit of the DSNA. So you see, unbeknownst to Schramm he fully understood the spirit of the award. He even went out on a limb and predicted I would claim my share of the awards. This never happened, although I did finish as runner-up six times and once was second, third, and fourth in the balloting.

Some of the winners and co-winners might surprise you, although it did not surprise us or them if they were being honest with themselves. They included talented sportswriter and columnist Frank Luksa Jr., nationally known sportscaster Verne Lundquist, *Dallas Times-Herald* Cowboy beat reporter Steve Perkins, and the extremely clever, beloved publicity guy Doug Todd.

Unlike some of us, Steve never slept on the job while covering the team. Unlike some of us, he did tend to sleep on many other occasions. Steve, working for an afternoon newspaper, was in the habit of waking up at dawn's early light to bang out stories. So he was known to

often drop off to sleep at unusual times, such as during dinner. This would happen in mid-discussion or even in mid-sentence when he was giving his opinion regarding anything under the sun. We would be having a drink or three before dinner, and suddenly his head would drop to his chest as he dozed off, snoring rhythmically. With all due respect I must admit when he did snap awake he'd jump right back into the conversation as if he'd never left or finish the sentence he'd started. Never-never land did not seem to affect his thought process.

Steve was never aware we had a pot going with the winner being the person who most accurately guessed the time Steve would doze off. And Steve's act was also an inspiration for Doug Todd, Mosher's assistant at the time. Whenever a conversation dragged, which was more often than not, Doug's head would drop to his chest and he'd pretend he was snoring. If the dullest contributor to the conversation didn't realize what was happening, he automatically became a candidate for the DSNA.

Mischievous as kids, perhaps even devious as hell, we'd sometimes leave Steve snoozing at the table and once even pinned a card to his lapel, giving his name and hotel and asking the finder to please bring him home. Nobody ever did. Yes, Steve's performance at dinner was good, real good, but never seemed to meet the Big Play requirement that often propelled candidates to actual victory in the DSNA. Finally he did, with a little help from his friends.

On the eve of the Cowboys game in Buffalo in September 1971, our dinner group was so large that a bus was chartered to take us to a restaurant in Niagara Falls. The night was especially long, travel and all, and so predictably Steve fell sound asleep at the back of the bus on the return trip to the hotel. Steve had been a little preachy and obnoxious that night but, hey, that happens. He also had scooped me on a story, but I certainly didn't hold grudges. As we started to get off the bus at the hotel, Mosher and I learned Steve was sprawled out asleep on the backseat. The driver had stepped outside, and

we began shushing everybody as we filed off the bus. Well, Steve needed his sleep and should not be disturbed.

There was a gamble that the driver might notice him, but he obviously didn't because the guy drove the vehicle back to the bus barn and left it, presumably heading home. Steve woke up alone inside a pitch black, empty bus among other dark, empty buses.

He later described the scene in his subtle way. "I had no idea where I was, you SOBs! Geeze, I thought I was dead or in the twilight zone! It was frightening. I almost had a heart attack! Geeze!"

I was raised a Southern Baptist, which means you feel guilty if you don't feel guilty. So you can imagine how I felt, for a brief while anyway, upon learning the toll our prank had taken on one of our own. Another weird thing happened. After our return to the hotel, we'd picked a bar at random for an after-dinner drink to toast our coup. We were laughing and talking as we visualized what Steve's reaction might have been when in he walked. There were a lot of gin joints in Buffalo and no way he could have known where we were going. Yet there he was, standing over our table, his eyes Dracula red and his face a squeezed lemon. He did not know how he found us, explaining when he realized he wasn't dead he'd hailed a taxi and demanded to be taken to some popular bar. He immediately picked me out as the culprit, which I felt was totally unfair as Mosher sat there, grinning. "You did this, you *#*#**!" Steve remarked, pointing at me.

"I know I've done a lot of sick things, but I'd never do anything like that to anybody," I answered, my sincerity inspired because I thought he might punch me out. We all agreed that we hadn't noticed he was asleep on the back of the bus or we'd surely have awakened him. This certainly qualified Steve for the DSNA. When told he was up for the award, he said that we were stupid and silly and he wasn't going to play childish games with us. So after Steve fell asleep again we called an emergency session of the DSNA board and voted him the unanimous winner even though it was only the first week of the regular season.

— ❏ —

I greatly admired Verne Lundquist, who I first met when he was a young television sports anchor in Austin, and I was working for the *Austin American-Statesman* in 1963. Verne, who worked his way to national prominence on the networks, was always just one of the guys no matter how much acclaim he received.

Unlike some in his trade, he could laugh at himself and didn't take himself so seriously. He was the sports guy for Channel 8 in Dallas and also the voice of the Cowboys on the radio when he became a fairly consistent prospect for the DSNA.

During a mid-December trip to snowy Cleveland in 1970 Verne and a couple of us were in a taxi heading back to the hotel after dinner, always a dangerous time. We were humming Christmas carols but Verne wanted more. As we stopped at a red light we noticed a group of carolers walking down the street singing, "God rest ye merry gentlemen...." Verne was overcome by the Christmas fuzzies, bid us adieu, got out of the taxi, and not only joined them but, like a drum major, took the lead as they marched onward to the next neighborhood. He wasn't seen until the next day. He was very hoarse. And in the unforgiving light of day, he reflected that perhaps the carolers weren't whispering and staring at him because they thought he was a wonderful leader with a fine voice. Rather they likely wanted him to leave but were afraid to ask.

Later that year we were in San Francisco for the playoffs. Verne went for a walk. He smoked in those days and was puffing away on a cigarette while pondering life. The wind was up, whipping into his face. It also blew ashes onto his new leather overcoat. By the time he got to the hotel a big hole had burned into his coat.

He confessed, knowing we would be forced to furnish the facts for him if he didn't. "Probably the only thing that saved me from a worse fate was that a passing car paused. A woman inside the car had apparently been drinking because she threw a beer on me to stop a possible fire. I never did get to thank her."

On the return flight home from San Francisco, Schramm served as master of ceremonies for the presentation of the DSNA to none other than Verne Lundquist! "Wear it proudly," Schramm told Verne, who kept protesting that he didn't deserve it. Frank Luksa, the only member of the board to ever vote on himself, applauded like the good sport he was and asked Verne to say a few words.

Verne responded, "This is a setup! I'm not going to stand for this! I want a recount! Mosher and St. John once again fixed the balloting!"

As the presentation concluded, Verne was walking down the aisle back to his seat when he bumped into a stewardess holding a food tray. Food got all over both of them. He turned

> "A woman... threw a beer on me to stop a possible fire. I never did get to thank her."

back, faced us, and added, "Okay, I see what you mean."

— ❏ —

We were looking down from the balcony of the Cowboys hospitality suite in a Chicago hotel at 2 A.M. prior to the Cowboys' first regular season game that September afternoon in 1973. Inspired by Carl Sandburg, we kept trying to recall some of his poem *Chicago* but the best we could do was, "...Stormy, husky, brawling, City of the Big Shoulders." Soon the Chicago spirit caught fire. An unidentified guy pretended to tilt an imaginary hat in a casual Sinatra way and sang, badly, "Chicaago, Chicagoooo, that toddlin' town...." Lundquist, who hands down had the most impressive voice, began speaking in his deepest Shakespearean tones about that "City of BIGGGGGEEEE shoulders" and then did an unknown soliloquy.

Subconsciously, I leaned over and shut the sliding glass door separating the balcony from the suite, and then turned just in time to see Verne spread his arms, sweeping them across the city below, and shout into the

night, "AH YES, ONE DAY THIS WILL ALL BE MINE!" He then spun around, said goodnight, and walked into the sliding glass door. He muttered "Ugh," his knees buckled, and he grabbed his nose.

For an instant those of us on the balcony weren't sure what had happened, but DSNA board member Andy Anderson was inside the suite. He was about to join us when he became an eyewitness. Andy, with the *Fort Worth Press*, fell on the floor laughing and kicking. Later regaining his composure, he said, "Verne...he looked like he'd...he'd been scared by a ghost." Naturally, Andy became a DSNA candidate himself for being a middle-aged man who fell on the floor laughing and kicking or perhaps it was because he regained his composure. However, Andy immediately nominated Verne as a two-time winner of the DSNA and also seconded the motion. Verne, ever the good sport, shook the cobwebs out of his head and remarked graciously, "I would like to thank my parents and Carl Sandburg for this honor."

Above: The *Fort Worth Press* was always trying to find ways to cut costs. Here's *Press* sportswriter Andy Anderson on his way to Cowboys training camp in Thousand Oaks, California.

— ⅃ —

Frank Luksa Jr., whose father was a distinguished college professor, appears to be a distinguished, reserved fellow himself. No doubt his colleagues today must think of the bespectacled graying columnist as a trusted elder statesman, one who is talented, knowledgeable, objective, and ready to offer advice on any subject whether asked or not. They just do not know what lurks behind that persona. He is a devious madman, suddenly becoming like a soulful Hamlet portraying Charlie Chaplin. So as you will see, his performance in those days made him yet another constant threat to retire the DSNA.

Luksa struck a blow for the DSNA on the final day of 1967 when we were in Green Bay for the historic Ice Bowl game. The wake-up call was foreboding. "Good morning," said the operator. "It's 9:45 and 16 degrees below." Somehow, as often was the case, Luksa and I were late leaving the hotel and consequently missed putting our luggage with that of the team so it would be loaded on the plane after the game, and we wouldn't have to fool with it. Life was never easy in those days as a sportswriter. So we had to tote our suitcases, portable typewriters, briefcases, and selves to the stadium, store the luggage in the press box, and be responsible for getting it on the plane. Oh yes, besides a suitcase Luksa also had a garment bag.

A taxi let us out by the parking lot so, our hands full, we had to walk across the ice, snow, and tundra to get to the stadium and WARM press box. I complained, but Luksa stared at me briefly and said the weather wasn't that bad for a real outdoorsman such as himself. "Follow me!" he shouted and took the lead. Now there was a ditch not far off our path, and the way we were slipping and sliding it certainly was to be avoided. Luksa, for reasons not even known to him, walked

precariously close to the ditch as if daring fate, which had always taken him up on a challenge. There was this blood-curdling yell, and he looked like a rooster trying to fly before sliding into the ditch, his luggage like an anchor quickly taking him to the bottom. Fate 2,000, Luksa 0. Gamely, he righted himself. He picked up his baggage and started up, only to slide down again.

I was seized by laughter as he yelled bad words at me. These decisions are tough when you have to leave somebody like that, but I could not attempt to rescue him, slide into the ditch, and thus be late for the important kickoff. But I did promise to send help if and when I got to the press box. This humane offer wasn't needed. Two local women helped him out of the ditch, and he was in the press box before the kickoff. He later denied being helped out by two women, but I verified the facts in my column so it must have been true.

There were heaters and blowers at each end of the press box, but if you didn't chugalug your coffee it would freeze. You took notes with pen or pencil clutched in a gloved fist. You had to keep blowing on your hands to type the game story. Andy Anderson, noting how the *Press* survived on an extremely low budget, tired of our griping and remarked, "How 'bout me? I've got to chisel my story in stone."

Vince Lombardi had told us at a press conference the previous day that there was no way the field would freeze because heating wires had been installed under the turf. Sure. Temperatures had warmed to 13 below by game time so of course the field was frozen stiff by halftime. By late afternoon when the Packers won, 21-17, on Bart Starr's two-yard quarterback sneak with thirteen seconds left, the temperature was eighteen below, the chill factor in the minus thirties. There were reported cases of frostbite among the players, and the NFL would never play a game under such dangerous conditions again. Frank Luksa strongly supported that stand.

— ◻ —

New England was a wonderful place in mid-November of 1975

when we were there for the game between the Cowboys and New England Patriots. We had dinner in a nice restaurant in Foxboro, Mass., and dined in a reserved room, primed to gorge ourselves on the wonderful New England fare of fresh lobster, crab, and oysters, and with the proper beverage, ordered by Doug Todd in his inimitable way.

"Hear ye, hear ye, good sir!" he told the waiter. "Wine! Wine! And fresh horses for my men!" Then he closed his eyes, his head dropped, and he pretended to snore. This brought chuckles from everybody but Perkins, who had already dozed off. But generally things were quite tame, warm, and friendly. Well, Luksa WAS having some problems breaking the hard outer shell of a huge crab leg in order to get to the delicacy inside. He was muttering to himself, and before we knew it he was out of his chair and in what appeared a life-and-death struggle with a rogue crab leg, its pincerlike claw seeking his throat. It was mesmerizing! "You'll not defeat me, you devil!" he shouted, twisting and turning as he pushed and pulled the claw at his jugular as they fell to the floor.

At last Luksa got the better of the crab leg, hovering over it on his knees as he pounded it into submission. "I've saved mankind from this beast!" he said and then, as if nothing had happened, calmly took his seat at the table, put the crab leg back on his plate, and proceeded to eat it. He received sporadic applause. A waiter came into the room, no doubt expecting some kind of madness had occurred, and politely inquired if everything was all right. "Certainly," said Luksa, "but how good of you to ask."

— ☐ —

Sometimes new people would join us, but rookies just didn't have the experience to ordinarily qualify for the DSNA, no matter how hard they didn't try. Such was the case when James Davis, now one of the vast number of editors at *The Dallas Morning News*, started covering the team for the *Garland Daily News*. It was tough for him, being among seasoned veterans, and he seemed to feel a little apprehensive and out of place

until that night he sat next to me when our group was at the Copa Cabana in New York to see Nat King Cole.

We were horsing around at the table, and James made some comment that I deemed *gauche*. Then he was feeling his oats after some drinks, which called for a reality check. I had been examining one of the little silver cups on the table. Then it dawned on me that with my unselfish help James might actually become a DSNA candidate.

I tapped unseasoned James Davis on the shoulder and said with great excitement, "Look! Isn't that Raquel Welch over there?" As James turned to gape I snatched the silver cup by his plate and placed it in his overcoat, which he hadn't checked at the entrance. Nearby Verne Lundquist smiled encouragingly. And as we prepared to leave I picked up another cup. Near the door I approached the host who had shown us to our table. I held the precious little silver cup before him and innocently asked, "Are these free souvenirs?" He was surely thinking "here's another stupid tourist" but politely said, "No sir, they are not."

Pointing at poor James, I continued, "I'm sorry. We thought they were so he put one in his coat pocket." He looked at James who appeared confused and then reached into his pocket and produced the cup, which he juggled as he tried to hand it to me. James wasn't someone who showed a lot of emotion, at least in those days. He seemed puzzled and then stared at me with Orphan Annie eyes. There was a slight problem, but the host was understanding even if James wasn't. "St. John," said James, unfairly assuming I was responsible for his great embarrassment, "I ought to whup you." Oh yes, it was James' lack of understanding that disqualified him for the DSNA.

— ❑ —

During the height of the DSNA there was still a heroic deed by one of our own, which bears mentioning among our frivolities. Yes, Blackie Sherrod's unselfish act on that December day in 1971 will forever be remembered by those of us who were there and shared the frightening experience in Yankee Stadium.

It happened during the time before the "House that Ruth Built" was renovated and updated and the New York football Giants had moved to the stadium in the Meadowlands to play games. Home teams furnish various kinds of food for sportswriters before and often at halftime during early afternoon games. The menu used to range from the classy fare furnished by the Cowboys to the awful, all you dare to eat hotdogs in Yankee Stadium.

However, food wasn't our primary concern after we'd entered the press box an hour or so before the game. A couple of uniformed guys began walking around, checking bags, looking under tables, chairs, feet, and so forth. The perceptive people that we were, we finally inquired what in the devil was going on.

"There's been a bomb threat in the press box," we were told. "But we're sure...uh...everything will be all right. Just doing a little checking, ha-ha-ha. That's all."

Good grief! Someone joked nervously that somebody had certainly wasted a perfectly good bomb on the likes of us.

But frankly we were a little apprehensive as we took our seats and began gnawing on the cold hotdogs, which had previously been burned. In this tense atmosphere, Blackie wiped his mouth on a napkin and shouted, "Don't worry about the bomb, men! I just ate it!"

Our minds a little more at ease, we put the bomb scare aside and began doing our jobs, although you could have heard a pin drop when a guy screeched his chair as the second half started. We approached Tom Landry after the game and asked him what might have happened had the press box blown up during the game. He pursed his lips and said, "Oh, we'd have stopped the game about 30 seconds and then continued with great enthusiasm."

— ❑ —

The spirit of the DSNA had begun to wane in 1977, the last season I covered the Dallas Cowboys. Perhaps we were blindsided by reluctant maturity or had begun to act our age. Oh, there was some drama but nothing like in the old days where on any given day, any given road trip, anyone could make the Big Play.

There was a little action on a road game to Washington D.C., but that was more of a team effort and didn't count toward an individual award. After dinner we returned to the Marriott Hotel and headed to our rooms. My experience, I expect, was not unlike the others. The key wouldn't fit the lock but I kept trying, and soon the inhabitant of the room opened the door and asked just what the heck I thought I was doing. Apologies followed and I went back to the lobby to find other members of our group.

Soon it was determined we'd gone to the wrong Marriott. I only mention this because it seemed to serve as a kind of forewarning for a life-threatening situation in which I would cross paths with two ladies in New York. But first, another Philadelphia story.

It was mid-season that year before we got a performance good enough for serious DSNA consideration. It happened in Philadelphia, which consistently seemed to bring out the worst, or best as it were, regarding the

Not one to miss an opportunity, Tom Landry makes his one and only bid for the Distinguished Soup Nose Award. He was disqualified for not being a member of the media. In spite of a lengthy protest by Frank Luksa, so was Smokey. (Dallas Cowboys photo)

DSNA. In the early morning hours a number of us were huddled in the Cowboys' hospitality suite very possibly sounding like ducks as we talked at the same time. About 3 A.M. we dispersed to our rooms, ports in the night. There was, frankly, some drunkenness involved. Doug Todd found his room, quickly dropping into slumber on his bed, a direct hit. But he did not close the door. Frank Luksa misplaced his balance and perspective and staggered through that same open door to what he thought was his room. He then collapsed on the bed occupied by Doug.

Both described the experience when they heard a wake-up call the next morning. As they awakened back to back, each, obviously disoriented, felt movement on the opposite side of the bed. One muttered, "Oh my god, what have I done?" They slowly turned and looked into each other's face. It was a horrible experience. Foul breath, horrible twisted faces, hair askew, blood-red swollen eyes. Each one screamed, one leaping to his feet and the other falling off the bed. Each swore off

booze. They became co-winners of what turned out to be the final DSNA.

— ❑ —

Many, especially Luksa, felt I should have finally won the honor a couple of weeks later on that terrible time in New York. A great benefit of being a sportswriter covering a professional football team is that you get to go to New York and thus the theater. Also for cultural purposes, more often than not when the Cowboys played in Philadelphia we'd catch the train to New York, go to the theater, and then hop the late train back to Philly. Anyway, that particular time we arrived late to New York and there was a rush to get to the hotel and then make the theater on time. I hurried into the hotel, grabbed my room key, and not even waiting for help from the bellhop, lugged my suitcase and typewriter, etc., onto the elevator and down the hall to my room. My plans were to quickly dump the baggage into my room, hail a taxi, and head for Broadway.

I put the key in the lock, opened the door, and went into

the room. Two women were there on the bed. "OHH, PLEASE DON'T HURT US!" said one, sitting up in bed. "You get out of here, I'm calling the police," said the other, reaching for the telephone. "Operator! Operator!"

It became an unreal blur. I was trying to leave quicker than a heartbeat but had trouble getting through the door, which automatically closed as I reached down to get my suitcase and typewriter, which I had dropped. And I was saying, "Oh, excuse me...I...I must be in the wrong room" and a woman was saying that somebody had broken in their room and at last I stuck my foot in the door to keep it from closing and slung my suitcase and typewriter into the hall, gathered them up, and ran for the elevator and...the elevator stopped in what seemed a day as I thought a house detective or security guard would collar me at any second and I heard or imagined I heard a woman's scream and got on the elevator....

An older, well-dressed couple were on the elevator. The woman gave me that are-you-sure-you're-all-right look and I said, "Good morning" only later realizing it was early evening. I hurried from the elevator through the lobby to the front desk, explaining in a voice much higher pitched than usual, that I'd been given the wrong key and scared the devil out of two women. Apologies were offered, and I made sure a bellman accompanied me to my room. I made the theater on time but kept imagining scenes where one of the women had shot me or that I was arrested and, when asked if anybody in the Cowboys party knew me, Luksa, smirking, would say, "I've never seen him before in my life. Sick people like this should be taken off the streets."

The DSNA seemed mine that last year when I left sports after covering the Cowboys' 27-10 victory over Denver in Super Bowl XII. But in the final voting I failed to win because the majority of the board determined my performance wasn't unusual but normal and to be expected. It was given to the lovely couple for their performance in Philadelphia, but I was awarded a second, third, and fourth place.

Other Acts, Other Rooms

Now rookies were intimidated and frightened when the veterans came to training camp because they were confused, worried, and just never knew what was going to happen from day to day. But Sims Stokes, out of Northern Colorado, was more paranoid and excitable than most when he appeared in Thousand Oaks in 1967. Really, the only time he seemed happy, relaxed, and felt welcome was during afternoon practice when he believed assistant coach Ermal Allen was enthusiastically waving "Hello" to him. Sims smiled broadly and waved back at Ermal, thinking what a nice, cheerful man he was. Then Ermal, disgusted, cornered Sims and explained he was calling him to another practice drill. So he became jumpy and excitable again.

On a dark, still night when not a creature was stirring, not even a sportswriter, Sims and Rayfield Wright were fast asleep in their room. Sims was awakened by a loud, frightening scream at the door and then saw this figure, distorted by the dim hall lights, coming into the room blowing fire, and he screamed, "Oh, Godddddd, help me!" Then he bounded across the room and jumped on top of Rayfield, causing the bed to creak and almost collapse.

It was only Walt Garrison, doing his fire-breathing act. What Walt would do was put lighter fluid in his mouth, strike a match a foot or so away from his face, then blow the fluid at it for instantaneous flames. He scared a lot of rookies a lot of times. "Once I got too close," Walt admitted, "and singed Pete Gent's eyebrows."

Those of us who covered the Cowboys in those days were lucky because there always seemed to be something to write about besides the usual football stuff. Of course we looked for unusual and humorous situations to lighten things up, whether it be in training camp or during the regular season. You don't see humor that much on sports pages now. Maybe the players are just more serious. Maybe the writers are just more serious. Maybe the world is just more serious.

— ▢ —

Oh yes, on a more somber note, the finale of Walt's fire-breathing act happened when he decided to scare the hell out of a friend who was resting against a trailer. Walt's plans were to sneak into the trailer and blow fire out a vent near the guy's head. Only thing, Walt started laughing, got fluid on his face, and it ignited when he blew at the match and burned the heck out of him.

As you know Walt was a real cowboy of the rodeo kind so fortunately a horse blanket was around, and Walt was able to put out the flame, which scorched his nose and lips. "Went to see my ol' wife Pam in the hospital when she was having a baby," Walt said. "While I was visiting, a nurse walked in and got all excited about my burnt face. Pam got to leave the hospital and they kept me seven more days."

Walt kept everybody laughing except rookies and was the team's funniest guy. But when you have him, a quarterback like Don Meredith singing "It wadn't Gawd who made honkey-tonk angels" in the huddle, a mischievous Roger Staubach, basketball players becoming pro football players, and injuries occurring in unusual ways, such as wide receiver Mike Montgomery falling out of a tree one night during a get-together at Charlie Waters' place, you're likely to have unusual things to write about.

And unlike all the embarrassing off-the-field problems the recent Cowboys had, the former group really didn't have that much trouble, and the culprits were soon gone. Walt Garrison, who always seems to have a line for everything, remarked about the problems the players had in the 1990s by saying, "Ninety-five percent of the Dallas Cowboys give the rest of them a bad name."

Oh, Ralph Neely did roar around on his motorcycle and break his leg. Ralph would take a sip or so but wasn't drunk or on dope, so the mishap just came naturally to him. And among the more usual happenings involved Toni Fritsch, an Austrian all-star soccer player who was anointed a Cowboy kicker. Especially in his early years with the team, Toni couldn't speak or understand a lot of English. He also didn't exactly look like an NFL player because he was chubby and stood about 5'6".

So one night in Thousand Oaks his teammates sent him out to get a pizza. He had to wait in line and then drive like mad to get back to camp before curfew. One of Thousand Oaks' finest stopped Toni for speeding. Toni hadn't brought his wallet containing his driver's license.

He knew enough to know the officer had him, but the Cowboys were extremely popular in Thousand Oaks, and Toni told the officer in broken English that he was "Koyboy keeker." The officer asked him to repeat what he said and Toni did, "Es Koyboy fam-us keeker."

The officer looked at Toni, laughed, and said, "Sure and I'm Bob Lilly." Then he took Toni to jail. I would venture an educated guess it was Gil Brandt who quickly got him out.

Not knowing the language worked out sometimes for Toni. During a tense moment when Toni was trying a last-minute field goal to beat St. Louis, the Cardinals started yelling at him, "Hey, you're going to miss it!

Don't choke! You're gonna choke!"

"You're wasting your time," said Dave Edwards, in to block on the field goal. "He doesn't understand a word you're saying." Toni just smiled, and his kick sailed right through the uprights.

— ❏ —

There weren't journalists like locusts in camp then so players were more accessible to us, and after camp you could always catch them at practice or even go over to their houses or apartments or meet them for a beer. It certainly helped that Schramm was a former public relations guy and sportswriter so he made sure we had such advantages, even if he couldn't sway what we wrote, which doesn't mean he didn't try. I doubt the exchanges between the writers and the players are the same now.

When Ed Jones decided he wanted to be a boxer in 1979, an experience that lasted one year, he called Carlton Stowers and said, "I just called to let you know I'm retiring and going into boxing. By the way, do you have

Coach Landry's telephone number? I need to let him know too." And the players were good about returning calls at home (we had all their numbers) with some exceptions. It was during the off-season that Dave Edwards didn't return my call. I was a little upset and called again, and he answered the phone.

"Listen, I'm sorry I didn't call you back," he said. "My wife wrote your number down on a Kleenex and I blew my nose on it and couldn't read your number."

— ❏ —

Charlie Waters was and is a super guy, a pleasure to be around, and even in his early years with the Cowboys he'd tell funny stories and was always a good interview. One particular training camp he showed a more serious side to the media, hoping to change his image. He stopped being funny, telling good stories. When I talked to him in training camp he was pleasant and helpful but just a little bland. Frank Luksa listened to my interview for a while and said, "Charlie, you're dull now."

"Come on," said Charlie. "What do you mean?"

"Sorry, Charlie, I like you and all that but you, well, have become bland."

Charlie takes things to heart, and naturally we couldn't let him off the hook. The following day I saw him walking across the street and yelled, "Hey, Charlie, can I talk to you?"

He said sure, and when we met I said, "Oh, never mind. You probably wouldn't have anything to say anyway."

"You rat."

"Charlie, there's something I've been meaning to ask you," Luksa told Charlie on the sidelines at practice the next day.

"Sure, Frank, what do you want to know?"

"Oh, well, I've got to be going. See you later," Luksa told him as he put his pen and pad away.

"Both of you are rats," said Charlie in an apt description. Unfortunately, vengeance was his.

I had good play with *On Down the Road* in the Sunday *Los Angeles Times*, and TV guys from an LA station had run out of interviews that day with players, coaches, scouts, club officials, trainers, equipment guys, ball boys, fans on the sidelines, and Moon Dog, the animal the team adopted because he hung out around the practice field and ran the fastest time in the 40. So the TV guys decided to interview me about the book. They would do it outside by the practice field, just like a player's interview. I've been so dumb in interviews that I really was going to try to be philosophical, astute, and all those things. The guy doing the interview introduced me with camera rolling and asked a question. I paused briefly for effect and started to answer when Charlie Waters jumped out from behind the cameraman and started clowning.

I doubled over laughing. The interviewer didn't see the humor but tried twice more to get a comment before I finally finished the interview, blabbering aimlessly as usual. "What a choker!" yelled Charlie as he walked away. Later as I was walking to the dorm Charlie yelled at me. I was trying to think of what I was going to say if he tried to apologize.

Is Charlie Waters ecstatic, frustrated, or demonstrating how a short official signals a touchdown? (photo © 1999, NNNN)

"Oh, never mind," said Charlie. "You probably wouldn't have anything to say anyway."

Charlie didn't blow fire out of his mouth, but he scared me silly one day when I was at my desk in the sports department, pondering life's problems as I stared out the window. Suddenly Charlie, who had been hiding behind my desk, leaped up and yelled, "Boooo!" I lost my dignity and almost flipped over backwards in my chair, but after a quick check felt somewhat better because my pants weren't wet.

— ❏ —

Below: Cliff Harris and Charlie Waters failed to find a bench to sit on. (photo © 2000 XTASY)

Luksa and I went after Bob Breunig as he stood on the sidelines during practice. Now Breunig was one of the toughest players on the team. He was playing with a badly injured knee but refused to miss a game. Tom Landry remarked, "He's so tough you can't ever tell when he's hurt."

Breunig was in sweats and actually being held out of practice to rest his knee. Flick and Flack, Luksa and myself, stood within hearing distance. "Well," I said to Frank, "some people can practice when they're hurt and some can't."

Breunig, towering over us vertically and horizontally, kept looking out on the field, but a grin crossed his face.

"Well, some guys just fake a knee injury so they can get out of practice," continued Luksa. "Some guys just can't play hurt."

Breunig moved closer to Luksa, noting Frank had a pen and pad in his hand, and said, "Frank, can you write hurt?"

— ❏ —

Troy Aikman, certainly a super player, was mostly portrayed in the media as a serious, no-nonsense guy who didn't loosen up until his retirement speech. I can't remember many funny Troy Aikman stories being written. Roger Staubach was different and made good copy for things other than his football heroics. He certainly was all business on the field, although not always on the sidelines and otherwise. As you no doubt know by now he not only had a prankish side but, at least when he was a rookie, was fair game for his teammates.

Roger was twenty-seven, married with kids, and just out of the Navy when he joined the Cowboys in 1969 at training camp. A devout Catholic, he didn't exactly run around in the wild, crazy circles of Southern California. One day this extremely sexy girl was watching practice. She had on tight shorts, a revealing blouse, and an, uh, effective walk. Actually, she was dating one of the players, and after practice the guy called Staubach over and said, "Roger, you're a Catholic so I thought you'd like to meet Sister Teresa."

Roger Staubach was always scrambling and finding new ways to make yardage. Here he tries passing off the back of a camel. (Dallas Cowboys photo)

Roger was very polite and respectful. But later he said, "I knew I'd never seen a nun who looked like that. But I kept thinking, maybe she really was. So I fell for it. The girl told me she was on leave from a convent. I went around the entire camp thinking she was a nun. Whenever I'd see her, I'd say, 'Hello, Sister Teresa.' Can you imagine how those guys were laughing at me?"

Craig Morton sneaked two lovelies into Roger's room in the dorm one night. The lights were out and he was sound asleep, dreaming of throwing touchdown passes or some such. He felt something pressing on the foot of his bed. He woke up. He smelled perfume and, realizing the situation didn't have anything to do with throwing touchdown passes, opened his eyes. His eyes bugged, his heart jumped. He pulled the covers up to his chin.

"Uh, uh, uhh, I'm married and have kids," he said. "What are you doing in here?"

"Oh, so you're Roger Staubach," one commented. To which Roger answered, "Can I show you pictures of my kids?"

His teammates in the hall doubled up laughing as the girls left Staubach's room. When he recovered, he laughed too. A teammate said, "I wish somebody had sneaked them into my room."

Roger later got big laughs from his teammate when he was retired and said, "Well, guys, the things I'll miss most are the booze and broads."

— ❏ —

Staubach used to drive defensive players crazy scrambling, especially during his early years. He'd start this way, come back the other way, retreat, etc. Asked how in the world you blocked for Staubach, Garrison commented, "You just stay where you are because he'll be back sooner or later."

It took Roger twenty years, but he finally retaliated at a roast in 2001 for Walt. "If you needed a yard, you always gave Walt the ball," said Roger. "If you needed a yard and a half, you gave it to somebody else."

Even Landry didn't escape Staubach's pranks. Tom was a determined guy who kept jogging and working out in spite of having a terrible knee. I can still see him jogging with a discernable limp around the track. Sometimes if a player showed bad technique or wasn't executing a play exactly as Landry wanted, Tom would step right in and demonstrate the proper way.

He didn't like the way Staubach was running a play in practice. "No, no, no, Roger," said Landry. "Let me show you how to do it." Landry showed Roger how the play should be run and told him, "Now do it exactly as I did."

"Yessir," said Roger, who then ran the play with a limp.

During a game in Texas Stadium, Landry's arms were folded and he seemed to be staring at the sky showing through the hole in the roof at Texas Stadium. Staubach, standing nearby, said, "Now I know where you get your plays, coach."

— ❑ —

One afternoon in the summer of 1976, Roger was in the club's offices, which were then on the eleventh floor of the Expressway Towers. He was waiting to see Schramm. And waiting and waiting. Finally Roger took

matters into his own hands as he tended to do on the field. He located a side door in the hall, which led out onto the ledge surrounding the building. He went through the door onto the ledge, about three feet wide, and slowly made his way around to Schramm's office window.

Typically, Tex was leaning back in his chair, staring out the window while talking on a conference call, this particular time to two NFL owners. He noted the clear blue sky, chatted idly, and briefly pondered cloud movements. Then he gasped, his eyes widened, and his heart skipped a few beats and he shot up in his chair like he was being ejected. There was Roger Staubach, the franchise quarterback, looking through the window at him from the eleventh floor ledge! Schramm dropped the telephone.

"I had walked around the building and was behind a pillar out there," said Roger. "Then I just jumped into his view. He did turn a little white. I guess I got his attention. Oh no, there was no danger out there. I had plenty of room, except maybe when I went around that pillar."

Schramm regained his composure somewhat, motioned Roger off the ledge, then picked up the phone off the floor. When the caller asked him what happened, Tex told him, "Oh nothing. My quarterback is just jumping around on the ledge outside my window. Eleven floors up!"

— ❏ —

In training camp Schramm would have let his hair down if he'd had any. Tex was hardly the tower of unyielding innocence, but there were two episodes in which he was certainly in the right place at the right time and then innocently in the wrong place.

A small gathering was with Schramm at the "Levee" in Westlake after midnight. Schramm liked to sit outside on the patio, adjacent to the lake, and ponder and philosophize. It was peaceful and quiet, and when nobody talked you could hear faint sounds from the condos and apartments across the lake. Then a yell broke the peace, the tranquility.

"NELVA! NEEELVA, COME BACK!"

There was a faint splash in the water, and as the yells for Nelva continued, someone was approaching the shore right at the Levee. A sea-maiden rose from the water near Schramm's chair. She was naked.

Schramm blinked, then coolly grabbed a tablecloth from a nearby table and handed it to the woman. "I was, sure, a little shocked to discover she didn't have on any clothes," he later explained. When grilled what he had said to her, Schramm noted, "Well, hell. Just what am I supposed to say to a naked woman who suddenly comes out of the water near my table. I couldn't think of anything to say." Sorry, the story ends. Nelva left, disappearing into the night.

Schramm and club officials were invited to a poolside party in Thousand Oaks and were friendly, mingling with all the guests who couldn't get enough of the Dallas Cowboys. Schramm was entertaining a group when he was told this woman wanted to meet him. Obliging as usual he met the woman and sat down to chat with her. He felt something hit him over the head and was soon on the ground. He looked up to see this man with a crazed look holding a chair. In this instance Cowboy officials were as quick as the players as they pulled off the attacker and ushered Schramm away.

Schramm was treated for his injury and had a bad headache the next day. It was later learned that the man was the hotheaded, jealous estranged husband of the woman. He had been drinking heavily and followed her and her escort to the party. He'd sat outside the house, sipping some more, as he stood all he could and then charged into the midst of the party. He saw his wife talking to a man he presumed to be her escort. He did not know it was Schramm so he clobbered Tex with a chair. Schramm was glad the guy didn't have a gun, and he never saw the lovely couple again.

— ❑ —

Craig Morton was one of the good guys who looked the part of a star. He was 6'4", 215, and had dark, handsome features that women, I believe, call devilish; he dressed fashionably, drove a nice car, and to borrow a

Jimmy Webb phrase, lived in "that beautiful balloon."

I think Ray Shafer, a personable little guy who printed programs, brochures, etc., for the Cowboys, captured Craig best. Ray had just undergone an eye operation, was wearing a patch, and was not feeling all that great. His wife had to drive him around. She parked their used Volkswagen in front of the Cowboy offices, and Ray was just getting out of the car when Morton strolled past. Craig sauntered over to his new flashy car and got in beside a most ravishing member of the opposite sex and drove away.

Ray, shaking his head slowly, turned to his wife and said, "Honey, tell me one more time that all men are created equal."

I'll always remember chatting with Craig after practice one afternoon and mentioning one of my sons, Rob, was playing football on a kid's team. Craig asked the location of their practice and showed up one afternoon. The kids freaked out as Craig hung around for over an hour, talking to them and throwing them passes.

— ❑ —

Tom Landry, Craig Morton, and Don Meredith discuss strategy, while Pete Gent ponders life and scratches his neck. (Dallas Cowboys photo)

Craig was in a supporting role with Lance Rentzel, who devised a dummy with coat hangers and extra pillows and covered up so they could sneak out of the dorm undetected. In darkened rooms they figured Dick Nolan, the assistant who checked rooms to make sure players didn't break curfew, would be fooled. Their cover was blown when Dick came by a little early and Rentzel, in the process of sneaking out, leaped on the bed with the dummy and was in the process of pulling up the covers when Dick walked in.

"I bet you're wondering why I'm in bed with my clothes on with coat hangers and extra pillows?" said Rentzel who, like Morton, was fined.

Once I was jogging up the hill, more like a small mountain, behind the practice field at Cal Lutheran in Thousand Oaks. Groups of players ran the grueling jaunt up the trail, which went behind a huge rock at the crest and then led back down near the practice field. As I got to the top behind the rocks, there was Craig, sitting down smoking a cigarette. He'd planned to rest then blend in with the next group. He grinned and said hello, and I went on around the rock and down the hill. A headline today might read: Cowboy Quarterback Puffs at Conditioning.

— ❏ —

I was fortunate to be around Don Perkins the final two years of his career. He was a very intelligent guy with a straight-faced sense of humor, which he dropped like a thunderbolt at the strangest times. There was certainly prejudice in Dallas during those days of the late 1960s, and Don would speak out against it. But around the team he was just Don Perkins, a well-liked teammate.

Once in the Cotton Bowl against New Orleans, Don was tackled and sent skidding face down across the white chalk lines marking yardage. He got up and trotted back to the huddle with the chalk all over his face, and his teammates started laughing about how funny he looked.

Without changing his expression, Don said, "Well, I finally made it."

In a game against St. Louis, Danny Reeves was hit hard on the sidelines and knocked out of bounds by the Cowboys bench. Suddenly one of the tacklers reached down and grabbed the soft part of Danny's leg and squeezed the heck out of him.

"Ouch! Ouch! Stop that!" said Danny. Landry looked at Danny calmly, paused for a few seconds, and walked away.

Danny went back into the huddle as 70,000 fans in the Cotton Bowl cheered his grit, his desire. Teammates asked him what happened, and Danny told them, "Why, that sonuva-buck pinched me. It hurt."

There were a few snickers and Don said, "Oh that's all right, Danny. I'll goose him on the next play."

— ❏ —

In the early days of the team, Mount Vernon native Don "Dandy" Meredith served as quarterback punching bag because blocking was mostly a state of Landry's mind. Once, Don was blindsided and knocked flat to the ground, twisting slowly in pain as trainers Larry Gardner and Don Cochren rushed on the field to get the remains.

"Why oh why...oh why did I ever do it?" said Don.

"Geeze, Dandy," asked Larry, "tell us. Why what?"

Meredith lifted his head, grinned, and said, "Why did I ever leave Mount Vernon?"

There was the time when Don was a rookie that he uttered the immortal audible at the line of scrimmage. Don's worst nemesis was New York Giants middle linebacker Sam Huff, one of the league's toughest, give-no-quarter players. When he would blitz unblocked or supposedly blocked and crash into Don, it was a shot heard round the stadium.

Don was at the line of scrimmage calling signals as Huff crept closer to blitz. Don looked at him, tried to think of what to do, and said, "Red right...uh, oh, s---, time out!"

When Don had torn stomach muscles, he wore a bag of reddish fluid around his waist. This would at least keep the muscles warm and allow him to operate in less pain. Sure enough, Huff broke through and not only blasted him but busted the bag. Red fluid was all over Don's stomach.

"My God!" said Huff. "What did I do?"

"Looks like you killed me, Sam," said Don. "Looks like it's all over."

"No! I'm sorry, so...."

Then Don started laughing.

Don was quick and sharp and never at a loss for words. Well, there was the time in training camp when brash rookie running back Dick Smith furnished us with some ink. Meredith missed Dick on a passing route, and the rookie came back to the huddle and said, "Hey man, I thought you were supposed to be an NFL quarterback! Can't you throw!"

All Meredith could say was, "I don't believe this. I just don't believe it."

Dick didn't make the team. What a shame.

— ❏ —

I was not completely beyond exaggerating or otherwise for

the sake of a lighthearted story. I was sorry Pete Gent left the team after my first couple of years covering the Cowboys because he was such a clever guy. Pete, like Cornell Green, didn't play football in college but rather starred in basketball. In those days Gil Brandt was finding basketball players, trackmen, and good athletes who would make excellent football players.

Pete had tremendous hands as a receiver and was fearless catching the ball crossing the middle. He had a local television show, and once after he'd been benched he was pointing out things to viewers on a blackboard. Then he marked an X completely off the blackboard and said, "That's me here."

Once he told a rookie not to bother finishing Landry's huge playbook "because everybody dies at the end anyway." He was funny but when I couldn't find him once he later told me it was okay to say whatever I wanted as long as it was funny.

— ❏ —

When I was a senior at North Dallas High School, I decided to read a chapter of *Something of*

Value, a fine book by Robert Ruark. I couldn't put the book down and read to daylight before studying fast and furious for a test. Somehow I passed the exam, probably because of a benevolent teacher.

At the beginning of the book Ruark quoted a Basuto proverb: "If a man does away with his traditional way of living and throws away his good customs, he had better first make certain that he has something of value to replace them."

I never forgot that quote and sometimes would make up Basuto proverbs and sneak them into my sports column. When Pete Gent visited Honduras, he bought a banana tree. Sadly, the tree died. So I led a column on Pete with an italic lead which went something like this: *"If you seek a ba-na-na tree in Honduras and it dies, den you havv no ba-na-nas. – A Basuto proverb."*

— ❏ —

A Cowboys game with the Bears in Chicago was interrupted when a rabbit, of all things, ran across the field. Vicious, mean, brutal Dick Butkus was the terror of the league. After he tackled somebody he tried to gore them. So I wrote he stomped the rabbit then picked it up and ate it before play resumed. One night when I was watching "The Tonight Show" with Johnny Carson, he used the line about Butkus.

It's great flattery when your lines or ideas are pilfered, and like most writers, I've been on both sides of that issue. Curt Mosher and Cowboy scout Bob Griffin, with a lot of help from Walt Garrison, started collecting lines from C&W songs, such as "I bought those shoes that are walkin' out on me" or "I offered her my ring and all she gave me was the finger." When Doug Todd came along, he took it to another level and even collected them in a book. So I wrote a couple of columns about the C&W lines, which was a stretch for a sports column.

Later John Anders used my idea with some of the same C&W lines in a column, which was mentioned on "The Tonight Show." Any ideas I've stolen from him never got mentioned on the "The Tonight Show."

— ❏ —

Besides being a constant candidate for the Distinguished Soup Nose Award, the late Doug Todd was one of those unforgettable people loved by all. I doubt there was a more popular public relations director in the National Football League. He had the best, quickest sense of humor of anybody I've ever met. This even overshadowed the fine job he did for the Cowboys, including being instrumental in bringing about the title "America's Team."

Doug came up with phrases that we all use today. If somebody such as overweight Frank Glieber studied the menu too long, Doug would tell the waiter, "He'll have Page 2, medium rare." Doug stopped drinking after having liver problems, but when he was still downing the sauce, he'd hold up four fingers to the bartender and say, "I'll have one more."

Another favorite trick was when a particular member of our group would arrive late for dinner at a restaurant. Doug would have everybody ready, and when the tardy guy would sit down, everybody would get up and leave.

If someone became upset because Doug didn't have enough details about a situation, he would reply, "I deal in concepts, not details."

I loved the John Wayne movie *True Grit* and so did Doug. He could do a great impression of John Wayne and Robert Duvall, playing Rooster Cogburn and Lucky Ned Pepper during the showdown. "Aw call that bold talk for uh one-eyed fat man." He could also mimic Schramm, Landry, Joe Bailey, and probably the rest of us.

Doug lost his job when Jerry Jones took over the Cowboys and brought in his own people or hired new ones. He and his wife, Marti, moved to Chicago, and he died at the age of fifty-three on June 3, 1997. His humor didn't.

— ❏ —

When Cornell Green was a rookie, he kept complaining of a sore hip during training camp. Equipment manager Jack Eskridge finally checked it out. It turned out Cornell wasn't that familiar with football equipment because he'd been a basketball player and had been wearing his hip pads backwards. That's a true story.

I can't remember how it started, but I once wrote that Cornell, who had become one of the NFL's outstanding cornerbacks, said he had never been beaten on a pass. When reminded that indeed he had a number of times, Cornell purportedly said, "Well, if I did I talked myself out of it coming off the field." The quote was repeated in newspapers around the country.

"Cornell was a good guy and an outstanding player, but all the years I talked to him I never got all these funny anecdotes you did," said Luksa. "I wonder why?"

— ❏ —

The most obscure, ignored inner team organization was the exclusive, lethargic Zero Club, which glorified anonymity and enlightened indifference. Members were Larry Cole, Blaine Nye, and Pat Toomay. They banned together because generally they felt ignored by fans, their teammates, and coaches. Seldom were they asked for autographs, and when one of

Cornell Green prepared for his football career by playing basketball. He became an All-Pro when he stopped wearing his hip pads backwards. (PR photo Utah State)

them actually signed their name for a fan, he or she would respond, "Who?"

Meetings were held during training camp in a member's dorm room, but nobody ever really had the floor because they would assume a prone position and do nothing. On occasion someone would speak, just above a whisper, but one of their mottoes was the less said the

Larry Cole sadly ponders his lost anonymity as a member of the Zero Club after scoring yet another touchdown. (Dallas Cowboys photo)

better spoken or something like that.

Cole was elected official non-spokesman for the group and forever optimized its spirit when he ran for city council in Bedford, where he then resided. When asked what the results were, Larry said, "I got just what I went after. I was defeated."

Their chronicler was none other than my roommate Frank Luksa, and I can vouch he was the perfect, understanding person for the job. Sadly, the ugly face of notoriety reared its head, and the Zero Club dissolved as Toomay was traded and became an author, guard Blaine Nye made one of the All-Pro teams (1972) and was named to the Pro Bowl (1974), and Cole started scoring touchdowns.

You've probably forgotten, but during Cole's thirteen years with the Cowboys he scored an unheard-of (for a lineman) four touchdowns, all coming against the Washington Redskins, which stacked their offense to stop him. His final gallop for pay dirt came his final season in 1980. He said it was no accident, that a great deal of planning and work went into the timely execution that resulted in the score.

As Redskin second-string quarterback Mike Kruczek tried to pass, tackle Randy White crashed into him. The ball squirted out, hitting a charging Cole in the face. Larry, who said he had it all the way, reached up and managed to pull the ball out of his facemask and take off like a bear on ice skates for the goal line, forty-three yards away. As he headed in turtle speed for the goal line and big No. 4, he claimed his jealous teammates from the defensive line were the most dangerous tackles after him. But he broke loose from Jethro Pugh, Randy White, and others and made the end zone. Once he scored there was some question as to whether he spiked himself or the ball. Later watching films, he modestly commented, "I must say I was impressed with myself."

— ❏ —

I did a lot of stupid things when I covered the team, but my smartest moves were to make friends with the team physicians, beginning with Dr.

Marvin Knight and later working my way to Dr. J. Pat Evans, who is still my friend as is Dr. J. R. Zamorano. You'll probably be surprised to learn I was always getting hurt so I latched onto Dr. Knight when I was first on the beat.

Dr. Marvin Knight was a character in his own right. He was a nationally respected orthopedist and had won the Legion of Merit for innovative surgery while serving in the Army Medical Corps in the South Pacific during World War II. So he was a crusty, straightforward guy who had little sympathy for complaints of the players.

For Bobby Hayes the thought of pain was worse than the pain itself. Dr. Knight inserted a wire-like pin to hold Bob's separated shoulder together while it healed. Knowing how fearful Bob was about having it taken out, Dr. Knight walked up to him one day and started manipulating his shoulder. Then he suddenly jerked the pin out. It was over before Bob could hurt.

Pete Gent had drawn Dr. Knight's ire several times with his joking around attitude and because he wore his hair long. Pete had an ankle injury, which required surgery. Just as Pete was being put to sleep, Dr. Knight put a pair of shears on his lower stomach and smiled.

My personal experience came after Dr. Knight operated on my back in 1970. It had been bothering me for years, but I decided to get it fixed when I went up for a jump shot and froze in mid-air. He kept me in the hospital for a long time, and I started growing a beard. When it was time for me to check out, he came into the room, looked at my beard, and said, "I'm not letting you out of here until you shave that stupid-looking beard."

I laughed and said, "Sure."

"Goodbye," he said and started walking out of the room.

"Come back! Come back! I'm shaving right now." And I did.

With Dr. Knight's permission, I wrote a column about him. The American Medical Association didn't like some of his methods and wrote him a letter. When I heard about the letter I asked him about it, and he said, "I don't give a s---!"

Friday Night Madness

"Can you believe that? They hanged me in effigy."

—Burle Pettit

The first real baptism of fire for most sportswriters is covering high school football, which in many parts of Texas ranks right up there with the flag, motherhood, honor, and apple pie. You develop a number of characteristics that certainly help you in later life no matter what field of endeavor you might pursue. You learn such things as humility, flexibility, sleight of hand, how to keep your sense of humor when all about you are losing theirs,

and that perspective blinds reality.

High school football in small towns is a social event, the most important happening on any given Friday night. A town will literally vibrate for a game played by, say, the Hereford White Faces or the White Face Herefords. Nicknames of high school teams abound, but you'd best not take them lightly around the local gentry. When John Anders, tongue in cheek, decided to give schoolboy teams new names in his column, some small-town residents thought he'd insulted the American flag. His list included Odem Golden Slippers, Hellena Hand Baskets, the Eden Ups...well you get the idea. Anyway, towns are fiercely loyal to high school players and even their team mascots.

During his younger days Tom Williams, then with the *Waco News-Tribune,* had a most unusual experience covering the Fighting High School Goats one Friday night in Groesbeck, a small town just east of Waco. As well might happen in a small town, Tom found the press box filled to capacity with school officials, relatives, various citizens, pet animals, and perhaps a member of the local media. So Tom improvised and gallantly walked the sidelines with pen and pad, scribbling notes.

During the course of the game he suddenly felt something tugging at his pants leg. It was none other than the team mascot, the Groesbeck goat, pulling and chewing on his trousers. Tom tried to jerk his leg free, but this only angered the determined animal, which then bit him on the leg.

"OUCH-OUCH-OUCH!" screamed Tom, his voice lost amid yells of the nearby cheerleaders. So there was Tom hopping and trying to jerk free from the beloved goat. The way one of the cheerleaders saw it,

Tom was kicking the Groesbeck goat. "Hey, leave our goat alone!" she yelled. Gradually, people in the stands saw this stranger attacking their goat.

The cheerleaders got the crowd behind them, and everybody started booing poor Tom, calling him names, and some even chanted, "RAH-RAH-RAH, LET OUR GOAT GO! LET GO OUR GOAT. RAH-RAH-RAH." Well, fans helped the goat escape the grasp of Tom's pants and led it to safety. There were threats of reporting Tom to the humane society. Finally he was warned in uncertain terms to get out of town and never come back.

"That was the fastest story I ever wrote," Tom observed. "And I never gave a thought of going back to town."

— ❏ —

Burle Pettit, longtime executive editor, who retired in January 2000 as editor in chief of the *Lubbock Avalanche-Journal,* was the only guy I ever heard of covering high school football who was hanged in effigy, ordinarily a fate for coaches, politicians, and straying husbands. But Burle suffered the wrath of fans at Idalou, near Lubbock, and learned to have a thick skin while covering high school football, if not to turn the other cheek. He too had trouble finding a seat in the press box and failed in his effort to nudge between two school officials. As a young man Burle often bragged about his ability to keep cool so he kicked an occupied chair, stunning the occupant, and uttered choice words as he stormed out of the press box, refusing to walk the sidelines. He went back to the *Avalanche-Journal*, and instead of a game story wrote about the problems covering a game in Idalou with press box seats reserved for everybody but journalists.

Shortly thereafter Burle received a picture in the mail from Idalou. It showed his likeness swinging from a tree with a note reading, "Sorry you couldn't have attended this hanging in person."

"Can you believe that, being hanged in effigy in Idalou," he said.

Previously Burle, six months removed from graduation at North Texas, saved his money after a Spartan college life and purchased the best $25.50 suit money could buy. He had a degree; he had that new suit and wore it proudly to a high school game in Amarillo. That night he was especially slow finishing his story, trying to capture the essence of the game in words. Other reporters were gone. Burle Pettit was alone in the press box. Suddenly all the lights went out. So did the lights in the stadium. Pettit cursed, yelled. Had a fit. He got his gear, stumbled in the dark out of the press box, and by the light of no doubt a full moon, found his way to the gate in a ten-foot cyclone fence. It was locked tight.

There was no choice. He started climbing while carrying his briefcase and thirty-five-pound typewriter. Near the top he almost fell, swinging out on one arm and managing to toss the typewriter over the fence. "I hate my life!" he recalled yelling into the darkness. But gamely he made it to the top. Unfortunately barbed wire was around the top of the fence, and as he climbed over to the other side he heard this ripping sound. He had torn the heck out of the best

$25.50 suit money could buy. He started yelling again, and finally the night watchman came. I cannot tell you what Burle told him because, heaven forbid, children might read this book.

— ❏ —

Popular *Fort Worth Star-Telegram* columnist Randy Galloway once covered high school football and learned a valuable lesson about the better part of valor, which of course he soon forgot. Randy had written a story telling how Frisco had won a particular game on a "fluke play." The backlash of the term he used was evident when he returned to Frisco for a game the following Friday. Now in order to reach the press box in those days you had to climb a shaky ladder, lugging all your equipment. As Randy got halfway up the ladder he heard this voice from above saying, "That story you wrote last week was the worst trash I ever read. Pure trash." Then he felt someone shaking the ladder. He almost fell but managed to hang on and make it to the top, angry and out of breath.

Randy was about to tell the guy what he thought of him when he noticed his adversary was maybe 6'4", 250. The man was a bear, someone who could certainly shake a man with a typewriter off a ladder. "Uh," said Randy, "that was the worst story I ever wrote. Trash. Pure trash."

— ❏ —

Jim Brannan, who covered high school football for the *Dallas Times-Herald*, was dispatched to Wichita Falls to cover a high school playoff game. This was the town in which *Wichita Falls Times and Record-News* sportswriter Ted Leach once so adamantly disagreed with an official's call against the hometown basketball team that he charged on the court and got into a fight with the guy. It's not that Ted was prejudiced toward the home team, but if you called him a "homer" he thought it was a compliment. Jim was more objective.

The superintendent of schools had sent him a press pass for the game. But the super hadn't signed the pass, which was only a formality at best.

Now Jim had driven from Dallas to Wichita Falls and had to walk a mile to the stadium lugging his equipment because the media area of the parking lot was full. Only local high school writers had parking privileges. So the guy at the gate told him he couldn't enter because there was no signature on his pass.

"To heck with you, I'm going in," said Jim. The man said, "No you're not." Jim started through the gate. The man drew back and smacked him upside the head, knocking him to the ground. Stunned and shaken, Jim righted himself and decided it was best to try to reason with the man. He finally was able to contact an official in the press box and allowed to cover the game. As best as I can determine the guard was never reprimanded for punching Jim. Had it been the other way around, I suspect Jim would have been in trouble.

— ❑ —

I had worked my way through school on the night shift at the Corporation Court in Dallas and was on a first-name basis with officers, lawyers, criminals, and street people. When someone was arrested for whatever crime, we'd check to see if they had any outstanding tickets or warrants on their way to jail. So after graduation I took a job, which paid less than I was making as assistant supervisor of the night court, as a hard-hitting crime reporter-feature writer for the *San Angelo Standard-Times*. Hey, I'd been around detectives and criminals in my job so I knew a thing or two about solving crimes. Instead of being an ace crime reporter, as there were no murders or such, I mostly wrote obits. However, I was to become the most notorious, talked-about obit writer in the history of the newspaper.

The publisher and owner of the *Standard-Times* was Houston Harte, who also had interests in other newspapers with the Harte-Hanks group. Once one of Mr. Harte's dear friends died, and the man from the funeral parlor happened to get me when he called in information for the obit. I took down the data, including survivors, pallbearers, and the day, time, and place where the funeral would be held.

The story, still told today by those who worked on the paper at that time, becomes hazy and the different versions have taken on a life of their own. One that seemed most accurate was that Mr. Harte showed up at the funeral in great mourning. His dear deceased friend had been rather well-to-do, as of course was Mr. Harte. Yet people at the funeral did not appear to be so well off. But perhaps that was just Mr. Harte's imagination. One version had him actually viewing the body of a total stranger and almost going into shock before he stormed out of the funeral parlor. I'd gotten everything in the obit right except the day of the funeral, although I was close, informing readers such as Mr. Harte that it was on Wednesday when actually it was on Thursday.

Fortunately, I was off that day when he came charging into the office, yelling for the hide of the stupid reporter who got the wrong day on the obit. Managing editor Ed Hunter, who went on to hold that position at the *Houston Post*, saved my job. Thanks to sports editor Dub Brown, shortly thereafter I switched to sports. Nothing special happened, and anybody could have been driving one of Mr. Harte's three staff cars to a track meet in Eldorado, missed a turn, and flipped the vehicle down an embankment. Well at least everybody knew who I was, and I was only there less than a year before Jay Harris at the *Lubbock Avalanche-Journal* called and hired me after my North Texas classmate Burle Pettit told him I was a good writer and very steady and dependable.

— ❑ —

In Lubbock during the early 1960s I covered the Lubbock High School Westerners, while Burle covered the Monterrey High School team. During that time of the linotype machines, copy was set in lines of lead type and then placed in the frame of a page to be printed. If you wrote a story and wanted the backshop to put statistics below a Lubbock High story, you would just write a tag line, "PU Westerners" for pick up the Westerners stats. So at the end of a Lubbock High game I wrote, "PU Westerners." Unfortunately for me somebody in the backshop had failed to take out the "PU Westerners" line. The next day a delegation from Lubbock High came to the office. They were very angry and suggested in heated words that I should be fired for saying the Westerners STUNK. I explained as best I could what happened and was forgiven, although I suspect never forgotten by the Lubbock High Class of '62.

So as you might gather, sometimes fact is stranger than fiction. Actually, in the wacky world of sportswriters in those days, sometimes fiction was stranger than fact.

— ❑ —

There was a fierce rivalry between the *San Antonio Light* and the *San Antonio News*, which sneaky *Light* sports editor Harold Scherwitz exploited every chance he got. A very important part of the competition was high school coverage in which a talented, concerned Perry Winkle threw himself heart and soul into the fray against the *Light.*

This did not go unnoticed by Harold Scherwitz, the sports editor of the *Light*, whose enthusiasm for his job was unmatched except, perhaps, by his penchant for mischief and scheming against the rival newspaper. Perhaps Scherwitz' greatest invention was a rip-snorting, hard-running fullback named Albert Stuneros of Agua Dulce, Tex. Stuneros became the greatest high school back never to have played the game. His legendary feats were eagerly documented by none other than Perry Winkle, who would take calls each week from an equally enthusiastic correspondent in Agua Dulce. Poor kid did not know the correspondent was Scherwitz, deftly disguising his voice and reporting how Stuneros had once again led Agua Dulce to breathtaking victory. Why, there was even a good chance at the end of the season that Stuneros would be named to Winkle's high school all-star team, which he called the All-Iron Man Team. This certainly wouldn't be easy because Winkle had set very high standards. A youngster had to be more than an outstanding athlete. He also had to be an outstanding citizen, an A-student.

Scherwitz made sure he was. He compiled outstanding statistics for the seventeen-year-old phenom and lofty comments from others lauding his fine character and contributions to the community. Then he had the art department at the *Light* touch up a photograph of an unknown college running back in case Winkle wanted to run a picture of the fabulous Stuneros. Well, Stuneros made poor Perry's heralded team. Scherwitz couldn't stop. He wrote Winkle a letter thanking him for his undying support of Stuneros and naming the lad to his All-Iron Man Team. He signed the letter, "Hokie Carmichael, head coach at Dulce High."

Winkle even invited Coach Carmichael to attend the banquet honoring the team and decided to check to see exactly where the proud community of Agua Dulce was located. It wasn't. There was, of course,

> **Perhaps Scherwitz' greatest invention was a rip-snorting, hard-running fullback named Albert Stuneros of Agua Dulce ...eagerly documented by none other than Perry Winkle.**

no such place. If you have not gotten the full impact of the legendary name, spell it backwards.

— ❑ —

In that memorable fall of 1968, Larry Powell was sent by his employer, the *Shreveport Times*, to cover the opening high school football game of the season at Fair Park Stadium on the state fair grounds of that fine city bordering Texas, just inside the Louisiana state line. Larry was twenty and had left his hometown of Texarkana to conquer the world. He smiled and nodded happy greetings to the early arrivals as he made his way up through the stands to the top of the stadium and arrived at the press box entrance. You've got to be kidding me, he thought as he looked at his route to the press box, a ladder-like staircase 100 feet off the ground in a steel cage welded to a wall of the stadium.

"It was death-defying, terrifying," he recalled. "But I took a deep breath and ventured into the abyss onto the shaky staircase." He slowly climbed the ladder, hanging on as if the ladder were the love of his life, while pondering the erratic reputation of some Louisiana construction companies. Maybe the concrete would crack and the whole thing would come apart. But he made it and figured the worst part was over before remembering that he who comes up must go down after the game.

"There was no way I could enjoy the game because going back down it would be dark, I'd fall to my death and splat on the parking lot with my damned portable typewriter in one hand and my other hand frozen like a broken wing because my final effort was to try to fly. And I'd miss my deadline, the ultimate humility."

Coverage was *heavy* with Larry and one other guy from the rival *Shreveport Journal* in a press box that seated 25-30 writers. The other guy had been there before and knew how to turn on the lights so they could see. As the game began they smelled smoke. Larry, using those quick, perceptive skills that would one day make him a proper columnist for *The Dallas Morning News*, immediately surmised it wasn't coming from cigarettes because neither of them was smoking.

He looked up. Smoke was coming out of a light fixture, which had shorted out. So were hundreds of red wasps, angry that the smoke interrupted their lives in nests they built during the summer when the stadium was empty. Larry froze momentarily, but his alert counterpart grabbed a newspaper, rolled it up, and swatted wasps as he courageously fought his way to the telephone, located near the flaming fixture. He phoned for help while asking Larry what was happening on the field. Larry didn't care because he was dodging wasps. They opened the windows because even sportswriters can't survive without oxygen. And about ten minutes later a fire crew showed up, spraying the wasps and dousing the fire.

After the game ended Larry was able to hug and kiss his way down the ladder, hurry back to the office, and write his story. He imagined the headlines: Sportswriter Defies Flames, Billowing Smoke, and Angry Wasps to Get Story. But there was no mention of the courageous young man in the story, much less the headlines. The experience inspired Larry, who had once read Grantland Rice, to ponder and compose his own immortal line:

"It matters not whether you win or lose but only the stupid difficulty in which the damn game was covered."

Becoming Unscrewed

When I was at *The Dallas Morning News,* we were caught in or rather embraced the madness surrounding our business and threw ourselves under the wheels of our profession and life in general. So it didn't take much coaxing for us to try to live up to, or down as it were, the image of the old-time sportswriters, the hard-drinking, hard-living guys, some of whom were excellent writers. Those who were bad or awful writers didn't know they were so it didn't make any difference.

Author Mike Shropshire (*Seasons in Hell*) escaped the profession with the Ghost Riders in the Sky posse on his tail and reflected back on those days. After leaving college he immediately attempted to become an extension of his predecessors. He'd read where Grantland Rice admitted in his autobiography he had gone to the first Jack Dempsey-Gene Tunney championship fight in 1926 too drunk to write and had to hire a wire service guy to do his story. Unfortunately, the wire service guy was a joker and wrote that the fight was fixed, not exactly endearing Rice to Tunney, the winner.

"If a legendary sportswriter like him had that attitude, why shouldn't I," said Mike. The thing was Mike tried to take it to a higher (or lower) level. One day he picked up a copy of *Readers Digest* in the barbershop and glanced at a story titled "Are You an Alcoholic?"

"There was this test of questions, you know, like, 'Do you occasionally drink to enhance your enjoyment on certain social occasions?' Stuff like that. So finally I go down the list and get to question No. 14 before I could answer, 'no.' The question was, 'Do you ever hide whiskey in your home?' No, why should I? A man's home is his castle and there was whiskey in every room. Then there was the usual stuff like, 'Did you ever drive over Niagara Falls? Did you ever set your hair on fire?' Well, I got four pretty solid 'no's' there at the end and was feeling pretty good about myself. Then I read if you answered ANY of these questions 'yes' you were really a screwed-up alcoholic."

A few years ago Mike started "Sportswriters Anonymous," which he said was dedicated to helping people kick the profession, although he added there was little need considering how sportswriters are nowadays. He remains the founder and only member at this writing.

Some drank more than others; some of us saved our madness for weekends on the road on Friday and/or Saturday nights and/or special occasions defined in the eye of the beholder. Our inner circle at the newspaper played, partied, joked, and laughed at ourselves and others within our reach. We married, had children, sometimes divorced, and survived, although it's difficult to figure out how.

We had a lot of fun, no doubt real and imagined, and I'm glad I was there at that time and place and got out alive. We were players, characters in our own right in the arenas we covered, not just businesslike professionals. We told stories about the antics of players and, to a degree, they told stories about our extracurricular activities. Our jobs notwithstanding, we also tried to

A person with various talents, Mike Shropshire visits with game show host Monty Hall after winning the world's smallest television set on *Let's Make a Deal*. Mike thoughtfully narrowed down the time the photo was taken, believing it was a twenty-year period between the 1960s and 1980s.

coach and scout. I remember arguing with Cowboy assistant Jerry Tubbs that a rookie named Thomas Henderson should start, and having a long discussion in training camp with a disgruntled first-year player named Harvey Martin, who was ready to leave. Harvey stayed. Thomas finally made the starting lineup and touched stardom with tremendous potential. Then he was let go after self-destructing on drugs and booze.

And Steve Perkins actually discovered Australian transplant Colin Ridgway, a soccer player and track guy from Abilene Christian, and strongly suggested the Cowboys sign him. Steve predicted Colin would lead the NFL in punting. The Cowboys did sign him, and Colin did indeed have amazing power. Known as "Boomer" for his long distance kicks in practice, he lost his career in San Francisco.

You see, Boomer had never played football, and gridiron pressure was a stranger. During a preseason game in that City by the Bay, the Cowboys were backed up to their own 15-yard-line so Landry turned to the young Aussie to kick his mates

out of trouble. Now there was a strong wind, not at all unusual in San Francisco, blowing into Boomer's face. But he planted his foot solidly into the ball. A beauty! Up, up, up it climbed.

"That sonuvagun's hit pretty darn good, by jove," Boomer recalled thinking. Films showed Harold Hays taking off on punt coverage as if being chased by a pack of wolves. Hayes gradually began to slow down and bend backwards as he looked for the ball. The wind had stopped the ball's flight and sent it back toward Colin. Soon Hays fell flat on his back. Kerplunk! Others stared upward as if looking for flying saucers.

Meanwhile, Colin was thinking, "My god! That sonuvagun's coming back. Save me soul!"

What could Boomer do? Nobody had taught him how to signal for a fair catch. He stood frozen in his tracks while a stunned 49er lineman picked up the mysterious football that had dropped out of the sky and ran it back to the 16. The ball had traveled five yards, a club record. Sometime thereafter coaches stopped taking our advice, although we were always ready to give it.

— ❏ —

By socializing with club officials I learned things about the nuances of pro football. For instance, Tex Schramm was always ready to enlighten a person over cocktails after practice or at dinner during training camp, although disagreements did arise. But he would offer helpful insights into players, scouting, operation of the club, and the NFL. However, he was not always so insightful about other matters.

There was the time at dinner during training camp when we got into a discussion about how our nation was divided by the war in Vietnam. Tex volunteered that things were different during his time, World War II, because the country was united regardless of race, creed, or religion.

"Well, right here in your native California, the government took Japanese-Americans out of their homes and placed them in internment camps," I said. "These included mostly people born and raised in the United States."

His face reddened as it does before he erupts and he said, "You're commenting on something you know nothing about!"

Curt Mosher, then the team's publicity director, said, "I think he's right, Tex. I had this Japanese friend in the army, and he was very bitter about what happened to his parents during the war!"

"You don't know either!" yelled Tex. "You be quiet! Why, the Japanese-Americans understood! They didn't mind!"

The following morning the *Los Angeles Times* had a story in which former Justice Earl Warren remarked that the low point of his service on the Supreme Court came when he advocated placing Japanese-Americans in internment camps during World War II. We pasted the story on the door of Schramm's room. Schramm laughed when he saw the newspaper.

— ❏ —

Again, Tex and I certainly did have arguments about the Cowboys and the NFL, and he had his own way of getting back at you when he didn't like what you'd written, such as the time

Tex Schramm and Bob St. John smile after each tried to tell the other how to do his job. (Photo by Bob Griffin)

I wrote the Pro Bowl was played as if the participants were out for a beer. He called me at 7 A.M., knowing that was about 5 A.M. in sportswriter's time, and began cussing me up and down before I could even wake up. He said I'd defamed my family, God, and the NFL and had shamed Dallas. He didn't laugh when I said, "Don't be so subtle. Speak your mind." Slam! Disconnect! He did that a number of times. He'd get mad as hell, ready to kill me. But by the next day he'd act as if nothing had happened.

Long after I'd stopped being a sportswriter for the *News*, I visited Schramm in Key West, where he had a condo and kept a fishing boat. We got into an argument on his boat, and he threatened to have me thrown overboard. I was glad we didn't have to wait until the next morning for cooler heads to prevail.

— ❏ —

We didn't make much money in those days in the sports department, although some of us compensated by free-lancing for magazines and periodicals and/or writing books. Socially, you didn't need to make much money. We were welcome at the best places around town and invited to important functions and parties at the homes of such people as Clint Murchison Jr. and Lamar Hunt. We were the power of the press, celebrities in our own right, albeit with frayed collars. Okay, we also were compelled to drink a bit at these functions to maintain the image of our profession. It did not take much compelling.

One of the annual freebies was the Cotton Bowl New Year's Eve Ball, preceding what was then one of the biggest of the Bowl games. While other noted guests wore the traditional black tux, we'd rent bright blue, maroon, or green ones, feeling we looked stylish when in actuality we appeared more like French Quarter barkers in front

of strip joints in New Orleans. Who cared? We didn't. Ah, perspective of the times.

We knew the biggest names in sports and also came in contact with a variety of celebrities such as Willie Nelson, Carol Burnett, Don Rickles, Natalie Wood, James Garner, George Plimpton, and Barnaby Conrad; George Bush, then head of the CIA, would greet the Cowboys when they played in the nation's capital. Long after I'd left sports, current President George W. Bush, as an owner of the Texas Rangers, was on a first-name basis with Randy Galloway and many of the survivors of our generation of sportswriters. As far as celebrities, the one that got away was Ursula Andress, who lost her chance to meet sportswriters John Anders and myself.

Our desks in the sports department were by the third floor window overlooking Ferris Plaza, a picturesque place with benches, a fountain in the middle, and lines of trees inhabited by grackles who dropped poop indiscriminately on those walking along the surrounding sidewalks. They became known as Poop Droppers or PDs. So on one of those unusually quiet days in the sports department I gazed below on Ferris Plaza, looking for inspiration, when I spotted none other than Ursula Andress, who was immortalized for many of us when she stepped out of the water wearing a bikini in Sean Connery's first James Bond movie, *Dr. No.*

"My God, it's Ursula Andress!" I calmly told Anders, who answered, "Sure" and ignored me. I finally coaxed him to look and bingo. "My God, it's Ursula Andress!" he said as we both ran for the elevator, then ignored it and raced down the stairs two at a time and out into the sunlight and across the street to Ferris Plaza. She was doing a commercial or some such by the fountain. Anders has written that I, a father and husband for goodness sakes, started doing cartwheels. In another version he wrote that I fell to my knees and started quoting *Romeo and Juliet*. Neither was true. However, I did wave at her as he duck-waddled in circles. Only once did she even glance our way, obviously looking at

me. John claimed she was looking at him. I believe he wrote that in his third version of the incident. Anyway, the magic moment was lost forever when the PDs, the mischievous devils, pooped on us. In retrospect that seems appropriate.

My other special memory of the PDs was when what seemed like hundreds were invited to speak at a roast for popular bar operator Joe Miller in the banquet room in Union Station, separated from *The Dallas Morning News* by treacherous Ferris Plaza. Randy Galloway and I and our wives left our cars at the newspaper and walked over to Union Station. Everybody was all dressed up, coats and ties and such. Randy and I were a little apprehensive about what we were going to say that someone who preceded us to the podium hadn't already said. As we walked past Ferris Plaza he stopped in mid-sentence. "Sonuvabitch! I quit!" he said. His sports jacket had been bombed by PDs, scoring two direct hits. We all hurried to shelter. PDs took no prisoners.

— ❑ —

Fans of Randy Galloway, of which there are many, would assume there was no way the popular, sometimes outrageous columnist and radio talk show host could be embarrassed. However, I must confess for him that there were indeed times that, unbelievably, he was, even momentarily, stuck for a loss of words.

During his younger, wilder days when Randy was a baseball writer for the *News*, he was assigned to interview Brooks Robinson after the Baltimore third baseman had won the Most Valuable Player Award in the 1970 World Series. Brooks was the toast of the sports world and came to Dallas on a promotional tour. His schedule was tight. He flew into town, had an appearance at Market Hall, and then had to go to the Fairmont Hotel for a luncheon. A publicity guy had agreed to set some time aside for Randy to interview Brooks between engagements. Randy hopped aboard the Blue Goose, formerly known as a 1962 Ford Falcon, and rode off from his Grand Prairie home hot on the trail of another penetrating interview.

Now the Goose had a personality of its own. The Goose smoked, fumed, shook, the passenger's door would jam, and as Randy recalled, "had a habit of dying at all times." Randy liked to point out to those critical of his pride that otherwise the Goose was a fine, dependable car. It just came naturally for him to get out, open the hood and readjust the carburetor when the Goose died, dislodge the door with a kick, and, oh yes, wrap up in cold weather because the heater didn't work.

As Randy stopped by the office that fateful day, temperatures in the thirties, before heading to Market Hall to interview Brooks, he got a hurried call from the PR guy. Brooks' flight was delayed and he was running late on his schedule and everybody was in a panic. Brooks wouldn't have much time to talk to Randy at Market Hall.

"Tell you what," the PR guy suggested. "Why don't you just pick him up and drive him to the Fairmont. You can talk to him on the way and then maybe have some time before the luncheon."

Randy's heart sank. "I gulped, thought, holy s---, I'd have to pick up Brooks in the Blue Goose!

"I got over to the Trade Mart and we talked about twenty minutes and then had to leave for the Fairmont. I went to get my car and came back to pick him up."

Brooks could hear and smell the Goose before he saw it. It was smoking, choking and Brooks, the nice guy that he is, didn't say a word while Randy tried to act nonchalant. "Brooks had on this light suit so I knew he was cold as hell," said Randy. "And wouldn't you know it. We got to the triple underpass leading to downtown and the damn thing died."

So here was Randy in heavy traffic jumping out of the Goose and opening the hood as motorists went around him, honking and yelling while Brooks Robinson, the toast of the sports world, silently shivered in the car. Quick as he could Randy adjusted the carburetor then jumped back in the car, started it, and moved on to the Fairmont, trailing smoke.

"I pulled right up to the valet parking," continued Randy, "and you could imagine what the doormen thought."

The doormen were accustomed to parking Mercedes and other top of the line automobiles, and here comes the Goose, smoking and rattling to the front entrance like the circus was in town. Doormen and young men working valet parking stared in disbelief. People entering the hotel turned to look. One of the young men carefully approached the car, was shocked to see Brooks Robinson in such circumstances, but quickly tried to open the door for him. It would not open. He jerked and jerked. Finally, he yelled at Randy, "The door is locked!" Randy said, "No it ain't." He got out of the car, went around to the passenger's side, and kicked the whey out of the door. It opened.

A crowd watched. It grew larger when somebody said, "Hey, there's Brooks Robinson!" Brooks very nicely thanked Randy for the ride. "Anytime," said Randy. Brooks smiled weakly and in his dignity got out of the car and walked toward the hotel. There were little balls of foam rubber from the tattered car seat all over the back of his suit. Randy put his hands over his face but could not disappear. The bellman escorting Brooks also noticed the little balls on his suit. Randy didn't say a word. Neither did the bellman. I mean, what can you say to a superstar with little balls of foam on the back of his suit? Randy got out of there as fast as he could. The Goose didn't die.

"Years later after I got to know Brooks, he was a broadcaster for the Orioles," said Randy. "I went up to him in the booth one day and reminded him of that day and the Blue Goose. I told him I really appreciated him not saying anything. And all he said was, 'I hope you got rid of that thing.' Well I did. Two years later I couldn't sell it so I gave it to my brother."

— ▢ —

Steve Pate, a carryover from our hellion days in sports, actually worked for a while for Dave

> **What can you say to a superstar with little balls of foam on the back of his suit?**

Smith with the new generation of writers. He learned times had changed. When Steve returned to the office in 1981 after a month on the road covering the baseball playoffs and World Series, he turned in what he considered a very conservative entertainment bill for $500.

"That wasn't nearly what I spent drinking and visiting with my sources, but I felt a little guilty," recalled Steve. "Dave called me into the office and said he didn't pay for drinking. I told him that was how I got half my stories. We would go out with the players and coaches. They trusted you. The next day if you got a big story, you'd double-check to make sure it wasn't off the record.

"I got nowhere with Dave. So I went back into the newsroom to fortify my position. I asked one guy how much he turned in for drinks. He said he didn't drink. Then I asked another. He said he didn't drink. The same thing happened with Barry Horn. I knew the profession had all changed. It was a different world."

— ❑ —

Maybe some of the sportswriters preceding us were more wild and crazy than we were, and certainly the heyday of madness of Gary Cartwright, Bud Shrake, and Co. at the *Fort Worth Press* and *Dallas Times-Herald* might rank at the top of that category. But a good example of the bygone days of the profession was our inner group of rascals at *The Dallas Morning News*. It was a last hurrah, bridging the gap between the old and the new. We suffered life's ups and downs, physical and mental injuries if not in the line of duty, then close by. Yet along the way that familiar unseen force with a sick sense of humor seemed to sometimes punish us for our indiscretions. But at least we didn't kill anybody. Well, that's not entirely true.

No matter what your standing might be, Walt and Assistant Sports Editor Sam Blair notwithstanding, you were required to serve time on the dreaded rim. You might write columns, special features, have a major beat, but you also did rim duty, meaning you read and edited copy, wrote headlines, answered the telephone, etc.

Walt would post the weekly schedules on a clipboard in a tray on his desk. You could tell who drew the rim by the cussing and slamming of the clipboard. If that person was Mike Jones, it was best to take cover as you snickered or possibly get hit by a flying object. It was funny if your cohorts worked the rim. It wasn't if you did. Some will gripe that I drew very little rim duty, perhaps four hours a week on the early rim and an occasional late rim during the off-season for the Cowboys. But in my perspective little was too much.

There would be a slotman such as Ed Knocke or John Barker, who did the layouts for the sports pages and doled out copy to a couple of reluctant rim guys to read and write headlines. For the morning paper rim work began about 4 P.M. and lasted until the slotman said it was okay to go home, usually around midnight. Sometimes rim duty was split, so you only worked an early schedule or a late one.

And there were even times where you wrote stories while working the rim. Say there was late breaking news. This naturally played havoc with your concentration. Such was the case when John Anders killed SMU assistant basketball coach Bob Prewitt. Legendary Mustang basketball coach E. O. "Doc" Hayes was the one who had died but John, rushed and overworked, wrote a story that legendary SMU assistant basketball coach Bob Prewitt had passed away. The error was caught just before the paper went to press, but you could imagine the shock poor Bob Prewitt would have had when he read the newspaper and found out he was dead.

Had John been writing this book, he no doubt would have given more prominent display to some of my mistakes over the years, such as calling Congressman Jim Wright "Jim Collins" in a column and later referring to NFL player turned broadcaster Alex Hawkins, with whom I'd just partied on the road, as none other than then New York

Giants coach "Alex Webster." I had nothing to do with the worst *faux pas* of all credited to me. But as some believe what goes around comes around, everything eventually evens out, nobody gets away with anything, or something like that. I usually do not believe these things. Yet perhaps what happened was my comeuppance from that unseen force for some of the pranks and mischief I inaugurated.

— ❑ —

The Dallas Cowboys training camp in Thousand Oaks, California, was very peaceful in that summer of 1972. Dallas had finally put away ghosts of the past, the stigma of not being able to win the Big One. Dallas had won the biggest one, beating Miami, 24-3, in the Super Bowl that January. Prior to the Super Bowl, Calvin Hill, who had been injured much of the year, and Duane Thomas were both healthy and played in the same backfield for the final few games of the regular season. They were a magnificent combo as Dallas won by scores of 52-10, 42-14, and 31-12. Calvin subsequently injured his knee again and was unable to start the Super Bowl. However, when training camp opened, fullback Walt Garrison, one of the team's stars, felt a little uneasy because of speculation that Calvin and Duane might be the starting running backs. So I wrote a column about Walt and his situation. Asked just how he really felt, Walt said, "I feel like the bastard son at a family reunion."

I used the comparison in my column. About 6 A.M. (8 A.M. in Dallas) on a cruel, heartless morning the telephone rang in my room. It rang and rang. When I finally answered it was Frank Clarke, a player turned broadcaster who was one of the good guys. "I didn't know you were like that," he said as I tried to clear my head. I had no idea what he was talking about. He repeated the statement and said, "I can't believe you of all people would do something like that. I guess I really didn't know you. I'm very disappointed in you, very let down." I still didn't know what he was talking about and kept telling him that. Exasperated, Frank read what was irritating him from my column,

which instead of "…bastard son at a family reunion" read "…black at a family reunion."

"WHAAATTT! NOOOO!" I said. Frank, all the readers would think I was some kind of racist for writing such a thing. Flashes. My career would be over. My life would be over. I wanted to die. Then I tried to explain as best I could to Frank that I didn't write that, somebody had changed my copy without my knowing about it and I'd make sure there was a retraction. I was never sure if he really believed me. People assume if it was in your column, then you wrote it, not allowing for screwups elsewhere.

I called the newspaper and found out what had happened. Knocke, working the desk, believed "bastard" was offensive and without letting me know had changed it to "black sheep." Someone in the backshop, accidentally I hope, had dropped the word "sheep" while setting the type. The rim guys, the proofreaders, and Knocke failed to catch the error so it came out in all editions. I finally got Knocke on the telephone that afternoon after he came to work.

"Ed," I said, "I'm going to kill you when I get back to Dallas." At that instant I meant it. It didn't matter that he'd caught mistakes I'd made in my copy before. He should not have changed my copy in the first place and, at the least, should have caught the mistake that must be one of the all-timers in *Dallas Morning News* history.

The newspaper ran a short paragraph retraction on an inside page. I doubt many people saw it so I called everybody I could think of and told them I was innocent. By the time I got back from training camp, I'd decided not to kill Knocke and besides I could get revenge by making his life more miserable when I worked the rim for him. Frankly, I was vengeful in those days, but time has calmed me down, helped me take things as they come and then forget them. Mostly.

— ❑ —

If Walt ever found out any of us actually had experience in the slot, he'd use them to fill in for Barker or Knocke. So Harless Wade or Tom Williams would sometimes work the slot.

Knocke and I had worked together at the *Austin American-Statesman*, and he had unintentionally done me a favor by telling Walt I was an awful slotman and could not be trusted. In this case the truth didn't hurt. I had indeed gained some experience as both a terrible slotman and terrible rim man while also writing stories and columns at the *Lubbock Avalanche-Journal* and *American-Statesman*, both of which had morning and afternoon papers. For an afternoon paper in Austin you had to report for rim duty at dawn's early light. I was nearly always late, which caused the slotman, Bill Galloway (no kin to Randy), a great deal of frustration and grief. His frantic phone call would often wake me up. I'd wake Katherine, my wife at that time, who would explain I'd already left and should be there at any minute. I'd throw on my clothes, take a bite of toothpaste, splash water on my face, and run for the car. I eventually would rush into the office with clothes askew, hair looking like I'd touched a hot wire, and a ready apology and excuse. I might have used an excuse a copy boy once had for being late but couldn't think fast enough. The kid said he actually wasn't late, that he arrived at the office on time. "But I forgot to put on my shirt and had to go back home to get it."

I'll always remember Bill's poignant words once as I rushed into the office late and wished him a happy good morning. Staring at me coldly he said, "I hate you." I told him, "I understand," ducked my head, and started working.

I knew how he felt. Hey, I worked the slot once too. In one of those unimportant nights that nothing much was happening and anybody could handle the slot, I ended up by myself on late duty, putting out the darn newspaper. Only one thing could happen and that was bad. I'd sent the copy with headlines, or thought I had, to the backshop to be set in type. Somehow, the backshop never got the copy. I had no idea where it went. Maybe, as Anders would do later, I mailed them instead of my bills. It was worse than one of those dreams you sometimes have, like taking an exam you haven't studied for or, in the

case of journalists, drawing a blank when you start to write a story on deadline. But I didn't wake up. Fortunately, my friend George Breazeale happened to come by the office, sized up the situation, and went to work. He helped me grab stories off the wire, write headlines, and get everything in eight minutes before deadline. Maybe by about five minutes. George was highly intelligent and could do anything. However, I must point out that George wasn't wild and crazy, but his eccentricities qualify him to be mentioned.

— ❑ —

George Breazeale was a tall, straight, lanky guy with glasses. He looked like a very somber professor and some of the University of Texas athletes he covered referred to him as "Lurch" as in the butler for the *Addams Family*. But the guy could expound on science, philosophy, and about anything else you wanted to discuss. He just, well, had his idiosyncrasies. He drove a Model T, which you must admit was ancient even in 1963. Not only that but he shunned the newspaper's lot and parked on a hill two blocks away and three blocks from the railroad track. That was because the car would not start by normal means so he used the hill to give his car a running start. Each night when he got off work, he'd launch the car down the hill, run along beside it, and then jump in, slam it into gear, and the engine would ignite.

He missed one night. The car stopped on the railroad tracks, which didn't seem the best place to be because of possible passing trains, but no doubt George was the kind of person who knew the railroad's time schedule. When I left the office about 2 A.M. to go home, I heard these grunts and cries in the dark. There was George trying to get the car off the track. His well-rehearsed routine had failed. I asked him if I could give him a shove, and he said, "No. No, everything is just fine." Somehow he got it off the track and drove off in his merry automobile.

As I said, George might have been a little unusual but he was smart. He figured out this formula that proved if a person

bought more than $1 worth of gas at a time, it would evaporate to a certain degree. So he never bought more than $1 at a time. Of course you got more gas for a buck in those days. But not that much!

George refused to use office supplies at work. So he shunned the company typewriters and lugged his old portable into the office. There was, however, no truth to the rumor that it had only Roman numerals. And he would not use copy paper, claiming it was wasteful. So he'd write his stories on the back of press releases, which came in colors of orange, red, and yellow. That was just his way, and nobody thought anything about it except a new copy boy who kept giving him office paper to use. He'd give it back. And George had great concentration at work. He'd compose, bite his fingernails, then write some more without looking up no matter what was happening around him.

He had a surefire method of always catching his sources at home when he covered the area high schools. He would come into the office and call them about 1 A.M. to get information for his column. His opening line would be, "Oh sorry. Did I wake you?"

He used logic in explaining his method. "I don't see anything wrong with it. I seldom miss anybody."

That year we had this UT student working part-time. Just before Easter a shopping center had a contest in which eggs were packed into this old French car, a Renault I believe. The person who came closest to guessing the number of eggs got the car. The UT kid guessed 9,462. The car contained 9,460. The kid had himself a car, which had a mind of its own. Lights would go on and off on their own. When the ignition was turned "off" the motor would start. One night the kid was going home but couldn't get the lights to come on. We all fiddled to no avail. Then George showed up and asked what the problem was. We explained.

> He would come into the office and call them about 1 A.M. to get information for his column. His opening line would be, "Oh sorry. Did I wake you?"

George stared at the car, bit his fingernails, and stepped back and kicked the heck out of the thing. The lights came on.

"A simple process," he said, then walked into the night.

George was political, although we could never talk about such things because he was an ultra-conservative or as a friend said, "just to the right of John Birch." But he was once elected to the City Council in Westlake, a suburb of Austin. He won by two or three votes and immediately called his election by the people "a towering mandate." Soon he was voted out of office, although I suspect he saved the city hundreds of dollars on paper.

— ◻ —

Austin was a great place to be and work when I came there from Lubbock to work for the *Austin American-Statesman* in the summer of 1963. They used to say we had our own United

Nations at the newspaper. The staff included sports editor Lou Maysel, Charley Eskew, Joe Heiling, George Breazeale, Ed Knocke, Russell Tinsley, and a St. John. Knocke and I were the young guys, and there was another kid just starting out at a local TV station named Verne Lundquist. I wasn't that crazy then although there were signs I was headed in that direction.

We were more behaved in those days and were in love with the city and our profession. Austin was just the right size then with the State Capitol building and the University of Texas Tower the tallest structures, and instead of driving to the top of Mt. Bonnell, you had to park and climb up the last third of the way to the top. The view, the feeling of being there was worth the effort. In one direction downtown Austin spread out before you like a miniature city, and sunrise would give the capitol a pinkish glow. On the other side the Colorado River moved picturesquely, endlessly through hills thick with trees and shrubs, and you could hear the faint echo of faraway voices far below. And it was a time to

see and hear Ernie Mae Miller at the New Orleans Club on Red River, singing "Moon River," "Days of Wine and Roses," and "I'm a Womaaaan, yes I am, W-O-M-A-N."

Bill Brammer was our inspiration. His book *The Gay Place* had among its characters a politician remindful of Lyndon Baines Johnson. It was the talk of literary circles, and those of us would-be writers dreamed of one day doing such a book. During late afternoons into nights we joined authors, journalists, politicians, and teachers at Scholtz Beer Garten, sharing pitchers of beer while discussing our crafts and solving the world's problems.

As luck or fate would have it I rented Brammer's former residence on McCall Road up a hill from Caswell Tennis Center. It then belonged to his ex-wife Nadine and her new husband, state legislator Bob Eckhardt. I got along great with Nadine. She'd come by to see if anything was needed, hauling her kids with her. Once she left one of the kids there. She realized he was missing an hour or so later and called to see if he was there.

He was playing with my kids, who were there too so we were both relieved.

So many places that had a history are gone now, alive only in times of reflection about Austin. We'd go to the Hill's Restaurant for a steak, and I remembered my cousin C. W. Green talking about going there as a student at UT in the 1940s. We'd also spend a lot of time at the PK Grille, which was downtown and a place where generations of students and residents had gone and would go. And Freddie, the night manager, worked the late shift from 8 P.M. until 6 A.M. I believe his last name was Louden, but I'm not sure and couldn't find anybody who knew because he was always Freddie, just Freddie, and nobody asked. But he always knew the names of customers, who were varied and many. There were not just journalists but regular citizens, students, politicians, lobbyists, gamblers, pimps, prostitutes, taxi drivers, cops, and guests of the nearby Austin and Driskill Hotels. It didn't matter who you were. Freddie gave you a friendly greeting and escorted you to a table. And it seemed

like every time you took a sip of water Freddie was there to refill your glass.

When Lyndon Baines Johnson was elected president, Walter Cronkite, who went to UT, remarked in his national broadcast something like, "I bet LBJ and his gang are at the PK Grille. I wonder if Freddie is still there."

Austin is still a great place but it's so big now, seeming to be growing into another Dallas or Houston in size. But if you lived there during those times you never forget the way it was and to you always will be.

— ❏ —

I married Katherine, who now lives in my ex-house in Richardson, in Austin that year, and she quickly became indoctrinated to life with a sportswriter. I was young, enthusiastic and figured she'd be thrilled to learn shortly after we got married that she would see not one, not two, not three, but four football games in less than three full days.

To get into the spirit of the weekend we went to a party on Thursday night in Austin. It was a long party at an old house that had a porch, surrounded by a wooden balustrade and hedges. Frankly, there were some silly, immature guys there. Around midnight some of us were magic and began playing a game in which we'd stand on the top rail and attempt to leap flatfooted over the hedge into the yard without stumbling, much less falling. I quickly surmised I was the best athlete among the group and figured I could show them a thing or two. I announced that I would stack the deck even more. I would get a running start on the porch and not only jump over the rail and the adjoining hedge but also land safely halfway through the yard without stumbling. Dern. I'd have made it too if my foot hadn't caught on the hedge, causing me to tumble head over heels into the yard. My glasses flew out of a shirt pocket and broke, but otherwise I only injured my ankle, elbow, and pride. Yet I learned something that would come in handy as a sportswriter. You must be able to write hurt with hangovers, with bodily injuries, and during times of mental anguish.

We drove hurt to Dallas on Friday and that night watched the John Roderick-led SMU Mustangs edge Navy and Roger Staubach, 32-28. The next afternoon we saw Darrell Royal's Texas Longhorns with Tommy Nobis, Tommy Ford, and Scott Appleton demolish an Oklahoma team with Ralph Neely and Joe Don Looney, 28-7, en route to the national championship, and then drove from Dallas to Waco to watch Don Trull and Lawrence Elkins lead Baylor over Arkansas, 14-10, that night. Then we drove back to Dallas and on Sunday saw the Dallas Cowboys beat Detroit, 17-14. Katherine was so excited she slept most of the way back to Austin as I explained the finer points of each game. In the summer of that year of 1964, we moved to Dallas and I went to work for *The Dallas Morning News*, a paper I'd read much of my life.

After I'd been in Dallas for a while, Walt was looking for a full-time slotman. I recommended a very good slotman named Ed Knocke, which for me had its advantages and disadvantages. Ed proved adept at his work and Walt was pleased. Ed played by the book, which we'd never read. And after he upset some rimmers with his panic attacks and insistence they take the prescribed hour for dinner and caused other inconveniences, some of my friendships were in danger.

8

Wacky at the DMN

"I might have been able to handle one of you crazies. But not five!"

—Walt Robertson, *DMN* Sports Editor

We considered ourselves writers, and we might take criticism for our rim work with a certain amount of perverted pride, but our writing was a different matter. We would become upset at the slightest change in our copy unless, of course, we'd made some factual mistake. Once when Merle Heryford changed Bud Shrake's copy, the sports columnist sought him out the next day and said, "If you ever change my copy again I'll kill you." So we always used "kill," which when translated only meant we disagreed with any changes that were made.

Sometimes we also disagreed with headlines deskmen put on our stories. Sometimes deskmen disagreed with our stories. Once I wrote that Cowboy defensive line coach Ernie Stautner was not satisfied with the performance of his players. They'd actually played pretty well, but Ernie was hard to please. Merle apparently had watched the game on television and was much more upset than Ernie. So he wrote a headline, "Stautner Detests Linemen." I tried to explain to an embarrassed Ernie

Stautner that I didn't do it. He understood. Mostly. Another time I quoted a few lines from Jimmy Webb's "MacArthur Park" in my column. Webb's original lines were edited and re-punctuated by Knocke. But again, slotmen saved me a number of times by catching stupid mistakes. They didn't save me at other times by not catching stupid mistakes.

So writers were touchy in those days and certainly had more clout. We picked on rimmers and slotmen unless we were on the rim or in the slot. After covering my last game, Super Bowl XII, I got back to Dallas and saw that somebody had put the final score in the first paragraph, à la Associated Press style, of a game which an entire nation of sports fans knew the outcome, so I had a fit. It was the lead story on Page 1 of the newspaper, but nobody would just come out and admit doing it. Times changed.

Most everybody in this business wanted to be a writer in those days with some exceptions who preferred to work the desk or be editors. Then there were those who didn't show a particular flair for writing and were made full-time deskmen. Walt did believe people with special talent were a little, different shall we say, so he tended to give them more slack when they would become upset over copy changes or their behavior went far beyond the norm.

The parade began to pass for writers in the early- and mid-1980s on newspapers in Texas. A new breed of people who wanted to be deskmen and edit copy showed up and had a lot more authority over the writers. Some were excellent. Others, as were some writers, were only excellent in their own minds. We figured we knew more than they did. They figured they knew more than we did. But they became the final authority, and if you said you were going to kill them they just shrugged, ignored you, and told the boss you were out of line. We had become an editor's newspaper for better and worse. Ah, for the good old days.

— ❏ —

Above all, Knocke was a deskman, which he wanted to

be, although he also put in time covering rodeo. It was his job on the desk that often left him in a state of panic. He would get nervous at 4 P.M. if there was a late game coming in near midnight. He would even get nervous if his rim guys, such as Jones, Galloway, John Anders, Harless Wade, or the Dallas Cowboys beat writer, disappeared for a couple of hours on a dinner break. We were supposed to get an hour, but if we weren't back in sixty-two minutes, Ed would be on the telephone trying to locate us at various watering holes. I do not mean to imply that being late was a common practice but, hey, it did happen. Sometimes we'd be late just to rile him. He needed to be punished for getting upset and raising his voice.

Poor Ed Knocke (pronounced K-NO-KEE) wasn't a bad guy when he wasn't working the slot. Sometimes he was okay when he was working the slot. He was orderly, disciplined and just didn't understand the nuances of our weird psyches and, instead of accepting them, fought the inevitable. And there were times when he couldn't

locate reporters on out-of-town assignments. Galloway was reporting on the Dallas Chaparrals game in New Orleans with the Buccaneers. Randy was staying at the Governor's House Hotel in New Orleans, and Knocke needed to warn him there was an early deadline.

Ed called the *News* operator, told her where Randy was staying, that there was an emergency, and she needed to find him immediately. Thirty, forty minutes passed and an angry Knocke dialed the operator and said, "Hey, listen, you were supposed to get me Galloway! I told you it was important. I've got to talk to him!"

There was a moment of silence and then the operator let Knocke have it. "Don't you talk to me that way. I want to tell you something right now, Mr. Ed Knock-ee! First of all the home of the governor isn't in New Orleans. It's in Baton Rouge! And I've continually called and they don't seem to even know a Mr. Galloway!"

— ❑ —

Knocke labeled Anders and myself the "bottom of the

Mug shots of John Anders, Harless Wade, Walt Robertson, Steve Pate, Randy Galloway, Mike Jones, Carlton Stowers, Bob St. John, and Sam Blair during early years at *The Dallas Morning News*. (Photos courtesy of Walt Robertson)

barrel" rim men, a title we accepted with great pride and dignity. When we tied for the worst rimmers in the sports department, I believe Mike Jones and Randy Galloway were jealous. When Knocke was the slotman and Anders and I would show up to work the rim, he'd often say as loud as he could, "Man, I've got the bottom of the barrel!" When Anders finally won the tiebreaker I felt disgraced, while acknowledging perhaps he deserved the dishonor.

After you wrote headlines you attached them to the stories with a paper clip, put them in a tube, and sent them through the chutes to the backshop, where they would be set in type. Occasionally we had parties while working the rim, especially if Harless Wade was filling in as slotman because he was always ready for a party, no matter where or when, during lonely nights on the rim.

Even when there was no party, you tried to take advantage of rim duty, considered wasted time, by doing such things as making personal calls, reading books, or writing checks to pay your bills. So Anders claimed the dishonor of being the worst rim man when he did his bills, put them in envelopes, then sent them in a tube to the backshop to be set in type for the morning paper. Now John is no fool. He quickly realized what had happened when he prepared to mail the stories and headlines.

— ◻ —

Harless Wade, unsound of mind, unsound of body, was dragging himself reluctantly into middle age. He was between marriages in the mid-1970s and had become an after-hours fixture at James Bailey's popular sports bar The Point After. We identified with the place, and thus the proprietor, because James once escorted a rowdy customer outside and tried to squirt him with Mace when the guy came after him. Only thing was, James got confused in the action and Maced himself. And one night Harless, then our golf writer who also covered SMU, admittedly was skunk drunk. This became even more obvious to an SMU coed, young enough to be his daughter, after the third time he told her his life story with his heroics gaining stature with each telling. Harless, banned by circumstances from a family life in suburbia, was living in an apartment with an old buddy, Bill Perryman, who also was between marriages. SMU was nearby so the coed, who also had been drinking, was still aware that there was no way Harless could drive home. As instructed he followed her block by block back to her place, where he could recover, have some coffee, and hustle on home. Common sense, logic, etc., as usually is the case, was obliterated by booze. Oh yes, her place was a young woman's dorm room on the campus at SMU!

Harless as usual fell asleep. Slowly and painfully, he awoke the next morning on the floor of the young woman's room in the dorm. The impact was tremendous, the reality of his situation shocking. Here he was a dirty old middle-aged man, a known, easily recognizable sportswriter for *The Dallas Morning News*, in the middle of a women's dorm on the campus of SMU in the early morning hours.

"Oh man alive I've got to get out of here!" were his first words. The coed worried about being expelled. Harless worried about going to jail. The coed guided him down the stairs. Other coeds were leaving for class and an older woman, apparently matron of the dorm, walked past. Harless pulled his jacket over his face, apparently in his state of recovery feeling this would make him invisible. Amazingly, he made the door, hoping anybody who noticed him would be in denial. How could he be there? It was against logic, the rules, proving once again that people sometimes do not see the obvious when it's totally unbelievable. And undetected or at least unreported, he was outside to freedom in less than a heartbeat.

Harless always seemed to have a sense of timing, unplanned as it was. Years later at Joe Miller's, a famous watering hole for journalists, some of us were having drinks. I struck up a conversation with a couple at the next table. They were from England. The woman said, "We've heard this is a place where journalists hang out. Ah, perhaps we might meet one." As if on cue, Harless, leaning back in his chair, fell over backwards on their table.

"You just did," I told the stunned couple.

— ❑ —

As I mentioned, on slow nights on the rim you found unusual ways to entertain yourself. Merle Heryford, our baseball writer who was a real nut for the game, studied the *Ready Reckoner,* the baseball book of numbers with all the possible variables for figuring standings and averages. He concentrated on each page, sometimes looking like a kid with his first *Playboy* magazine. Sure enough, after searching for no telling how many years, Merle finally found a mistake in that heralded statistical bible. Mike Jones liked to search drawers in Walt's desk to see who was making what and what the chief's plans were for future assignments. Anders did his

You think sportswriters were tough in the old days. Here Harless Wade takes time out for a snack. (Photo by Bob St. John)

bills. And Harless Wade would crawl under his desk and go to sleep with only his feet sticking out. After Anders and I left sports and began our regular special section columns, we had adjoining offices. Oftentimes I would think he wasn't there only to find him asleep, his feet protruding from under his desk. I admit to some snoozing on occasion myself, but we were only amateurs. Harless Ainsworth Wade could sleep with the best of them!

Once he worked the slot until 2 A.M. and had an early meeting in the office for an interview at 9 A.M. Harless decided it would be ridiculous to drive home then turn around and come back. Anyway, the guy came into the office looking for Harless the next morning. Nobody could find him. Finally, after a desperate search, somebody saw two legs sticking out from under a desk. They belonged to Harless. He'd crawled under his desk, used two telephone books as pillows, and was snoring away.

During a siege of bad weather Harless decided to stay at my place, sleeping on the couch instead of driving home to Rockwall, some 25 miles away. He cooked himself a steak before tumbling off to never-never land. The next morning I found him sound asleep, his steak half eaten and the television playing. That was no big deal, but then I noticed he was holding a fork with a piece of steak on it. He had gone to sleep in mid-bite!

Long after Harless retired from the newspaper, he was often contracted to help with golf coverage. He covered a Texas Titleist championship event at Horseshoe Bay near Marble Falls. Harless always claimed the best exercise a man could get was riding around in a golf cart. So on a warm afternoon he took a golf cart up a hill and parked under a shade tree, where he could have a good view of the contestants on the green below. Naturally he fell asleep. At dusk a few hours later he was awakened by someone who had seen him, dead still, in the cart and hurried to see what the problem was. After he woke up Harless, the guy said, "I'm sorry. I thought you might be dead." Harless slapped himself on the face and said, "Whew. I'm still alive."

— ❑ —

Regular slotmen Ed Knocke and John Barker would duly report to Walt when rimmers would take extra time for dinner. We called them "Informers." Walt would warn the perpetrators, who would then take the designated hour for a while and promise never to do it again. But there was always a chance for a breach. Walt would issue another warning and then just shake his head in frustration.

Don't get me wrong. Walt was far from a passive person but even when he jumped you about something it was mostly in a controlled, even keeled way. If you REALLY challenged him over some matter, he'd get riled up, but after a short struggle with his temper he'd regain his cool and lower his voice. There were those times when we were late for work or coming back from dinner that I think Walt just got to the point where it was easier to ignore some of our madness than to listen to our long excuse stories, which were

at times even more creative than our writing.

Harless walked in an hour or so late one afternoon for early rim duty at 4 P.M. When Walt confronted him Harless said, "Whew" then sighed as if he'd just had a close call and explained that indeed he had stopped by a liquor store, which shortly thereafter was being robbed. Harless said the robbers had locked him and the manager in the cooler while they took the money and ran. He added in circumstances like that he might have been killed much less late for work. Walt pondered the circumstances, briefly unsure of his preference. The skies suddenly darkened, followed by thunder and lightning.

Harless had a poor grandmother who also died a lot, making him late for work or placing him in a situation in which he didn't show up at all. Walt later estimated Wade's grandmother had died six or seven times. And a most unusual thing made him late another time. With straight face, Harless said his dog had swallowed his car keys. The skies darkened, followed by thunder and lightning.

— ❏ —

Harless kept a bottle of vodka in a drawer of his desk for an after-hours medicinal cocktail before leaving the office. That was easy to smuggle into the office. The beer drinkers had more problems bringing in a six-pack. They'd get ice from the lunchroom after Walt left and put it in a trash can to keep their beer cold. Subtly, they'd put the empty cans into a large desk drawer by the rim. Once Walt came looking for a reference book. He opened the drawer in question and empty beer cans overflowed loudly onto the floor, clanging like they were tied to a frightened cat's tail. Of course, everybody blamed everybody else, and all agreed none of the beers were touched until the newspaper had been put to rest. Mike Jones felt it was very unfair when Walt approached him, uttered unpleasantries, and then said, "The least you could do was throw away the empty cans!"

There was the time the guys on the late sports rim forgot to empty ice out of a trash can when they left for the night. When Walt came in the next morning, empty beer cans had floated downstream around the department. Mike Jones felt it was unfair Walt approached him about this oversight.

"Once when I came to work with two six-packs in a brown sack, I happened to meet Walt on the elevator," said Jones. "He tried to peek over into the sack, and I kept trying to hold it higher so he couldn't. He was taller than I am so I kept edging up and was finally standing on my tiptoes. He never said anything. He was accustomed to unusual behavior."

I admit involvement in madcap rim activities one night when Harless and I had oysters on the half shell from Vehon's and drinks in the office during our dinner break. At least Tom Williams, working the slot, knew where we were. Tom finally said he'd join us for just one light drink. So I put a lot of scotch and a little water in a paper cup and handed it to him. The next one I gave him was scotch with just a touch of water. Tom, who stuttered when he talked, had a nice singing voice and did not stutter when he belted out a tune. He started singing in the slot and was feeling very benevolent when he told us to go on home about 10 P.M., that he'd put out the paper himself. When I got up the next morning, my drowsiness was quickly interrupted by thoughts of what might have happened to the newspaper after we left a tipsy Tom Williams. But after I rushed outside and got the paper, the sports page looked just fine. Tom had performed by rote!

— □ —

It is very pathetic that Mike Jones, Steve Pate, and Randy Galloway on a given day were better rim men than Anders and I. I include Galloway as a superior rim man because he did have a knack for writing innovative, in-depth headlines on two-paragraph stories. His most famous concerned a boxing match between two Japanese fighters. Randy penned the immortal "Jap Fighter Wins." Walt was furious and put a note on the bulletin board that the newspaper had had complaints about the headline, which he

said was totally inappropriate, with underlying racism and that he did not want to see a "Jap Fighter Wins" ever again.

A few nights later Anders was working the rim with Galloway. A story came over the wire about a boxing match in which a Japanese fighter lost. Anders gave the story to Galloway, who got this wild look on his face and penned the headline "Jap Fighter Loses." When Walt jumped him Randy claimed, and with some accuracy, that the headline was indeed not the same as the previous one.

Randy and I had this habit of eating paper. More accurately, we'd tear off corners of paper, roll them up like toothpicks, and chew away. In our defense I likened the habit to baseball players chewing tobacco. It had a calming effect. My worst moment came when I was conducting a serious interview. I'd chewed the paper into a little ball, and when something humorous was said, I laughed and accidentally sent the wad onto the face of the guy I was interviewing. It stuck and I was so embarrassed. But he didn't notice or say anything, and I sure didn't either.

When Randy was covering the Dallas Chaparrals for us, Jim Brannan was his *Dallas Times-Herald* counterpart on the beat. A game went into two overtimes, and they were under intense deadline pressure. They rushed to get quotes from players. Brannan beat Randy back to the press table and began looking for his notes about the game. When Randy returned, Brannan was on his knees desperately putting together wads of paper. Randy had chewed up the poor guy's notes!

— ❏ —

Randy and Jones were two hours late returning from dinner, and Knocke, as was his nature, was having a nervous breakdown. He not only was running the slot, answering the telephone, and making up the sports pages, but also writing headlines. I can see him sitting there now, shaking his head and muttering, "Those guys...I can't believe this. I can't believe this." Whenever somebody would come down the hall, he would look up, hoping, nay praying it was them.

Finally they arrived and met Ed, who was sweating, rubbing his hands together, and actually pacing up and down the hall. They slurred their words and walked as if they were in mud and had birds chirping in their heads. Ordinarily, news department people, Frank Reece excluded, didn't like to venture after dark into the corner of the office where the sports department was located. But Buster Haas, who would survive to become a *News* executive, was heading the news side night section. Knocke had tattled on them to Buster, the janitor, the operators, strangers who called for scores, and guys bringing in seven-page wrestling stories, regularly trimmed to two or three paragraphs. Buster, no fool, realized the state Randy and Jones were in and decided he'd just send the drunkest one home and hopefully get enough on the rim from the other one.

Randy was supposed to be the late guy, who might be there until midnight or 1 A.M., whereas Jones would get off at 11:00 P.M. or thereabouts. Sensing which direction Buster was leaning, Randy began acting even more drunk, if that was possible. When he began telling Buster and anybody who did not want to listen what was wrong with every major sports team in Dallas, Buster said, "Randy, you're too drunk. Just go on home!"

Jones's mouth opened wide and pain shot across his face. "Wait a minute," pleaded Mike, "I'm drunker than he is!" Case closed. Jones had to finish Randy's late shift while the Blue Goose escorted his pal home to Grand Prairie.

On special holidays when abbreviated editions of the newspaper were put out, Ed went to dinner with the other guys. Such was one Christmas Eve. He had Harless and Galloway on the rim, and they couldn't find anyplace open to have dinner. Nearby Boots Place was always open. It had beer, short orders, pool, and usually a lonely wanderer trying to dance with a chair. So Harless, Galloway, and Knocke decided if they must they'd eat at Boots. They were the only customers that night and ordered the house specialty, chili. As they sat there eating, Randy noticed this giant rat crawling along the wall near Boots, the proprietor. He pointed this out to his dinner companions, and as they watched, Boots reached over, got a baseball bat, and smashed the rat. He then grabbed the rat by the tail and took it to the back.

"There goes tomorrow's chili," said Galloway.

"None of us finished our chili," recalled Ed.

— ❑ —

Walt was considering hiring Randy Harvey in 1973. Randy had interned for us, and some of the staffers liked him and were pushing for him to become a valued member of our staff. However, Walt had heard rumors that Randy might be a little wild and crazy like some present staffers, so he chose instead a talented young man named Steve Pate. He did not know Harvey was a tame guy or that Pate was as crazy as we were...maybe even more so.

There were nights when Pate and Jones drew double duty on the rim and felt justified to buffer themselves from such distasteful duty. After all they were writers. So there were some nights when they prepared themselves for the rim by touring the line of strip joints on Harry Hines Boulevard. They'd start at the farthest one away and stop at each one for a beer en route to the *News*.

Pate was not only a wild man on the streets but also had that mischievous, madcap side that Walt had hoped to avoid. In fact Steve directed one of the more imaginative capers. When Steve, Jan Hubbard of the *Fort Worth Star-Telegraph*, and Richard Justice of the *Dallas Times-Herald* were covering the Dallas Mavericks, they became acclaimed in NBA circles with escapades such as their stellar performance in Georgetown, that popular residential area in the District of Columbia. They went into a packed club where the band was playing songs made popular by the Kinks, a group during the 1960s. Between sets Pate stopped the young woman who was the lead singer, engaged her in small talk, and then said, "See that guy over there? He's one of the original Kinks."

"Oh, hey, wow," she said. "Do you think he would do a song for us?"

"Sure, he'll even do you a Kinks song," said Pate.

"Swell! Swell!"

The so-called original member of the Kinks was none other than Jan Hubbard, who wore his hair long in those days and, well, during the heat of drinking, the crowd assumed he was indeed once a part of the group. So Jan was introduced, stood up, and got a big ovation. He hurried to the bandstand, grabbed the mike, and told the band he was going to sing a particular Kinks' song. "What key?" he was asked. "Any key, my man," said Jan. He sang and swayed, and the crowd loved it. Before leaving, it took a great effort from Steve and Richard to convince Jan he hadn't once been a Kink.

— ❏ —

I was proud of their performance at the club in Georgetown. I do not know why, nor do I care to know, but for more years than I can remember I've greatly enjoyed harmless shams in which you play somebody you're not. Perhaps it has to do with frustration from an ill-fated acting career when I played the tragic Don Jose in the J. G. Wooten Elementary School of Paris, Texas, fifth grade production of *Carmen*. In the climatic scene in which I stabbed Carmen, played by a girl named Nancy, I was supposed to stab her in the breast because she dumped me for the ratfink bullfighter. After I kept getting confused about the location of the breast, the teacher decided I could just stab her in the back with this little rubber knife, which was supposed to be a sword.

Anyway, I was really into the part and got carried away. I stabbed her too hard and she yelled, "Ouch!" and got tears in her eyes. Then the trooper that she was, she composed herself and fell to the floor dead as a doornail. I was supposed to cry "Carmen...Carmen...I loved you." But I messed up and cried, "Nancy...Nancy...I liked you."

The great failure haunted my life and acting career. I was only trusted with lesser roles in elementary school, such as being relegated to playing Mr. Sunshine in another production. And

I later learned the only reason I got the part was because I had a red face. A lifetime later I was able to rid myself of frustrations by taking on various, and might I add, successful roles while a sportswriter at *The Dallas Morning News.*

— ❑ —

When I lived in Richardson there was a picture of a Tarahumara chief in my house. I'd taken it in the late 1960s while in the Sierra Madres in Northern Mexico working on a magazine story. The chief was fat and had whiskers and long hair. Once at a party for a group of sportswriters and their wives, one of the women asked who or what that ugly face was on the wall. She was a very intelligent woman but had had a few drinks and was ripe for the kill. She laughed but stopped quickly when I did not laugh but rather quietly stared at the floor.

She was puzzled and didn't know what to say or what to do when I mentioned in a shaking voice that it was a picture of my mother. She stared at me, waiting for the punch line. There was none. I was on stage again. I told her to go ahead and laugh.

"All my life people have laughed at my mother because of her looks," I said. "She can't help it if she's a...a fat Tarahumara Indian." I then explained how my father, an Irish prospector, had met and married her while in Mexico and how she could never give up her native ways or dress.

"Lookit, all my life I've been ashamed of my mother. Just look at the picture! I was afraid to bring my friends home. It hasn't been easy."

She put down her drink and, bless her heart, said, "Why, in her way she's beautiful. You should never be ashamed of your mother. Be proud of her and your heritage." I didn't tell her the truth until later, and she didn't speak to me for weeks.

My greatest role during my sportswriting years was as Jill St. John's husband, an oft-repeated performance. The actress was a big star in the sixties and seventies and made a big splash in a comeback as the sexy redhead in Sean Connery's James Bond movie *Diamonds are Forever.* As I traveled around

people would hear my name and joke, "You must be Jill St. John's husband, ha-ha-ha."

I was on a commuter flight from San Francisco to Los Angeles, working on a magazine story on Cliff Hagan, the NBA hall-of-famer who was then coaching the Dallas Chaparrals. The Chaps had played in San Francisco and had a game in Los Angeles that night, and it was a perfect time to interview Hagan. A man kept coming across the aisle and interrupting our conversation. He was lonely, wanted to be our friend, and would not go away. Finally he introduced himself, and in self-defense we told him who we were. He eyed me, giggled, and asked, "Are you any kin to the actress Jill St. John?"

As if on cue, Hagan said, "As a matter of fact he's her husband." The lawyer started to laugh then stopped just to be safe and said, "Are you joking?" He looked at my somber face. Terry Stembridge, then the voice of the Chaps, was nearby and said, "He really is."

"Why," I said, coldly staring up at him, "anything wrong with that, Buddy?"

"Oh...no, of course not," he answered.

I looked into his eyes and knew I had him and continued, "Hey, it isn't easy being nobody, just a shadow, an object sitting on a shelf near her. We go out and people disturb us. They want her autograph, to get close to her. And ignore me...I'm like dirt. I have no identity, just Jill's husband."

"Easy," said Stembridge. "Easy."

I stared past Hagan through the window so the guy wouldn't notice me trying not to laugh. I was afraid he'd see through the obvious. After all I had failed as the tragic Don Jose. But the guy never realized what was happening. Before we landed in LA, the guy gave me his card and asked us to a party at his house.

"Hey, you're a nice guy," he said. "I like you better than Jill. You bring her to the party and I'll make sure you get all the attention and she's ignored. Then she'll know how you feel!"

> My greatest role during my sportswriting years was as Jill St. John's husband, an oft-repeated performance.

He paused then added, "Can I buy you a drink?" He couldn't. We were landing. I accepted the invitation to the party but we didn't make it. Jill had other plans.

— ▢ —

Unfortunately there was a full moon or the stars were askew shortly after a party ended at Casa Dominguez, my good friend Pete Dominguez' popular restaurant for sports types. It had begun to rain as the late crowd left the restaurant, and that strange feeling came over me again. There was a nearby fountain just across the street, so I raced over and started tap dancing in my cowboy boots. Up the concrete stairs I danced, then back down with a tremendous leap off the last step. Harless and a couple of amazed women started clapping and doing their musical version of the theme song. "I'm singing in the rain...singing in the rain ...what a wonderful feeling...."

The performance was interrupted when a squad car stopped and a puzzled officer got out. Pete knew the officer and talked to him. And besides, there is no known citation for singing in the rain so he told us to keep it down and drove off.

— ❏ —

Besides the schedule, Walt would sometimes leave notes for us on the clipboard. He had a certain style in the notes, which some of us would forge when we considered it a fair and dishonest time.

You were due in the office if you weren't out on assignment or didn't have rim duty. Pate figured a way around this. He'd come in, put his briefcase on his desk for all to see, and then leave. That way Walt or Sam would think he was in the building, perhaps in the library

Members of Walt Robertson's old sports crew share some laughs with his wife, Janice, and Pete Dominguez at the popular Casa Dominguez Restaurant. Left to right are Bob St. John, Sam Blair, Janice, John Anders, Randy Galloway, Pete, and Walt. (Photo by Clint Grant)

researching or in the cafeteria having coffee. Not so. He was out for a beer. Jones, of course, was aware of this. So in Walt's style, he wrote Pate notes, such as, "Steve, it would benefit this department if you'd spend as much time here as your brief-case does. Walt."

He'd also send derogatory notes to Bill Livingston, a young staffer who would grow up, sorta, to become a featured sports columnist for the *Cleveland Plain Dealer.* Livingston would later determine that Jones was indeed his "Svengali." When Bill, an undergraduate at the time, began working for us, he was very naturally unhappy when called upon to work the rim. Naturally Jones would encourage this attitude.

Temple Pouncey, a quiet, low-key, hard-working guy, would cover soccer and tennis and also draw some rim duty. Furthermore, he was even a dependable rim man for good-ness sakes! So on occasion it befell Livingston and Jones to be working the rim at the same time Temple would be off cover-ing the Dallas Tornado, which was the local version of the professional soccer league founded by Lamar Hunt. Tem-ple, very versatile, was chosen to cover the team for the *News.* Bill did not want to cover the Tornado. Jones did not want to cover the Tornado. But they re-sented Temple being out of the office and plotted their revenge. Jones egged Bill on...and on.

Temple kept his desk very neat and even had a nice little set of helpful paperback books enclosed in a holder on his desk. Temple liked those books, which included a dictionary, thesaurus, and an edition of synonyms and antonyms. So Mike and Bill began tearing pages out of his dictionary when Temple was off on assignment. They might attack the A's, then skip over to the J's. "Gimme an Rrrrrr!" one would say, and they'd tear out a page of R's. The pages were cleanly torn out, and when Tem-ple actually needed the dictionary he would become a little, well, puzzled. I will leave it to your imagination who got the idea to start kicking field goals with Temple's books but it became far-reaching.

At first they would just drop-kick a book and then it became much more elaborate, or rather devious. For instance if Anders were around, he'd be the snapper while Jones and Livingston alternated kicking. It was three points if the book sailed over Temple's typewriter. Once columnist and assistant sports editor Sam Blair walked into the office and raised both hands, signaling the kick was GOOD. Temple just figured they didn't make books like they used to and had no idea what was happening until years later when Anders, then a columnist in the Today section, wrote about the episode.

What they didn't know was that things weren't always so easy for Temple on the soccer beat in those days. The teams played wherever they could, including high school stadiums. Once Temple was covering a Tornado game on a schoolboy field in Dallas. He was the only person covering the game. After it was over Temple began writing in the tiny press box. The janitor came in, turned out the lights, and started locking up. He did not understand Temple's concern about writing a story locked up in the dark press box.

Temple got nowhere pleading his case.

"Okay, how much do you make an hour?" Temple asked him.

"Six dollars an hour."

"I'll give you $3 for 30 minutes."

"Okay."

When word got out the following day, a guy from the Dallas Independent School District offered to give Temple his $3 back. So did Sam Blair. So did the team. He refused. Had it been some people I know they would have collected $3 from all of them.

— ❏ —

Livingston was really getting into the spirit of the office as Walt watched sadly. Bill went with Galloway for what was determined a brief appearance at some baseball function. They'd go, have a couple of drinks, and hurry back to the office. They were gone three hours. Walt called Billy into his office the next day and said, "Billy, Galloway is not the last word here."

I always did well in our weekly pickup basketball games, but after Livingston came on the scene, he immediately beat me one-on-one in triple overtime. I mean the guy could shoot, and after he'd gone to work for the *Philadelphia Inquirer*, rumor had it he could outshoot some of the 76ers. I cannot remember if my defeat was behind another evil plan. Surely not. The Cowboys had detected some of George Allen's people spying on them prior to a Dallas-Washington game. Gil Brandt had gotten a license plate number and traced it to the Redskins. Allen retaliated by accusing Cowboys scout Bucko Kilroy of climbing a little tree to spy on the Redskins. Bucko weighed about 300 pounds. Poor little tree. So before the teams played again, Walt got this great idea. He'd send Livingston to the Cowboys practice field, posing as a Washington spy. Bill would carry binoculars and a clipboard and sneak onto the roof of the dressing quarters adjacent to the practice field. When seen he would rush off into the sunset with his innocent sidekick, photographer Jack Beers.

We all laughed. What a great idea. Then, knowing Livingston was a little frightened about the assignment, I called Landry assistant Ernie Stautner, noted for being tough and mean as a player. Ernie went along with my plan. He would spot Livingston, chase him down, and scare the daylights out of the kid and, as a bonus, perhaps frighten a few successful jump shots out of him as a delayed reaction.

Of course I warned Livingston to be careful, especially of Stautner, telling him Ernie had this terrible temper and had once broken a sportswriter's jaw, which wasn't true but seemed like something I should tell him. Livingston shook his head, with that "Why Me Lord?" look on his face. Bill and Jack arrived at the practice field. Bill, a smart guy, had known he'd need a ladder to get on the roof so he stole one from a nearby loading dock. Jack threatened to leave, but Bill reminded him he was there to take pictures and was expected to do so.

"I climbed onto the roof and got all set," recalled Bill. "But the sun had been out all day and I burned the hell out of my hands and knees. Then I looked out on the field and there were only a handful of guys there. Later I learned the team was practicing at another location." Bill had finally gotten into the spirit of the job and sounded a little disappointed. I was more disappointed.

So there was at times an underlying deviousness going on and, okay, some of our actions were indeed mean spirited. Even Jones, a master of the tactic, admitted that the most effective prank, and perhaps the meanest, was perpetrated by Galloway and, well, me.

— ❏ —

Sam Blair wrote the lead column, but besides covering our beats Roy Edwards and I also wrote three columns a week. Roy covered the Southwest Conference and was a good reporter and an all right guy. Our families even socialized a bit. But he hated pro football with a passion because it had infringed on the popularity of college football, namely the Cowboys being No. 1 in Dallas. To him the pros were corrupt and money hungry whereas all college sports were (puke) squeaky clean. In a fit of passion

with Old Glory waving and the *Star Spangled Banner* playing in his head, Roy wrote a column about his opinion on the subject and hinted that writers covering the NFL were on the take. Sam and I covered the NFL. Fortunately, Walt killed the column. It was okay. Roy was an innocent even in middle age.

He was not always an innocent when it occasionally came to wanting somebody else's assignment. When I first came to Dallas and was covering SMU, the basketball team had great success. When it came time for the NCAA playoffs, Roy told Walt he was going to Kansas to see a sick sister or aunt or somebody and would be there anyway, so he could just cover the games. Another time when I covered SWC baseball Roy said he was going to be in Omaha anyway so he could cover for us. Sometimes his tactics worked. Most often they did not. However, it was the spirit of the deception that mattered.

Roy loved SMU basketball. He'd covered the Ponies until I came on the scene and he took over the Southwest Conference beat. After I started covering the

Cowboys in 1967, Roy got his beloved SMU basketball beat back. He was all excited. He had several good out-of-town trips scheduled with the Ponies. Poor Roy, he was so happy. So Galloway, who also disliked brown-nosing to get assignments, and I wrote Roy a note, signing Walt's name and putting it on the clipboard. Walt always called Roy "Big Hoss" and if for some reason, such as economics, we weren't going to cover an out-of-town game, he'd use what he called a "phoner," meaning a correspondent in a particular place would do a story for us.

The note read: "Big Hoss, we're cutting corners for a while. So please arrange to get phoner for ALL of SMU's out-of-town games, Walt."

We figured Roy would go into momentary shock before he realized the note was bogus. We watched as Roy came into the office, read the clipboard, and slammed it down. Then he put a hand over his face, slumped, and hurried into the library in tears. We felt awful, never dreaming he would be so emotionally upset. I stopped writing notes

after that as nearly as I can remember.

Roy later had a falling-out with Walt and Sam and applied for the sports editor's job in Memphis. Roy and I were working the rim one afternoon when he got a call he'd been hired in Memphis. It was what he wanted, and John Barker, the slotman, and I congratulated him. He said to heck with Sam and Walt, in so many words, and that he was out of there. "I'll show them!" he said, walking toward the door. "Don't leave me here by myself!" I yelled. "You're hurting me and Barker, too." But he was gone.

Later when Roy was in Memphis, he suffered a stroke and lost use of an arm. I covered for him at a Super Bowl, feeding him information for some of his columns. I still felt worse about what we'd done to him that day than he probably did about trying to grab our assignments.

— ❑ —

One of the most favorite people I've ever met in my life was the late Henry Stowers, our Outdoors editor. Henry and his wife, Iris, were sweet, gentle souls and were always ready to help somebody. Henry was more interesting than subjects we'd write about. He'd been a young marine who had one of the ropes when they were pulling down the *Hindenburg* and was one of the marines taken prisoner in China when the Japanese invaded early in WWII. Furthermore, he was a member of the U.S. world championship shooting team and won trophies in rifle, pistol, skeet, and trap shooting. Hunting and fishing were his life.

Fortunately, Henry also had a sense of humor when we cut out a picture of Squeaky Fromme, who had taken a shot at President Ford, hung it on the wall behind his desk, and titled it "The National Rifle Association's Pinup of the Year." When Henry saw the picture he was puzzled, then he grinned and looked right in the direction of Jones, Anders, Galloway, and me.

— ❑ —

The thing the majority of us hated, except for Galloway who loved to talk, was answering the telephone on the late rim.

People were constantly calling in for scores, information, to settle bets. The phone rang constantly. You cursed the day Alexander Graham Bell was born. Walt always said we should be nice to callers, that they were our readers, our fans. Just give them an accurate, to-the-point answer. It was tedious, boring. So you made the best of it.

Ring, ring, ring, ring....

"Sports department."

"Can you give me the late scores."

"5-4, 7-2, 6-1...."

"Thanks."

Ring, ring, ring....

"Hey, good buddy, we're out here at the Point and got into this lil' bet. Can you tell me who won the 1946 World Series between Boston and St. Louis? I know it was the Cardinals."

"Congratulations. It was the Cardinals."

"All right! Wait a second. Can you tell that to my stupid, stubborn buddy."

"Hi, this is Larry Fluent."

"Congratulations, Larry. The Red Sox won that series."

Later there was the sound of a faraway ambulance. A coincidence no doubt, but there seemed to have been a number of accidents that night. Another thing I found somewhat entertaining was to pretend I was a recording, answering the phone in a dry monotone.

Good evening. You have reached the Dallas News Sports Department. We are unable to help you at this time but we certainly appreciate you calling. Please try again later.

"Thank you."

You are very welcome.

Late one night I was angry with Walt because he assigned me a late rim. I was trying to write a three-word headline and gamblers kept calling for late scores and lonely people called for conversation. "I can't stand any more of this!" I told Tom Williams and Harless Wade, my partners that night.

Finally, I answered the phone, *"This is a recording. The sports department is closed. If you want a late score, please call this number."* Then the low life that I was I gave out Walt's home number.

"Whose number was that you gave out?" asked a curious Tom Williams. Told it was Walt's, he put his hands over his face. Harless laughed.

"You've got to tell him it was you who did that," Tom said. "You'll get us all in trouble."

"Are you crazy? I can't do that. I don't think he'd understand."

— ❏ —

The best way to get around answering the telephone was to ignore it. But somebody had to do it when they worked the rim, although it never seemed to bother Merle Heryford if you took fourteen straight calls while he sat there pretending he didn't hear the ring. You were supposed to answer the telephones and, naturally, be nice to callers. But Merle would become grouchy if fellow rim men asked him to please help with the incoming calls.

"What do you want?" Merle would bark at a caller. Sometimes if a caller crossed him he would slam down the receiver, disconnecting the person without saying a word, or he might utter, "Screw you!" and then hang up. That Merle, he had a way with words.

Merle loved to talk baseball nonstop. Bob Lindley, with the *Star-Telegram*, could match him word for word. I watched them having a conversation in the press box before a Ranger game. They were looking at each other and talking at the same time.

Nobody doubted Merle was the reigning expert on baseball, and he loved the part. There were no television sets or radios in the sports department during the 1954 World Series when Don Larsen pitched an unprecedented no-hitter. It was just unheard of. I wasn't around in those days but was told somebody first noticed Larsen had a no-hitter going through the fifth inning by checking the Associated Press wire.

"Merle, Don Larsen has a no-hitter through five innings!" he told Merle, who without looking up from the *Ready Reckoner* said, "He'll never do it."

Later the guy said, "Merle, Don Larsen has a no-hitter through seven innings!"

"He'll never do it."

Eventually, the guy excitedly told Merle, "DON LARSEN PITCHED A NO-HITTER!"

"He'll never do it again," Merle replied calmly.

— ❏ —

The sports desk was right across the aisle from the news desk, where night editor Frank "Mose" Reese, a friend and one of the best people I ever knew in our business, prevailed. Reporters would check with him and Brenda Goodner, who sat next to him taking calls. An idle mind on the rim can be a dangerous thing.

There was talk about some obscene telephone calls coming in at night. I watched Frank and Brenda busily at work. Then I dialed the city desk. Brenda answered and I breathed heavily into the telephone then gasped, while watching her reaction. She reared back in the chair and said something to Frank. I hung up when he grabbed the receiver. I called again, breathed even more heavily into the phone, but Frank grabbed the phone out of Brenda's hand and said, "You crazy SOB! I find out who you are and I'll come kick your tail myself!" Then he slammed down the phone, had second thoughts, and looked over at me, knowing I was capable of such mischief. With the phone under my ear I moved my lips and acted as animated as I could while pretending to type a story I was taking over the telephone.

Once I did the same thing to Galloway, pretending I was an irate female reader. I'd practiced the high quivering voice at The Point After for, I believe, Harless Wade. I really got into the role and began carrying on a conversation with myself.

"Oh Bob, you're so wonderful and I have to have you this second. You're a terrific writer and soooooo sexy."

"Why thank you, little lady, but I'm afraid I have to be movin' on."

This went on for a while and then I noticed this couple at a nearby table staring at me. There was no way to explain.

But I had perfected my fake voice for Randy and called him the next day. "Mister Galloway, this is Lily," I began, sucking him in with sweetness. Then bang, "You are despicable, a sorry, no good...."

Randy replied in his own sweet way—"Screw you, bitch!" and hung up before I could get in another word.

Luksa, then working for the *Times-Herald*, was aware that I had been getting some irate calls

and letters from readers regarding a 1970 game in which the Cowboys, who would make the Super Bowl that year, were slaughtered during the regular season in Minnesota by the Vikings, 54-13. It was the fifth game of the season and the first the Cowboys had played on natural grass. I wrote that the grass died and women and children were evacuated at halftime. After naturally hearing from Schramm, I was called many things by others, and one guy wrote I was a disgrace to my profession and that he showed his little kid my column picture and told him, "This man will get you if you're not good."

Another caller with an unidentified accent (maybe part Spanish, part Russian) cussed me. He told me he was canceling his subscription to the newspaper and had collected 100 names on a letter he was sending to my publisher to get me fired. He was talking like a machine gun and I couldn't get in a word and my heart was racing...then I realized it was Luksa.

Frank did suggest I answer some of the crazier letters the

way he did. He would return the letter to the angry person and write, "I feel I must inform you that some fool is writing letters using your name. Sincerely, Frank Luksa."

— ❏ —

Easiest rim duty came when Harless worked the slot on occasion. He understood our attitude and psyche because he was one of us. If you were looking for somebody to do a story, Harless could usually tell you how to find that person. He had more sources than anybody on the newspaper because of the golf beat and also the fact he hung out at places sometimes frequented by the likes of Mickey Mantle. And Harless remained easy and calm in the slot and always let you go home early. As a slotman the only guy I ever remember him really getting mad at was Gene Wilson.

Now Gene was different. He liked sports, but his true ambition was to be handsome, dress stylishly, and rub noses with celebrities. Perhaps it riled Harless the way Gene dressed. While the rest of us dressed off the clothes rack and Harless always wore duds from some golf shop or other, Gene would show up as if he'd just stepped out of the pages of *Esquire* or *Town and Country.* He'd have on name-brand suits, fashionable sports clothes, and Italian loafers and seemed forever young. I once called him a "thirty-two-year-old teenager."

Harless and Gene had both gone to East Texas State and were from small towns. Harless grew up in Commerce and Gene in New Boston. Harless was known for keeping many of his country ways, being proud of it and saying things like, "It goes together like cornbread and beans." On the other hand, Gene came to Dallas, got his master's degree at SMU, dressed like a fashion model, and was always trying to put

> **One guy wrote I was a disgrace to my profession and that he showed his little kid my column picture and told him, "This man will get you if you're not good."**

aside his country background and be cosmopolitan.

Once in the office where guys would ask to borrow pens, pencils, paper, notepads, etc., Gene said, "Anybody in here have any shoe polish I could use?"

He drew rim duty with Harless in the slot and wasn't doing real well. After Gene had made a mistake or five, Harless told him he was ashamed they'd both gone to East Texas State. While coldly staring at Gene, Harless then took off his school ring and slammed it down on the desk. He claimed he'd never wear it again until Gene straightened out. Eventually, he gave up and put his ring back on because he didn't have forever.

So like Anders and myself, Gene was not a good rim man. And he didn't even drink! However, he did experience that one shining time on the rim while John Barker was in the slot. If you wanted to stay on Barker's good side, you had to continually go to the coffee machine and buy him a cup "with double cream and double sugar." We figured Barker's double cream and double sugars into our monthly family budgets.

I was supposed to be the other rim with Gene but didn't show up. Barker panicked, Gene panicked. Barker called Walt to tell on me. If Barker, one of the good guys, squealed on me, I figured I must have somehow once neglected his request for coffee with double cream and double sugar. He never forgot something like that.

"St. John didn't show up," Barker informed Walt. Walt asked him who the other rim guy was. "Wilson," said Barker. "Oh no!" said Walt, who panicked too. "We're in bad trouble."

My name was later cleared when it came to light that I had been experiencing stomach pains yet gamely started to work. Before I got there the pains grew worse so I stopped by to see the doctor and he kept me. My appendix had burst, and I was undergoing surgery at Baylor Hospital. Harless said that was a pretty lame excuse for not showing up at the office.

Gene, perhaps for the first time, did an excellent job on the rim, taking calls and writing headlines, while mandatorily combing his hair, straightening his collar, making sure dust wasn't on his shoes, etc. He finished his double duty without a hair out of place. Why, Walt even congratulated him.

Gene left the newspaper in 1968 and achieved his ambition of remaining handsome, dressing stylishly, rubbing noses with celebrities, and having his own successful public relations firm. But he never forgot that the evil Mr. Wade called him "Country" and remains in recovery even today.

— ❑ —

As Randy Galloway's readers and listeners are well aware, one of his main dislikes are "homers" in the media, the people who think of the team they cover as "we" and even have been known to cheer for the home club. There was no way even a young Randy Galloway would get personally involved like that.

During a Dallas Chaparrals game, Randy kept yelling at the referee making call after call against the Chaps. Finally, after a call he adamantly disagreed with, Randy leaped on the press table and duck-walked from one end to the other, yelling at the ref.

Hosting a talk show over WFAA-820 wasn't that big of a jump for Randy. He had a desk near mine in the sports department and was always talking to callers the same way he does on his show. "Hey wait just a cotton pickin' minute, my man, and I'll tell you the real deal!"

The fact is I used to think John Anders and Mike Jones would also get into radio. Goodness knows they practiced all the time, making it impossible to work. At an early age the broadcasting bug bit them all. So without any provocation they would suddenly launch into their versions of noted Golden Throats such as Harry Carey, Kern Tips, Red Barber, Alex Chesser, Connie Alexander, and other unidentified voices. To add color they would also be the Aggie band in the background.

Frankly, I thought they were funny at first, but after they did it again and again and again I made the mistake of mentioning I actually had work to do and would they please keep it down. Naturally that would only set them off even more. The performance would go something like this:

Anders would be working like a normal person hunched over his typewriter then suddenly straighten up, clear his throat, and give his rendition of Kern Tips.

"AND THERE HE GOES, WOW-OHHH-WOW! IT'S MR. GIB DAWSON RIDIN' THE SHOULDER OF HARLEY SEWELL TO THE 33 WHERE JACK LITTLE CLICKS HIS HEELS TOGETHER AND SAYS, DOWNNNNN YOU GO! AND NOW THERE'S A TIMEOUT ON THE FIELD AND WE'LL HAVE A WORD FROM ALEX CHESSER!"

Jones would immediately stop work, stand up, cup a hand over his mouth as though it were a microphone, clear his throat, and say, "Thank you, Kern, and may I say Humble wishes happy motoring to you all, including Bobby St. John. And nowww, let's go down on the field and pick up the music of THAT AGGIE BAND!"

Galloway might have been talking to a caller but would say, "I've got no more time for you, my man," hang up, and also cup

his hands over his mouth and begin playing a nose trumpet, an Aggie trumpet if you will.

"DE-TA-DA, DE-TA-DAAAAAA, DE TA DA-DE-TA-DA-DE-TA DA-DA-DA-DA-DAAAAA...."

Anders would then pick up his empty coffee cup, put it to his mouth, and blow air into it, becoming the crowd, getting louder and louder, and then give the Aggie yell, "AA, AGG, GG, GIE, AGGIES, AGGIES, AGGIEEEESSS!"

No matter whether I was sitting at my desk or innocently walking into the office, I was always open for attack. Jones, in a deep baritone, would say, "AND THERE HE GOES, LADIES AND GENTLEMAN. IT'S BOBBY ST. JOHN! HE'S AT THE 20...THE TEN, WHOOO WHEEEE...LOOK AT HIM GO...AND, AND HE SCORES FOR THE AGGIES! HE SCORES!"

Then without missing a beat, Anders would turn to baseball and say, "THIS IS RED BAR-BAAR...!" And Jones would say, "HOOLEEE COW, RED, DID YOU SEE THAT CATCH BY MAYS!" And Galloway, on the telephone again, lecturing some caller, would turn away from the receiver and start to do the Aggie band.

"The Aggie band isn't at Wrigley Field, fool!" Jones would correct. And Galloway would respond, "Sooo soreeee, ladies and gentlemen, we arrr experiencing technical difficulties...."

I would leave the room, get coffee, and return as Anders and Jones worked quietly at their desks. Galloway might be telling the mayor of Dallas, who called to get an opinion on the Rangers, how to run the city government. Anders would come alive, "AND BOBBY ST. JOHN GOES TO THE LAUNCHING PAD... WOW-OH-WEE, IT'S ANOTHER SUCCESSFUL MISSILE BY THE GUTSY LITTLE FELLER WITH A HEART BIG AS A TREE TRUNK!" And Jones would jump in, "AND MAY I POINT OUT, KERN, THERE WAS EXCELLENT COVERAGE ON THAT PLAY. EXCELLENT COVERAGE."

Anders would do the crowd noise, Jones the Longhorn band, and Galloway would be talking to another caller. "Now you just

wait a minute, big boy. Just get off the line with your BS." Then he would realize the live broadcast was underway, put his hand over the receiver, and do the Aggie band....

Jones and Anders would go for coffee. There was peace in our little corner of the sports department. Not really. If Randy had nobody to talk to over the telephone, he talked to himself while writing a story. One particular day he had been telling then Ranger owner Bob Short how to run the baseball team. Then he hung up and continued the conversation with himself while doing his story. "Now just a minute, Bob. Wait just a cotton pickin' minute!"

Anders and Jones would return, and Anders would be at it again. "AND JUMPIN' JACK FLOYD HITS THE LINE AND SAYS, YEEEESSSS I WILL, AND DON MANASACO SAYS, NOOOOOO, YOU WON'T. AND IT'S A CLASSIC PILEUP LADIES AND GENTLEMEN...."

It would be quiet for precious moments then Jones would start again. "HOOOLEEEE COW. IT'S A BEAUTIFUL DIVING

TRY BY BOBBY ST. JOHN! DID HE CATCH IT? DID HE? YES HE DID, LADIES AND GENTLEMEN...."

Wide-eyed, head spinning, I would start to walk out of the office and Jones didn't lose a beat. "A BIG SURPRISE! OUR HALFTIME GUEST IS BOBBY JOE ST. JOHN SR. YEEESSSS, HERE HE IS, THE DADDY OF THAT LITTLE GUY WITH THE, UNNNNN, HEART AS BIG AS A WATERMELON!" He would reach toward me, as if putting a microphone in my face, but I would keep going. Galloway would pass me on the way out of the office. "DE-TA-DA, DE-TA-DAA, DE-TA-DA-DA-DA-DAAAAAA!" I would follow him out. In the parking lot while looking for the Blue Goose he would say, "Well, I'll tell you one thang, Mr. Bob Short, SIRRR...."

John Anders never got over his nerve-wracking days on the sports desk. Even long after he left sports he sometimes became attached to strange friends. Sadly, this relationship didn't last. (Photo by Bob St. John)

— ❑ —

When I started getting complimentary copies of *Sports Illustrated*, I figured I was in the big time. Jones and Anders and Galloway did not get free copies. So they started stealing mine. I admit in those days I did have a temper, which, of course, played right into their hands. I was dumb enough to think it had just been misplaced for a few weeks but then started finding it in the trash can, locker room, and on Temple's desk. I knew Temple didn't get it. So I'd come in, my magazine would be missing, and I would subtly remark, "If I find out the SOB who is stealing my magazine, I'm going to kick his a....!" They would all be hard at work over their typewriters. But I knew Jones had a hand in it.

The thing you could count on in the sports department, Temple Pouncey notwithstanding, was revenge. An eye for an eye. Once staffers were invited to a

party in the press box lounge at Texas Stadium. As beat man for the Cowboys, I pretty much had the run of the place.

Mike, a Burt Reynolds-looking guy with real hair, was entertaining two of the lovely hostesses at a table in the press box lounge. They strolled over to the press area and gazed out the window onto the stadium as Mike continued to be his occasional charming self. One young woman looked at him with starry eyes. I sneaked around to where the scoreboard operator was and talked them into letting me put up this important message on the giant scoreboard: "Mike Jones, Please Call Your Wife!"

Even our crazy doings sometimes paled in comparison with those mad, crazy days when Edwin "Bud" Shrake, Dan Jenkins, and especially Gary "Jap" Cartwright rode fire-breathing horses through the Metroplex as their mentor, Blackie Sherrod stood by.

Blackie and the Wildest Gang

9

"They all started out as sportswriters but have gone on to loftier subjects such as dope smuggling, chicken-fried streak, and mass murder."

—Blackie Sherrod, inducting Dan Jenkins, Gary Cartwright, and Larry King into the "Walk of Stars" in Austin

The *Fort Worth Press* was a kind of poor cousin in the Scripps Howard chain and was located in an old two-story building between the railroad yard and farmer's market at a downtown intersection. The newsroom was on a cramped, cluttered second floor, where heating and air conditioning were part time at best and left to your imagination at worst. It was an environmentalist's nightmare, although nobody paid much attention to such things back then. Well there was the time when the company refused to acknowledge the women's restroom wasn't functioning. So the women called the Health Department, which pronounced it a disaster, forcing management to do necessary repairs.

The backshop and newsroom were cooled and heated by the same duct, which sent soot from the linotype machines into where the working writers and editors were chain smoking, a hardly noticed atmosphere that would send people today fleeing for fresh air or oxygen. Pencils were rationed and at times writers used the back of publicity releases to type their stories because copy paper wasn't always handy.

Across the street was the Gem Hotel, where late at night you might hear the sounds of music, laughter, screams, or an occasional siren and face the danger of being mugged, as one sportswriter was. He left the office early one morning and was confronted by an assailant who demanded his money. The request was obliged. Then the robber told him, "If you tell anybody, I'll kill you." The staffer kept quiet...for a year.

Pay was small in those days, with reporters' salaries just under $50 a week, and as *Press* alumni Mike Shropshire pointed out, "If you got a Christmas bonus, it came out of the vending machine. But we would get free whiskey from the Cowboys, TCU, and other sources."

For the understaffed, underpaid, inexperienced sports staff to compete with the well-heeled, fully staffed *Fort Worth Star-Telegram* might be compared today with Minnesota competing with the New York Yankees, which now pays its pitching staff more than the salary of the entire Twins' team. Circulation of the *Press* hovered around the 50,000 mark, never surpassing 60,000. But Blackie Sherrod's sports staff relished being David against Goliath and consistently beat the larger newspaper if not in content certainly in the written word.

And it was at the *Press* that a new age of sportswriting took roots under the influence of Blackie, who was purging young sports guys in his domain of the simple get-the-facts style of the Associated Press. His approach was to use humorous insights and comparisons of sports topics or characters to historical figures, movie stars, or whatever or whomever to make a point.

Expounding on the many contributions owner-showman Bill Veeck made to baseball, Blackie wrote that he'd probably be remembered as the guy who sent a midget, with a strike zone the "size of a Prince Albert can," to pinch hit when he owned the old St. Louis Browns. "This is like remembering Robert E. Lee because he rode a gray horse named Traveller."

Here's his description of Bobby Hayes, the World's Fastest Man: "Hayes wobbled and swerved and jerked. He ran with elbows pumping across his thick body like he was trying to force his way through a crowd at a supermart sale. His shoulders rolled and his head bobbed furiously. *Everything* moved, and not necessarily in sync. Bob didn't flow like a graceful speed machine. He looked more like a man trying to outrun a bull on plowed ground. To hell with form, just get me to that blasted fence."

He also spiced his columns with a language of his own, such as calling *Sports Illustrated* *"Sports Elevated"* and California the "Left Coast." At this writing Blackie was eighty-one and still doing his Sunday "Scattershooting" columns and inserting tidbits from his neighbor Jones. He was still hitting the point in 2001 when he wrote, "Our

neighbor Jones always told his son that anybody could become president, and now the kid is starting to believe it." And earlier comments include gems such as, "Our neighbor Jones sez that argument you think you won from your wife isn't over yet." And "Our neighbor Jones sez his wife drives like she wants to have her accident quickly and get it over with."

Larry King of *Best Little Whorehouse* fame admitted when he was a young sportswriter in West Texas he stole a lead from Blackie. But we all went to school on Blackie, and anyone who claims he didn't has forgotten, is fibbing, or is dumb.

On a minor, unimportant note that is used because this IS my book, Blackie had a great influence on me after I started reading the *Fort Worth Press* while making a name for myself as the worst engineering student at Arlington State College, now the University of Texas at Arlington. For the most part I'd been reading straight writing in sports journalism but discovered Blackie and guys named Jenkins and Shrake, who were not only excellent writers but also very funny.

Anyway, shortly after graduating from North Dallas High School, my buddy Mike McKeogh and I went off to Alaska that summer when I was Jack London. However, I wrote nothing and we worked for a group of engineers on a survey crew. The engineers drove nice Jeeps and had good-looking wives and/or girlfriends. So I decided I wanted to be an engineer. Some mistake was made on my entrance exam, and I was placed in an advanced chemistry class even though I'd never taken chemistry in my life. But I studied my tail off for the final and made a 27, a record which I suspect still stands.

So I read Blackie and the guys and figured they had Jeeps and good-looking wives or girlfriends so I switched to journalism. I quickly found success, winning first place in a journalism contest for game coverage by incorporating Shakespeare into my lead. I didn't even get a byline. As well as I remember I mentioned to the school sports editor what I was going to do in my lead and he liked the idea. I

guess he figured it was as much his story as mine. It helped prepare me for the profession. Oh well...I digress. Commercial over.

— ◻ —

Blackie has always been an avid reader of a wide variety of books ranging from Tolstoy to a collection of Red Smith's sports columns. He's mentioned being influenced by the words of such notables as Dorothy Parker, Damon Runyon, S. J. Perelman, James Thurber, and Max Schulman. And he grew up during the Depression and served in battle during World War II as a tailgunner on a Navy dive-bomber. Those experiences put life, much less sports, in perspective. His attitude was that sports was what it was supposed to be, just a game, and certainly not to be taken on the level of a moonshot, the Cold War, and civil rights, nor its stars poetically written about as courageous heroes.

He began work for the *Fort Worth Press* in 1948, and his ten-year run was unmatched as he put different twists on the way sports was written and influenced a crew of incredibly talented youngsters. When he was at the *Press* he saw the future. "There was one television per household," he said. "The husband ran the home in those days and had the set tuned in to ball games. The wife was sitting there and did not know what was going on or maybe have much interest. If you wrote so women could understand, you might get their interest. So we started using illusion, illustration, and comparisons to movies, art, Shakespeare, and so forth to catch women's interest.

"I also kept thinking the coming of television was going to eat us up. So we also started carrying television schedules for sports events, which some newspapers had refused to do. We tried to put the emphasis on good writing. That's something newspapers can give you that television can't."

He brought in youngsters Dan Jenkins and Bud Shrake at the *Press*, but contrary to popular assumption, Gary Cartwright didn't work for Blackie at the *Press*. Blackie had already moved over to the *Dallas Times-Herald* in 1958 when Dan

Jenkins replaced him as sports editor and hired Gary. Blackie took Shrake with him to the *Times-Herald* then hired Cartwright and later Jenkins. For a brief period at the *Herald* those four guys had to be the most talented group on any sports staff in the country. Then Jenkins went to *Sports Illustrated*, and Walt Robertson hired Shrake and Cartwright for *The Dallas Morning News*. In 1985 Walter, who was out of sports but working in various capacities for the newspaper, also was instrumental in talking Blackie into coming to the *News*.

— ❑ —

When Dan Jenkins was a senior at Fort Worth's Paschal High School in 1948, he wrote a parody about a *Star-Telegram* columnist. Blackie read the story and hired him. He once said Dan was writing the new journalism in high school but didn't know it. Bud had been friends with Dan at Paschal and soon joined him at the *Press*. Blackie considers Jerre Todd one of the more creative talents he had.

Dan Jenkins and Blackie Sherrod were on the cutting edge of a new approach to sportswriting.

Jerre had been told that the best way to impress Blackie was to shock him or make him laugh. So when he came in for an interview, he raced across the room to Blackie's desk and executed a perfect hook slide. "You're hired," said Blackie. Unfortunately, Jerre was impressed when color television hit the market and figured he'd never be able to afford one unless he took a more lucrative route in life. So he went into public relations, forming his own greatly successful business.

The thing that frightened them most was to get beat on a story or make an error, which usually brought on Blackie's wrath. They also feared his dreaded bulletin board upon which Blackie would tack up examples of overwriting, underwriting, and lapsing too much into Hemingway's or Fitzgerald's style.

Blackie was always suggesting books for his staff to read and also journalists he admired. He told a young Dan Jenkins he should check out Henry McLemore, a 1930s writer for the United Press who shunned the style of the time. Jenkins looked in the files and found a story by McLemore from the 1936 Olympics in Berlin. The lead was, "It is now Thursday. The Olympic Marathon was run on Tuesday and I'm still waiting for the Americans to finish."

So Jenkins wrote, "It is now Monday. Birdville played Handley on Friday night and I'm still waiting for Bubba Dean Stanley to complete a pass." Blackie tacked it to the bulletin board.

Bud Shrake once recalled, "We grew up under Blackie. We didn't tell him anything (about their capers). It would have been like going home and telling your mother... We were scared to death of Blackie."

"A myth exists in Texas newspaper circles that working for, or alongside, Blackie Sherrod at some early station in your life was the equivalent of a journalism degree. I wish to correct that. It was better than a doctorate," wrote Dan Jenkins in an introduction to one of Blackie's collections of columns, *The Blackie Sherrod Collection*. Dan also called Blackie "The best sports columnist in the history of Texas and one of the greatest in the history of the earth."

Shrake, Jenkins, and Cartwright all had interests beyond journalism. They wanted to be writers for magazines, do books, etc. They talked about writing all the time and wrote for each other. A successful story was one that amused their buddies.

"I think we were successful because we didn't take sports all that seriously," said Cartwright. "Sports was fun and games to us. We used to laugh at sportswriters who took it too seriously. It was a joke that all the New York writers always portrayed Yogi Berra as this witty guy with great charm. He was a moron. The greatest thing he ever said was, 'Uh, I don't know.' We appreciated the athletes and that they were good, but bottom line, it was still a game. A lot of our wildness was a reaction to the realization of not thinking sports was life and death."

— ❏ —

Besides the well-documented episodes of the Terrible Trio, others at the *Press* were, well, also different. There was

Delbert Garrett, the one-legged city editor, who Cartwright once wrote was forever in search of the Japanese soldier who blasted him in the leg. And there was Caroline Hamilton, who always wore cowboy boots, and of course Sick Charlie Modesette and Puss Ervin and my old buddy Andy Anderson.

Puss was a retired postman who became the bowling writer. He didn't let his job interfere with his pleasures and would come in early and compile what the bowlers had done while sipping vodka out of a paper cup. When Puss first saw Cartwright appearing late for duties, he stared at Gary, noting his Oriental features, and said, "Who's that Jap over there?" To this day Gary's friends still call him "Jap."

Sick Charlie Modesette was also a legendary drinker, which didn't have a positive effect on his health. Bob Trimble, who joined *The Dallas Morning News* staff after the *Press* folded in 1975, recalled when he got out of the army how he took a job on the news side but was called upon to help Charlie put out the sports page. They were supposed to be in early to put the Sunday paper to press at 4 P.M. on Saturday. Bob arrived an hour or so early because he didn't know the drill and wanted to warm up for the assignment. When Charlie didn't show up on time, Bob started writing heads and putting out the paper by himself. He admittedly was in somewhat of a nervous panic. A few hours later Charlie staggered in drunk.

Bob was angry and hungry as he said, "Dammit! What do we do about lunch?"

"Good idea," said Charlie, as he turned around to leave, "I'll go first."

Charlie was still there when Mike Shropshire worked for the *Press* in 1970. Mike recalled Charlie was in charge of picking the stories and putting out the sports section, but two days before the Super Bowl not a word about the biggest of games had been in the newspaper. When the managing editor Jack Mosely stormed into the sports department and pointed out in no uncertain words this oversight, Charlie calmly remarked with total indifference, "Yeah, I noticed that too."

Knowing Andy, I'm sure he disgraced himself like the others but he also continued the *esprit de corps* of the *Press* years later when he took over as sports editor. During a storm in Fort Worth that staggered traffic and caused all sorts of problems, Andy called the office and said he'd report for work one way or another. So when traffic stalled by the railroad tracks, blocking his route to the office, Andy parked his car and crawled under the train and walked the rest of the way. And out of the ashes of the craziness that was the *Press* rose another madman, Mike Shropshire, who will materialize later on a fire-breathing horse.

— ❏ —

Pictures and books line the walls of Blackie's office on the fourth floor of *The Dallas Morning News*. One picture is of Blackie and his staff of Bud, Dan, Jerre Todd, and Andy Anderson. They're smoking, wearing hats, suits, and ties (or shirts buttoned at the top) and look like the Untouchables about to go after Al Capone.

Blackie dedicated his second column book, *The Blackie Sherrod Collection*, to the old gang. "With a glass for the old *Fort Worth Press* rapscallions—Bud Shrake, Spanky "The Child Star" Todd, Dan Jenkins, Darwin B. Anderson, Jap Cartwright, Puss Irving, Sick Charlie Modesette—who came to work laughing every day, even though readership was limited to immediate families and payday was under a dim bulb so the ones would look like tens."

— ▫ —

Dan Jenkins certainly took part in some of the shenanigans, but the duo of Shrake and Cartwright were the main players. And they became even more rampageous when they came to Dallas, where they ruled the

Blackie Sherrod and his old crew at the *Fort Worth Press* in the 1950s. Left to right are Jerre Todd, Andy Anderson, Blackie, Edwin "Bud" Shrake, and Dan Jenkins.

madness of the night by taking outrageous behavior to a creative landmark.

The National Sportscasters and Sportswriters Association would send out ballots each year to sportswriters to choose the "Sportswriter of the Year" in their state. For instance, there were six on the sports staff at the *Press* plus Crew Slammer, whose stories mocking old-style sportswriters were popular reading around the office bulletin board but never made print. That was because he didn't exist except in the minds of Gary, Jerre Todd, and Dan Jenkins, his ghostwriters. Sports editor Dan Jenkins was away at a golf tournament when Cartwright and Jerre Todd intercepted the association's letter to Dan. Instead of sending in votes for the six staffers, they made up dozens more, including the ever-popular Crew Slammer, and mailed the ballots.

They were aware Bill Rives, then sports editor of *The Dallas Morning News*, actively sought the award. That year he finished second to Crew Slammer. Had people given "high fives" in that day they certainly would have at the *Press*. One of their own had

beaten all odds to be named the best sportswriter in the state! Rives failed to see the humor, blew the whistle, and captured the award in a recount.

— ❑ —

One of the most dangerous times for mankind and womankind was when first Shrake and then Cartwright got divorces and moved into an apartment just north of downtown Dallas prior to the assassination of President John Kennedy in 1963. They charged like the Light Brigade. Their apartment became a gathering place for visiting football coaches, athletes, strippers, entertainers, gangsters, musicians and you name it. Jack Ruby would even drop by with some of his musicians and exotics from his Carousel Club. Especially of note was a stripper named Jada. Beer, liquor, weird cigarettes, and goodness knows what else were handy.

In his book *HeartWiseGuy* Cartwright wrote Jada was "the most interesting and exotic woman I ever met." Apparently Shrake was also taken by her and vice versa because they had an affair. Gary's high opinion of

Jada might have increased when he married his second wife, Jo. As a wedding present Jada sent them a two-pound cookie tin filled with manicured marijuana.

Neither Jada nor Ruby was at the Colonial Country Club in Fort Worth the night Gary froze the audience. The Colonial National Invitational Golf Tournament at the hallowed grounds of the Colonial Country Club was not only a nationally respected sports event but also one of the most revered social events in Fort Worth. The rich, the celebrities, and the elite of Fort Worth were there to wine, dine, and watch the world's greatest golfers. Cartwright had a press pass for the golf tournament, but unlike Shrake and Jenkins, he did not receive an invitation to the first annual poolside luau and fashion show. He was a little bothered by this, and Shrake as usual urged him onward and downward. If Shrake wasn't actually going to take part in some madness, he would coax Cartwright into going solo. When Shrake suggested Gary dress up like a waiter and crash the event, his friend gladly did so.

Gary found out the waiters kept their uniforms in a linen closet in the basement and borrowed a jacket and emerged ready for action. A waiter passed by carrying a tray of rolls and Gary stopped the guy and said, "Let me take those." Why not. The guy gave him the tray of rolls and Gary headed poolside. However, club manager Virgil Bourland, no fool, stopped him. He looked at Gary then lifted a roll off the tray and said, "What's this?" Gary responded, "Them's rolls." Bourland asked, "What for?" Gary indignantly replied, "For hungry people."

Then when Bourland asked him if this was some kind of joke, Gary responded, "Hunger is never a joke" and hurried away. He hid in the hedges in case Bourland had sent somebody looking for him and then when it was safe to come out emerged again. Nobody recognized him but his bemused friends, Jenkins and Shrake. Models were being introduced as they paraded in their new, stylish outfits as Gary circulated among the tables, sometimes dropping rolls here and there as he neared the pool. He recalled someone from Dan and Bud's table saying, "My god, he's going to do it." And he did. He climbed up the three-meter diving board, delicately balancing the tray, and then leaped into the pool as a stunned crowd stared in disbelief and horror, wondering if what they'd seen really happened. As rolls floated among the orchids Gary climbed out and hurried away into the night. Thereafter, the luau and fashion show was not held.

Gary had the knack for bizarre reactions and popping up in curious ways. Perhaps some insight can be found in an episode when he was a mere child growing up in Arlington. Or perhaps not.

He had also been bored as a kid, and unknowingly might have trained for future rampages by putting on a bathing suit over his blue jeans, donning a T-shirt with a Big "G" written on it, devising a cape out of one of his mother's dish towels, and proclaiming he was a comic book character called "The Guinea."

He was joined by other bored kids, who would go into a five-and-dime store, scatter, and make sure a saleslady was watching as they lifted things off the counter. Then they'd begin putting pilfered items under their shirts and in their pockets while Gary watched outside through the window. Just as the saleslady moved in for the kill, Gary would rush into the store with a "Dum-de-dum!" His buddies pointed at him and screamed, "Look, the Guinea! Let's get out of here!" Then they'd take off with Gary in pursuit as the store employees watched open-mouthed.

Also the Guinea's pack would take their act to the streets as Gary climbed a nearby tree. His pals would stop approaching motorists by any means necessary and hover around the captured car. Suddenly, Gary would jump from the tree as the kids pointed at him and yelled, "The Guinea! The Guinea!" They then would run into the woods with Gary, his dishtowel waving in the wind, in pursuit.

"Even then," he once told me, "I wanted to see how people reacted to something shocking. I never changed a lot."

— ❑ —

Cartwright and friends occasionally made up stories that were printed in the *Press*. However, when he joined Jenkins and Shrake at the *Times-Herald*, they did perhaps their best work, inventing a town, a cast of characters, and naturally a football team. As Jenkins once said, "If you grow up in Texas and you're not interested in football, they drown you at an early age."

Previously, they had inserted make-believe Metcalf U. in the agate scores of the newspaper each week as the team beat opponents such as Indiana McGruder, and Southeastern Oklahoma Central. When the results of Metcalf, named in honor of the poet James Metcalf, was lost in the backshop and failed to appear in the Saturday paper, a reader complained.

And then there were the fabled Corbett Comets. Each week Cartwright, Jenkins, Shrake, and news columnist Dick Hitt created the story of the Corbett Comets as they fought their way to the state championship behind their twin halfbacks Dickie Don and Rickie Ron Yewbet. Their last name was in honor of late TCU coach Abe Martin who often used the word yewbet as in "Yewbet we're going to give it our all. Yewbet."

Each week the exploits of the twins and their Comets appeared under small type in the *Dallas Times-Herald*. They were gaining a following. Then just before they played for the state title in their unidentified division, tragedy struck. Dickie Don died of the mumps. On the eve of the big game things were gloomy in Corbett. But in storybook fashion Rickie Ron scored eight touchdowns as the team played one for Dickie Don and won the state championship over East Dozier.

The story of Corbett was too big to let go. They wrote a take-off on the University of Texas having the world's biggest drum by writing the Corbett High School band had the world's biggest tuba, donated generously by local Ford dealer E. O. "Shug" Kempleman. Later when Gary was working the rim for the *News*, he managed to slip in a story on the women's page that F. D. Orr defeated E. O. "Shug" Kempleman, 43 votes to 38 in the Corbett municipal elections.

Rives immediately blamed Gary. They never did understand each other.

— ❑ —

You might say what happened during a large Christmas party gathering at Blackie's house wasn't exactly one of Gary's impromptu, original ideas. That was the time he disappeared behind a curtain then reappeared nude. One account had him singing "Danny Boy" and/or various folk songs. Most agreed that he also dove into the pool and swam a few laps.

"I was very disappointed in the reaction," he said later. "Nobody seemed to notice that much." He recalled pulling the same trick at other times with the same reaction. So what was the use? Nothing ever had to be of use for Gary.

Gary was a fan of Bob Mitchum, who became his role model during a costume party in Hollywood. Mitchum reportedly showed up dressed as a hamburger with his costume consisting of ketchup on his body between two buns. Gary was also impressed when Mitchum became the first,

reported anyway, star to be busted and imprisoned for marijuana possession.

When asked about feelings he had while incarcerated, Mitchum remarked, "Just like Hollywood, but without the riffraff."

— ❑ —

Gary wrote about crime and dope smuggling for *Texas Monthly.* But it is doubtful anybody could have been more original than Gary when he tried to smuggle drugs INTO Mexico. It was another sordid tale of suspense and danger as Gary and a companion matched wits with an alert veteran customs agent. Gary and a friend were touring border towns for an article he was writing for the magazine. Halfway between Matamoros and Reynosa they were crossing the border at Progreso to eat lunch. The ever-alert agent paid little attention to their baggage other than a box labeled backgammon. He quickly found less than two ounces of marijuana. Ah-ha! Caught you! They were body searched and their luggage given a thorough going over. No more drugs were found. It puzzled the agent who thought he would find a large cache of pot instead of a dab of grass.

They were questioned thoroughly and the agent checked with the DEA in McAllen, who said to let them go with some exceptions. Their drugs were seized and their car impounded. It cost them $200 to get the car and then they were off after perhaps taking their place in history.

— ❏ —

Details are scarce and elusive as to exactly how, when, or why the Italian acrobatic team known as Le Flying Punzars appeared on the scene. Details are also elusive to founders Bud Shrake and Gary Cartwright whose minds were admittedly drifting into self-inflicted fuzziness in those days. Besides, the "whys" never were that much of a factor.

Apparently the Punzars appeared on the scene in a cloud of smoke, so to speak, and gained momentum. Slowly the mysterious duo (sometimes trio) took on a life of its own as did other madcap activities involving Cartwright and Shrake. The idea apparently came from the movie

Trapeze, starring Burt Lancaster, Tony Curtis, and Gina Lollobrigida. As in the movie, the ultimate goal for the Punzars was to complete the death-defying Triple Somersault WITHOUT A NET. The Punzars were reputed, by Gary and Bud, to have been on the Italian Olympic team in 1952 and sometimes in 1956 but were disqualified because they failed the gender test. Inexplicably they appeared in the Dallas-Fort Worth area. The first known performance occurred at the Riviera Club in downtown Dallas during the early 1960s when Lamar Hunt was operating the Dallas Texans, later to become the Kansas City Chiefs. Gary and Bud were at the club with Lamar, their friend Bob Halford, then publicity director for the Texans, and other unidentified guests who will not admit being present.

"We were stoned," admitted Gary, "and began speaking our version of Italian and dropping hints that we were international athletes touring the country."

"Pleeze speaka slow. No know much, how you say, En-gla-sa."

Gary Cartwright did have some calm, peaceful moments in the old days. (Photo by Doatsey Shrake)

Their group was wearing red Dallas Texan blazers and, well, looked like they might be touring the country. Soon their waitress began spreading the word that celebrities were in the audience. People stared at them. Gary and Bud grinned, waved. "*Ciao* to *tu* ... and *tu-tu*."

During intermission when the band and members of the floor show took a break, Halford approached the master of ceremonies and explained the internationally famous Punzars were indeed in the audience. If called upon they would put their lives at risk and attempt for the first time in public the Triple Somersault WITHOUT A NET. The emcee excitedly introduced them, and Bud and Gary stood up, bowed, and pranced to the stage.

"By that time we were so stoned we began to think we WERE the flying Punzars," said Gary.

As the drums rolled Bud, 6'6", crouched and prepared himself as the catcher of a much smaller Gary, who got into his running stance at the other end of the stage. Then Gary took off toward Bud as fast as he could but instead of jumping into Bud's arms, missed and hit him feet first in the chest, knocking him off the stage and landing on top of him as they crashed into the drums and cymbals, creating a crashing, banging noise as an apt finale to their performance. A great silence fell over the audience. Bud and Gary staggered to their feet, bowed, blew kisses to the audience, and returned with scattered applause to their table.

— ⌐ —

The Flying Punzars later became a part of Mad Dog, Inc., which was founded by Gary and Bud after they moved to Austin, put their days as sportswriters behind them, and became renowned authors. Gary thought the Mad Dog founding date was in the early 1970s. He said the reasons were fuzzy during those years, but it probably was simply because they thought it was a good idea. The Mad Dog motto was "Doing Indefinable Services to Mankind" with the credo "everything that is not a mystery is guesswork." They had cards and stationery printed, and membership grew to include some of the country's more noted writers and musicians and actors. Among the early inductees were Pete Gent and Jodi, his wife at the time, and Ann Richards and her former husband, David, who were later joined by Willie Nelson, Jerry Jeff Walker, Bill Brammer, and Jay Milner. Actors Warren Oates, Dennis Hopper, and Peter Boyle joined when they were in Durango, Mexico, making a movie written by Shrake called *Kid Blue*. Even Larry McMurtry was a corresponding if not active member.

Anyway, they took over the movie set, leaving scorched smoking earth behind them. They even had bit parts in the movie with Shrake's role as the town drunk very convincing.

Friends thought he was a natural.

In those days they boozed and did drugs but while running crazy also produced outstanding literature and music and established Austin as capital of the arts. As Cartwright wrote in his book *HeartWiseGuy*, "We prided ourselves on living on the edge. Some would say we lived delusionally, but from our perspective, reality covered more than a single dimension and Mad Dog reflected that perspective."

The group would diminish when too much partying and booze, too many drugs, and staying up all night caught up with them. Shrake had liver problems and diabetes and quit drinking in early 1983, and Gary suffered a heart attack and triple bypass and straightened out his life in the late 1980s. Their old pal Dan Jenkins also suffered a heart attack and bypass or as the trio called it, "Hit the wall." Others also slowed down or cleaned up their acts before reaching that point.

Ann Richards grew up faster, stopped drinking, divorced her husband, and became a political force among liberal Democrats and ultimately the governor of Texas. When she was running for governor she admitted making bad choices in her earlier life, but reporters wouldn't let it go. They kept asking about those days. I sent her a note, although I don't know if she got it, suggesting that the next time somebody asked her if she did drugs just say, "I don't remember. I was drunk."

Mad Dog, Inc. was not a group of sportswriters although two former ones were founders. So I'm not going to dramatize the escapades of the group because it would take an entire book. But you can read about the Mad Dogs in more detail in *HeartWiseGuy* and Milner's *Confessions of a Maddog*.

However, it is worth mentioning that after Shrake started dating Governor Ann Richards, another story about the Flying Punzars surfaced. Before Ann's political career took off, she was asleep in the early morning hours when suddenly the Flying Punzars, which then included Gary, Bud, and Jerry Jeff Walker, burst into her bedroom and announced they were going to do the ever-elusive Triple Somersault WITHOUT A NET. They tried and tried but, as usual, didn't make it. Now that they are older and gone straight perhaps they might try just one more time... no, it wouldn't be the same.

— ❑ —

And out of the ashes of his predecessors appeared Mike Shropshire. When he came on the scene at the *Fort Worth Press*, Blackie, Dan, Bud, and Gary were gone, which was probably better for all concerned. At the *Press* one fine day a woman appeared and told Mike she was a second grade teacher and her students had drawn some really cute pictures. She hoped the newspaper might use a couple of them. The drawings were terrible, even for second graders, recalled Mike, although he felt duty to his profession dictated that he at least check out the situation. Offices of the *Press* were very crowded and obviously no place to probe the possibilities of using the pictures. So he suggested they go some place where they could talk, maybe the Ramada Inn.

The next week a little six-year-old got her drawing in the newspaper. In the *Scripts Howard* magazine, sent to members of its chain of newspapers, the *Press* was cited for such an innovative idea as running a drawing by a youngster. Mike modestly accepted the credit and said it was just a lucky idea.

At the outset of his career Mike fell into the same trap a lot of us did when we came to Dallas-Fort Worth where the big hitters in the profession were. Public relations people were always giving you booze and buying you drinks, which also flowed freely at various parties. It did not occur to us to turn them down. We wanted to be one of the guys, part of the group, but we did so willingly so, dammit, it wasn't their fault.

"I was a guy in my mid-twenties who developed profound alcoholic tendencies," Mike admitted. "I'd rather forget some of the things that happened."

When the Texas Rangers came to town, Mike was hired away from the *Press* by the *Star-Telegram* to cover the team for more money, benefits, and all those things. "I still felt like I had thirty pieces of silver in my pocket for going to the enemy," he said. However, by then he had gained momentum for his own personal brand of wacko stunts such as the time he covered a Rangers game in Kansas City against the Royals. Mike, an extremely fast writer, finished his story ahead of the herd, which was dangerous because he had nothing to do. He got an early start on drinking and rumor had it some weird weed. So as everybody else worked away, Mike appeared walking along the ledge outside the press box. He then made his way to the broadcast booth of the Chiefs, where the radio team was doing a wrap-up on the game. It was said Mike then blew smoke into the booth, leaving them to explain when they got home what that weird smell was on their clothes.

"Honestly, I can't confirm that," said Mike. "I just don't remember, although that doesn't mean I didn't do it." Sure, there were times when he found unusual ways to cover out-of-town games but didn't we all.

10

Beat Experiences

"I couldn't tell any difference."

—Doug Todd after Cliff Harris and I had our bells rung

Sportswriters face many obstacles while on assignment, whether they are under or above and beyond their control. There can be missteps, false steps, tumbling over backwards steps, real steps, and dream steps. Yes, the road to the press box can be long and winding, and sometimes the road *from* the press box can be the same way. But we are what we are, rather were.

A recurring nightmare sportswriters have or used to have is when, due to circumstances beyond their control, such as beverages forced down their throats and oversleeping, they actually miss covering an assignment. Often I dreamed such a thing and still do every once in a while, along with taking an exam for which I hadn't studied or getting lost en route to some place, which come to think of it often happens when I'm awake.

In my eleventh and final season covering the Cowboys most cities, outside of New York or San Francisco, seemed to take on a sameness. After a night with fellow revelers I forgot to leave a wake-up call and woke up bleary-eyed with a headache and feeling misplaced. I looked at the clock, which lied that it was 2:45 P.M. As I started to go back to sleep the clock became the ugly face of reality and I screamed, "Oh no!"

I don't really cuss much unless it's at myself for doing something stupid, which means I swear far too much. So I was cussing myself as I stumbled to the window and looked out on the gray day and knew it was Philadelphia. Often games in the East started at noon, but maybe, just maybe I'd gotten the time wrong and it was a second game that started at 3 P.M. I checked the schedule: Dallas vs. Philadelphia, 2:30 P.M. By the time I got dressed and threw my clothes in the suitcase and hailed a taxi, I'd miss three quarters, but at least I'd be on the scene and improvise as best I could. Maybe I could tell Walter Robertson I'd stopped by a liquor store that was being robbed and...never mind.

I called myself a stupid so-in-so, dropped back onto the bed, put my hands over my face, and then that dim, blinking light came on in my head. I was in Pittsburgh for the game, not Philadelphia! The Pittsburgh game didn't start until 4 P.M. I was almost giddy as I packed, grabbed two packages of M&Ms with peanuts for energy, and made the kickoff with time to spare.

— ❏ —

I was going by the office en route to covering the 1976 playoff game in Texas Stadium between Dallas and Los Angeles ...or was it the St. Louis game near the end of the regular season? I planned to stop by the newspaper and then head on to the game. A few blocks away from the *News* a woman ran a red light and knocked the whey out of my car and me. I'd suffered a minor concussion and seemed to be in and out of a dream as an officer interviewed me. I apparently convinced him I was okay and he kindly dropped me off at the newspaper. The sports department was on the third floor but as I entered the lobby on the first floor I felt like I was walking in slow motion. For seconds I had no idea where I was. That should have been a clue something was wrong but I've always had trouble recognizing clues whether I've been knocked cuckoo or not. I didn't remember getting a ride to the game or going to the Cowboy dressing room to get quotes after it was over and talking to Cliff Harris, who didn't remember talking to me either because he'd had his bell rung during the game. Cowboy PR guy Doug Todd witnessed the scene.

"There you were in the dressing room standing almost face to face with Cliff," said Doug. "Both of you were talking at the same time, a mile a minute, and acting strange. On the other hand, I couldn't tell the difference."

Naturally, I had a terrible headache that night and the next morning but did rush to grab a newspaper to see what I'd written. But it turned out to be one of my better stories that year written in a state of fugue, not unlike a situation in which you're driving on a long trip, making all the proper moves, and suddenly realize you've driven for miles without realizing it. Now that I've gotten older a state of fugue seems to occur daily without a blow to the head.

Word got around that my bell had been rung and everybody teased me, but this was only fair after what I'd once tried to do to Golden Richards. Golden was knocked out in a game with Chicago and sat on the bench grinning as birds sang in his ears. After the game his head cleared and he couldn't remember what happened. I mentioned it was just as well after what he'd done.

"What? What are you talking about?" he asked. I hinted that he'd mooned the crowd. He had a puzzled look on his face, and quickly I added, "Ask Ron McAlister (a radio guy) and Frank Luksa if you don't believe me."

After seconds of terror Golden realized I was joking. That was a shame because I'd already briefed McAlister and Luksa to back up my story.

— ❑ —

Truth seemed worse than a bad dream during the final regular season game of my rookie year (1967) when the Cowboys played in San Francisco. The 49ers then played in Kezar Stadium, near the Haight-Ashbury section where the hippies, dropouts, and runaways had established their own idea of a perfect neighborhood with love (all you need is love), music, sex, drugs, long hair all over, and dressing in what appeared to be charity rejects. They protested against the establishment for LBJ and his boys to get out of the war in Vietnam. So there I was dressed in a suit and tie carrying a large suitcase, a briefcase, and portable typewriter making my way through Haight-Ashbury.

I'd planned to stay over in San Francisco so wasn't concerned about hitching a ride with one of the team buses to the airport. I could go down to the dressing rooms, get quotes, and take my time writing my game story. After I'd finished I could grab a cab and go back to the hotel. It was getting dark by the time I called a taxi. A guy answering the phone asked where I was, and when I told him he said, "We're not going out there now." When asked why, he said, "Hey, we're not crazy."

Naturally I was aware of the hippie movement and even sang some of the songs and also wanted peace and wasn't exactly

the hated Establishment but was certainly dressed like I was. Burning cabs and being beaten senseless with crude placards with peace signs flashed through my mind. But the only way to get out of there was walk and then find a phone booth and call a taxi.

I periodically had to stop, put down the heavy suitcase, which I couldn't drag because it had no wheels, rest, and then move on. The smell of marijuana permeated the air and people were outside on front steps, curbs, and everywhere, shouting and then laughing.

"ALL YOU NEED IS LOVE! AHHH-HA-HA-HA."

"LOOKS LIKE HE NEEDS MORE THAN THAT."

"YANKEE GO HOME!"

I looked straight ahead, picking up speed, and when somebody said something I can't print, I shot him the finger. This gesture brought on more laughs, and somebody said, "GET OUT OF VIETNAM!"

"HEY, CAN YOU SPARE A HUNDRED."

And singing, "ALL YOU NEED IS LOVE...LOVE... LOVVV...."

I eventually made it to a phone booth out of the area and called a taxi. I don't wear a suit and tie much anymore, but I wonder how many people from Haight-Ashbury that day might. It was a little frightening but nothing like what would happen later.

— ❑ —

Snow had begun to fall in New York that late afternoon in mid-December of 1968 when the Dallas Cowboys charter prepared to take off after the game with the Giants. There had been a two-hour delay, and the snow and ice got heavier after the 747 lifted off the ground to gain altitude for the trip back to Dallas.

Steve Perkins had mentioned on a previous flight something optimistic like, "Do you realize a major professional sports team in this country has never crashed? Every time we make it successfully, the odds go down."

"Thanks for sharing that with me," I said.

There was a sudden noise, like an explosion, and the plane began to rock and lose altitude and then dropped, causing that stomach in throat sensation. A stewardess, who soon would disappear from the charter flights, screamed, "We're going to crash! We're going to crash!"

"That's it! That's it!" yelled Bob Lilly.

D. D. Lewis, then a rookie, was sitting next to Meredith, who was calmly having a scotch and water. "Dandy, Dandy, aren't you scared?"

"Naw, D. D.," said Don, commonly known as Dandy. "It's been a good 'un."

The 747 straightened and leveled out as it gained altitude, and we had a smooth flight home. We were told one of the engines, while the nose was pointed upward, sucked in ice and became locked at low altitude. Joe Bailey, assistant general manager, told me years later the situation was a lot more dangerous than we thought.

Joe then added that had the plane crashed it would have been the biggest worldwide story in NFL history with all the big names aboard, adding, "They would have mentioned you at the bottom in 'others were'."

— ❑ —

Walt used to give me great assignments but also some difficult ones. He once sent me out to interview Mickey Mantle's kids. We sat around in a circle and stared. When one would say "Yes" I would quote him as saying, "Yes, we are very excited about Dad hitting all those home runs." Anyway, you get the drift.

> ... had the plane crashed it would have been the biggest worldwide story in NFL history with all the big names aboard, adding, "They would have mentioned you at the bottom in 'others were'."

Another time he called me early one morning in the 1960s and said Muhammad Ali was preaching at a Muslim church in South Dallas. It was my day off, but he said I was the only staffer he could find. Great. Ali had forsaken his name of Cassius Clay and become a Muslim and refused to be drafted during the Vietnam War, and racial tensions were high.

Cars lined the streets around the church, and a huge crowd was on hand. Outside the church they were selling sandwiches, and a man asked me if I wanted one. I told him no thanks, but he kept insisting. Soon people were around us, and I nervously said I didn't want a sandwich. Soon the crowd started moving back and Ali appeared. He put his arm around my shoulders and said I was there to talk to him and meant no harm. We had a nice interview. I liked Ali as a fighter before that day, although I wasn't crazy about his antics in the ring. I was crazy about him after that day no matter what he did in the ring.

— ❑ —

It was snowing that winter of 1969 in New York, and most cabbies were on strike and so it was important that we all catch the Cowboys team bus to Yankee Stadium. That way our luggage would be loaded with that of the team and we could pick it up back in Dallas rather than wagging it to the game and storing it in the press box. Naturally,

Saturday night dragged into Sunday morning and I overslept, woke up at noon for a 1:30 P.M. kickoff, and went into the fool's rush, throwing my things together and hurrying downstairs to the lobby. The team buses were gone, and with the problem with the taxis and all, there seemed no way to get to Yankee Stadium. There was a mild consolation because my rival on the Cowboys beat at the *Times-Herald*, Steve Perkins, came stumbling through the lobby like he'd just escaped the desert and was looking for a water hole. Not thinking, we stupidly surmised we might get a cab and asked the doorman for help. "No friggin' way," he said. But miraculously we saw a taxi stopping across the street to let out a body. We yelled at the cabby and slipped and slid after him before he drove off.

"Hey, cabby," yelled Perkins.

"Hey youse self," answered the cabby.

"Let me handle this," I said, pushing past Perkins, who in such pressured, frustrating situations can make Archie Bunker look like Mother Teresa.

"How are you, sir?" I said, making myself feel warm toward my fellow men.

"Whatsit-to-you?" he answered.

"Would you take us to Yankee Stadium?"

"Are you friggin' kiddin' me?" he answered and started driving off. I did not like my fellow man and threw my portable typewriter at the cab. It hit the trunk and slid down into the icy street.

A friendly, very perceptive officer of the law was standing across the street. He had been watching the pathetic scene and was laughing. "I bet youse guys are from out of town."

We explained our predicament, and he suggested our only hope was the subway, which would take us right to Yankee Stadium. No sweat. No problem. It sounded like his directions were "Godownthestepsoverdaretothethirdtrackfrom...." So we just went down the steps and decided we'd wing it. We discussed our predicament and surmised the best scenario we could hope for was to miss the kickoff, which no doubt would be run back for a touchdown. By that time Perkins, who knew a thing or two about leadership, had taken over. We didn't know which subway to catch. We asked a gentleman of foreign descent standing nearby. "Do we catch this subway to Yankee Stadium?" The man smiled and said, "Oh jes." Puzzled, I asked him, "Or do we catch the subway over there?" He smiled and said, "Oh jes."

We caught the first subway that came by, transferred with other passengers, and at 1 P.M. got off, and when we made our way to daylight we did not see Yankee Stadium. Rats! We were in Brooklyn. Then we saw a guy with binoculars boarding a bus. You had to get up pretty early in the morning to fool us. Binoculars. Football game. So we followed him and arrived at Yankee Stadium minutes before the kickoff, which was not run back for a touchdown. We looked awful, were nervous, but were there. There at last in the press box!

"Knowing you, I'm shocked that you're so calm," said Curt Mosher, then PR guy for the Cowboys, after I told him what had happened. A guy who turned out to be named Lou Sahadi

walked past. Mosher introduced us, and I said calmly, "Glad to meet you, Bob." Oh well, I already knew Lou anyway.

— ❑ —

If Frank Luksa had been with us, I'm sure he'd have handled the cabby much better. Hey, I give him credit for knowing how to deal with cabbies. Once we were in a taxi in another NFL city and were talking politics, one of the few things we usually agree on unless he's wrong. Without being asked, the cabby joined the conversation and Luksa asked him how he voted. The guy said he didn't vote.

"You're telling me that you, a grown man, didn't take the time to vote?" said Luksa.

"Hey, I was busy, okay," said the guy, who then volunteered another political opinion.

"Don't tell me your opinion if you didn't vote," said Frank. "You have no right to have an opinion."

"Hey, I've got . . . ."

"Just shut up and drive."

Years after John Anders and I had gotten out of sports, we met Luksa in New York. John was on holiday, I was there promoting a biography on Tex Schramm *Tex* (forgive the shameless plug), and Luksa was covering a Cowboys game. We had dinner, went to the theater, and afterwards discussed world problems over toddies. Frank had dozed off during the play and was fully energized afterward. Anders is a frequent visitor to New York and knows his way around the nightspots. We hit a couple of places and very late went to an Irish pub. Before closing we were singing Irish songs. When we got to the part where "and when Irish eyes are criiiieeeying" we all had tears falling down our cheeks.

However, we composed ourselves, managed to get through the door, and I walked up to a cabby by the curb. He was going to charge us only $50 to take us back to the hotel. I mentioned this to Luksa, who was humming a song in the shadows behind me.

"You fool," he said, using his favorite name for me. "Just get out of the way and let me handle this."

"Listen," Luksa told the cabby, "we're not paying you one dollar over $65. Take it or leave

it." He took it and Luksa got this pleased look on his face as Anders and I looked at each other in disbelief, although we shouldn't have been surprised considering the source.

— ❏ —

We took a taxi in New Orleans to Tulane Stadium (the Super Dome was in the future) for the Cowboys and Saints game with our suitcases, portable typewriters, and briefcases. Luksa had a larger than usual suitcase and also a suit carrier. He also wore a heavy coat in case the warm day suddenly turned cold. I figure he was lugging about fifty pounds. The driver couldn't get closer than two blocks from the stadium so after walking the distance with bent backs we arrived at a stadium gate. We were really dragging by that time, especially Luksa with his heavier burden.

I showed my press credentials and went inside. Frank couldn't find his. He searched through all his pockets, his baggage, carrying case, typewriter, briefcase, pant legs, everywhere. No press pass. He explained the situation to the guy at the gate who said, "Well sir, we can't let you in without proper credentials."

Luksa fumed while I resisted the urge to say I didn't know him and tried to get the guy to let him inside. Then Luksa got this twisted grin on his face and said, "Listen, you fool. Do you think I'd carry all this s--- to get in this f------ game free!" The guy's face turned red from the outburst. But we were holding up the crowd and an officer came over, was told the problem, and said, "You're at the wrong gate. The press entrance is around that direction. Just look for the sign."

Off we went again, and Luksa seemed to be in a state of fugue. When we got to the press entrance, the man in charge said I didn't have a proper ticket because the stub had already been torn off. He understood when I explained but told Luksa he couldn't get in without credentials, even a stub. If memory serves, Luksa berated everybody in talking distance and then sat on his suitcase while I went up to the press box, got credentials, and brought them to him.

— ❑ —

I never missed a kickoff, but in 1972 I did miss one of the most exciting finishes in a big game in Dallas Cowboys history. Dallas was trailing San Francisco 28-16 with some four minutes remaining. Some of us, including Luksa, then of the *Fort Worth Star-Telegram,* decided to leave the press box and head down to the field to watch the Cowboys' death rattle from the sidelines. At first the elevator stuck, delaying us for a few minutes, but we weren't going to miss anything important anyway. We walked to the tunnel leading onto the field, but a security guard wouldn't let us pass until after the game was over. About that time some media guy with a transistor radio mentioned that Dallas had come back and had a chance to win. The guy still wouldn't let us pass.

Wells Twombly of the *Houston Chronicle* tried to organize a coup in which we would storm past the guard, but it failed when we couldn't decide who would go first. Fortunately, Sam Blair had been a step ahead of the rest of us and had gone down to the field earlier and witnessed the unreal finish. He filled me in

On a fishing trip during Super Bowl XIII week Bob St. John landed a 9-foot, 111-pound white marlin. Frank Luksa caught a 7-foot sailfish. To this day, Frank swears his fish was bigger. (Associated Press photo)

on the details as we made our way to the dressing room. With 1:48 left Roger Staubach had run like crazy and thrown a twenty-yard touchdown pass to Billy Parks. Dallas recovered an onside kick and then Roger ran and passed for yardage, and Dallas won the game, 30-28, with 42 seconds left, on a ten-yard toss to Ron Sellers. So I didn't have to go into the dressing room and, like Luksa, ask players how they scored the touchdowns. I talked to Staubach, Landry, Sellers, and so forth and put all the drama I could into the finish I never saw.

When I got back to Dallas people were phoning and complimenting me on my game story. It was judged the best game story that year by the Pro Football Writers Association. That not only taught me something about myself but also about contests.

— ❑ —

It will come as no surprise that Mike Shropshire also set some new standards of his own while covering the Texas Rangers in their early days. Shropshire was a master of

improvisation. He had to be. The Texas Rangers were playing an afternoon game in Cleveland. He woke up with a terrible hangover and decided to turn on the television, watch a few innings, and then head out to the ballpark. He shut his eyes and fell asleep. When he snapped awake a voice on the television informed him the game was in the top of the ninth and Fergy Jenkins was shutting out the Indians. Before he could escape his room, Fergy, who did not waste time or pitches, had blanked Cleveland 1-0 in a game that lasted only 1:36, unheard of nowadays. He rushed to the stadium in time to catch Fergy for a few quotes and then head to the press box to do his story.

"It occurred to me the Rangers had scored a run and it might be important to mention how," recalled Mike. "Russ Snyder was covering the game for the *Cleveland Plain Dealer,* and the other guys from Texas had left. Russ hated Texas. He hated me worst of all because I was admittedly a little odd, and I think my seven-year-old daughter had once spilled a drink on his typewriter. But I swallowed my pride and asked him how the run had scored. He told me Jeff Burroughs had hit a home run in the first. I wrote the story and sent it to the paper. Then I got to thinking how Russ hated me and might have given me false information. I was pretty nervous but then talked to Rangers public relations guy Bert Hawkins, and he confirmed what had happened. Thank you, God."

Another time he was covering the World Series between the Oakland Athletics and Los Angeles Dodgers in 1974. He decided to stop by a bar two hours before the game to dull his skills. After a while he noticed there was this big television in the bar; he had a ballpoint pen and plenty of bar napkins for notes. So what the heck. He would cover the game live in a bar. He rationalized he might even get a different angle by watching over television.

"One thing led to another and I was discussing life with this person while everybody else was yelling about the game action over television. I couldn't see what was happening from my table and asked the bartender."

"Reggie [Jackson] just poked one out," the bartender told him.

"So I went back to my room and turned on the TV and made sure I had the right score," continued Mike. "I was so drunk I could barely hit the typewriter keys. I had some leftover quotes like, 'The team that makes the fewest mistakes wins' and stuff like that for my story. I sent it in to the paper. Then I got up the next morning and grabbed all the newspapers I could find to make sure my facts were straight. They were reasonably close. What do you expect? What I didn't expect was that I'd win an Associated Press award for my game story."

— ❑ —

When Dallas played Baltimore in the 1971 Super Bowl in Miami the team stayed at the Galt Ocean Mile Inn. The hotel was near the ocean so Deane Freeman of the AP and I decided to take a stroll on the beach one afternoon. We came upon Duane Thomas staring out at the ocean. That was Duane's rookie year, and he hadn't yet completely vanished into himself and become what we called the Sphinx. I was aware that he'd become upset with me when I wrote in a game story that he made a fine run but, "Only thing, he forgot the football." But he was pleasant enough. So we asked him a tough, penetrating question.

"Uh, what are you doing, Duane?"

"Looking at New Zealand," he said, mentioning that's where he wanted to go. We almost looked out there for New Zealand but quickly realized it would be fruitless. So we asked him another probing question.

"So, Duane, are you psyched up for the Super Bowl? What are your feelings about the biggest game, huh?"

"If it's the ultimate then why do they play it again?" he said, continuing to look at New Zealand.

We had quotes from Duane Thomas! Then he repeated the same things at a press conference, although I can't vouch that any other writers walked down the beach looking for New Zealand. But Deane Freeman might have taken his wife there.

Perhaps it was the fresh ocean breeze, salting his mind for adventure, but Deane suddenly saw a vision of himself whipping across the ocean in a sailboat. Now he'd never been on a sailboat, much less operated one, but it would be a cakewalk.

So he rented a sailboat, told his wife, who couldn't swim, to relax, and off they went to sea. "We were doing okay and then the wind switched directions," recalled Deane.

Naturally, he didn't want to admit he was out of control, that he couldn't handle a little sailboat and tried to fake confidence by looking stern. He blew his cover when he noticed the Galt Ocean Mile Inn was disappearing on the horizon.

They were out of control, lost at sea. Then he spotted a shrimp boat and took off his shirt and frantically waved it at the crew. The shrimpers towed him back to shore. If only I'd been there with a camera!

"But hey, we were alive," Deane said later. "So I went to pay the guy for renting the sailboat. I figured under the circumstances he might give us a break in the price. So I told him why we'd been gone so long and I was sorry our time had expired. But, hell we could have floated to Cuba on this damn thing."

The guy looked at him without expression and said, "Yeah, well it would have still cost you ten dollars an hour if you'd taken it to Cuba."

Deane recalled the episode after watching the movie *Perfect Storm* about a boat and crew being lost at sea in a massive storm. "It dawned on me again that I had had no proper instruction, was a flat-lander, and that we were in real danger." But there are always hidden dangers not only to players but sportswriters covering a team.

— ❏ —

Oh yes, Baltimore won Super Bowl V with 15 seconds left on Jim O'Brien's 32-yard field goal. It should never have come down to that. Dallas took a 13-6 lead just before halftime and when

> Perhaps it was the fresh ocean breeze, salting his mind for adventure, but Deane suddenly saw a vision of himself whipping across the ocean in a sailboat.

Baltimore fumbled the ensuing kickoff, the Cowboys recovered and drove to the Colt one. Duane Thomas fumbled on second down and films clearly showed Cowboy center Dave Manders recovered the ball. But the officials were confused, and when Baltimore tackle Billy Ray Smith began yelling, "Our ball! Our ball!" official Jack Fette signaled it was the Colts' ball. He made that decision even as Dave Manders got up holding the ball and handed it to an official. In the press box the recovery was given to defensive back Ned Duncan, which would have been a surprise even to him because he wasn't close to the play. Then the recovery was officially given to Billy Ray, a Plano resident who later told friends there was no way he recovered the fumble. His teammate Bubba Smith said, "We ought to give Billy Ray the game ball because he conned the official right out of the Super

Bowl." Even Landry admitted if Dallas had gone ahead 20-6, the way his defense was playing, he didn't see how the Colts could have won.

Fette's error was so blatant that I mentioned it in my story. Not that I hold grudges but every time Jack would come to Dallas to call a game, I'd write that he would be officiating and remind the reader of his call against Dallas. I also mentioned it in books on Landry and Schramm and the Staubach biography I wrote with Sam Blair.

Years after I'd left sports Tim Cowlishaw came back from a Cowboys game and told me an official named Jack Fette had asked if I was still around. I felt a little bad about what I'd done, but it was good that at least somebody remembered me.

After I'd been writing a Metro column with my ugly picture on it for maybe a dozen years, a prominent judge approached me in Joe Miller's bar. "Well, I miss you writing sports," he said, shaking my hand. Then he added, "By the way what are you doing now?" Ah, the importance of the sports page.

— ❏ —

One thing that used to drive me crazy, okay crazier, was the awful ticket business. People always assume sportswriters have an endless supply of game tickets, which is far from true. You get calls from your best friends you haven't seen in twenty years and relatives and total strangers asking if you can get them tickets. As with most things, I learned the hard way.

On a trip to Laredo-Nuevo Laredo to do a series of columns on *coyotes* who smuggled illegal aliens across the border, I made friends with this guy who said he'd love to see a Dallas Cowboys game sometime. I told him to let me know and I'd get him a ticket.

"You understand I'll have to pay for the ticket," I said.

"Oh sure. I just appreciate you getting it."

He later called and asked if I could get seven tickets because he had friends who had never seen a game. That would be difficult but I told him I'd try. I bought the tickets and sent them to him, explaining again, "You know I'll have to pay for the tickets. Just send me a check." When I didn't hear from

Above: Bob St. John and Willie Nelson having a beer and a bad hair day during an annual Super Bowl party in January 1978.

him after ten years, I figured I'd just write off the debt.

I crossed paths with Waylon Jennings early in my sports-writing career in Lubbock. He had a radio show I believe and had not yet become a superstar. Years later I was a big fan of his, especially when he did an award-winning version of "Mac-Arthur Park" with his wife,

Jesse Colter. So I was sitting in the press box just before a crucial, sold-out Dallas Cowboys game started. I was handed this message. "Waylon Jennings wants you to get him twenty tickets." I said, "Just tell him there's no way in the world that I can do that." I always hoped he didn't hold that against me.

Early one week I got a call from an out-of-town relative. He asked if I could get him a couple of tickets so he could take his wife to the Cowboys game that weekend. Sure, I told him and why didn't they just come by the house and ride to the game with me, saving a parking hassle and all that. I didn't even tell him I'd have to pay for the tickets. The day of the game I waited and waited and had to leave or be late for the kickoff. So fearing there had been an accident I called his house.

"Oh, it's been raining and we decided not to come," he said. Silence. "But I'm sure you won't have any trouble getting rid of a Dallas Cowboys ticket." I ended up giving them to this kid and his dad waiting in the ticket line at the game.

I had an extra ticket the night John Anders and I went to see the Dallas Mavericks because somebody who was going with us backed out. There was this soulful-looking kid outside Reunion Arena. I chatted with the kid for a minute and found out he didn't have a ticket. So I gave it to him.

After the game started, this belligerent drunk sat down in the empty seat next to Anders. He spilled beer on John, screamed, cussed, and yelled all during the game. It was a miserable experience for John. As the game progressed I realized the poor kid had sold the ticket I gave him to the drunk. Good grief! Snookered by a mere child. I truly believe many times no good deed goes unpunished. On the other hand, it was amusing watching John squirm. He would have felt the same way had it been me.

— ❏ —

I got along with most of the players even when I'd write negative stuff. Well, once I had written that kicker Efren Herrera probably would lose his job. Shortly thereafter I was in the Cowboys dressing room after practice, and he braced me and got right in my face as we hit each other with bad breath. Lee Roy Jordan, who probably had to bite his lip to keep from laughing, got between us. I was wrong. Herrera was the Cowboys kicker again in 1977, but Rafael Septien took over a year later.

I was out of sports after the Super Bowl in 1978 when I went to Laredo to do that series of columns on illegal aliens being smuggled across the border from Nuevo Laredo. I picked up the

Laredo newspaper, and there was a story about Efren Herrera. He talked about being let go by the Cowboys and said they were prejudiced against Hispanics. This might have come as news to Septien.

— ❑ —

Carlton Stowers, who took my place on the Cowboys beat, had a better idea on dealing with irate players. Carlton had been especially critical of the Cowboys defensive line, and Harvey Martin was furious. He cut Carlton to pieces over the radio on "The Beautiful Harvey Martin Show." He closed by saying, "It'll be interesting if he shows up at the practice field and has to face us."

Carlton did indeed go to the practice field. But he was there earlier than the players and borrowed a helmet from equipment manager Buck Buchanan. When the players walked in, there was Carlton, sitting on the bench wearing the helmet. Harvey looked at him, paused, and started laughing.

— ❑ —

Naturally Landry was always ready for the press. Carlton, Deane Freeman, and Frank Luksa all grew beards during training camp and looked pretty shabby when they approached Landry after practice.

Tom looked them over and remarked, "I don't know whether to call security or talk to you guys."

— ❑ —

After I first joined the *News* in 1963 I covered SMU for a few years. Some of the most enjoyable times were covering Doc Hayes' basketball team, which had a great run of success during those years. I had long admired Doc and had gone to North Dallas High School with his son Dick.

Besides being an outstanding basketball coach he was very clever. Once when asked why he didn't put a rug or something over his bald head, he said, "God only covered up the heads he was ashamed of."

When we were in a cab in Nashville, where SMU would play Vanderbilt, we saw a poor bum staggering down the street.

"There goes an old basketball coach," said Doc.

I also got along fine with football coach Hayden Fry, although some members of our staff didn't. We did disagree at times, and he would always say he wasn't upset but that I ought to stay away from his wife because she was really mad about what I had written.

Hayden had some good teams but will forever be remembered around these parts for bringing in Jerry Levias, the Jackie Robinson of the Southwest Conference, to play for the Ponies, the first of his race ever signed by a conference coach. Hayden did everything he could to get the ball to Jerry and ran all sorts of wild formations, which I called his "playground offense." Shortly after SMU had beaten a mediocre Rice team, I went into the dressing room with other writers, and Hayden, eyes blazing, pointed at me and said, "Now I guess you'll say we have a playground offense!" It was embarrassing and made me mad or as they say now, I allowed myself to become angry. So I made some bad gesture and walked away. As I was going

down the ramp and heading back to the press box, Hayden caught up with me and I had a momentary fear he might beat the heck out of me, but he hugged me and said, "Don't get so upset. You and I are buddies." So we made up. I never did know what his wife thought.

— ❑ —

My predecessor on the Cowboys beat, Gary Cartwright, did get into a fierce fight with Norman Van Brocklin, then the fiery-tempered coach of the Minnesota Vikings. It happened in a bar in Birmingham, Alabama, where Dallas and Minnesota were playing an exhibition game. For some reason that Gary forgot he took a swing at Norm and missed. Gary said he really didn't see what happened after that because he was in his coward's crouch with his eyes closed and his hands over his face.

Gary still kids me about when he was leaving the *News* and it appeared I'd take over the Cowboys beat. I told him I wasn't sure I wanted to leave the Southwest Conference because I could go to places like Austin for the Texas Long-horn games, stay in Austin and drive to College Station the next morning for the Texas Aggie games, and go to Houston and.... Anyway, I took the beat and didn't mind going to New York, San Francisco, Miami, and such, and I never took a swing at a coach.

— ◻ —

There were some rowdy guys in Houston. During a Houston Oilers press conference, Jack Gallagher of the *Houston Post* got into an argument with club owner Bud Adams. Soon they were on the floor wrestling but were pulled, or rolled, apart by cooler heads.

Jack didn't back down from anybody in print or in person, but knew when he'd had enough. When he was in Austin working at the *American-Statesman*, he went out with fellow staffer Tex Maule to have a few drinks. They got into an argument with a group of large UT students and went outside to

> For some reason that Gary forgot he took a swing at Norm and missed. Gary said he really didn't see what happened after that...

settle it. They were getting beat up and the students kept asking Tex if he'd had enough. "No!" Tex would yell. Finally Jack said, "Dammit, let me answer for us."

I met Dan Pastorini, the Oiler quarterback, during the American Airlines Celebrity Golf Tournament in San Juan, Puerto Rico. He was very polite and cordial and we had a few drinks and so forth. So it was surprising to later learn that Dan would take offense about something the *Houston Post's* Dale Robertson said to him. Words were exchanged and Dale ended up on the ground. There was confusion as to whether Dale was smart and dropped to the floor or was pushed.

— ◻ —

Sam Blair told me a story about a cool performance by Lindsey Nelson, who was a sportscaster but deserves mentioning. Sam was writing for the University of Texas' *Daily Texan* and also picking up an extra $5 a game to spot for Nelson and Jerry Doggett in the broadcast booth.

On Thanksgiving 1951 the Aggies and Longhorns were playing in College Station. It was such a hot day that they put the windows down in the radio booth. The stadium was packed as usual for the rivalry, and the game got very exciting near the end as the Aggies ran out the clock on a 22-21 victory. A fight also broke out on the field, and the Aggie fans had already started celebrating. With chaos everywhere Lindsey continued to calmly describe what was happening for the radio audience. Then a drunk Aggie made his way from the stands to the broadcast booth and was apparently trying to climb inside. He had pulled himself to the ledge and was getting inside as he yelled, "The Aggies beat the ...." He never finished. Lindsey reached out with his left hand, threw a mean stiff-arm, and sent the guy tumbling back into the stands. It is not clear whether the guy ever tried to climb into a broadcast booth again but I doubt it.

— ❑ —

Joe Heiling was one of my buddies in Austin and later was with the *Houston Post* and *Beaumont Enterprise*. He experienced a couple of tough interviews along the way. Once before Bobby Layne would consent to an interview he insisted Joe play "Cardinal Puff" with him. That's a drinking game with variations. Basically players sit around a table with a mug of beer. One will say, "Here's to Cardinal Puff the first time." Then everybody takes a swig of beer and hits their mug on the table. This continues with Cardinal Puff the second time, etc., with the bartender or waitress keeping the mugs full. By the time you get to "chug-a-lug" only the most resilient, such as Layne, remain. During this process Joe was swigging beer and interviewing Bobby.

"For some reason I had trouble reading my notes as the night progressed."

President Johnson had been known to sometimes answer questions while seated in the bathroom, which seems a little gross even for a president. Joe went to talk to Clint Courtney, a former major leaguer who had fallen back to the minor leagues. They were talking when Clint said he had to go to the bathroom. "Just come on and we can continue our interview," said Clint.

"Are you kidding me? See you later," said Joe.

— ❏ —

But hey, the most dangerous experience covering a game was when Terry Stembridge, then the voice of the San Antonio Spurs, was staying in a New York hotel prior to broadcasting a game. Two guys carrying guns followed him into his room. They handcuffed him and put him on the floor.

"Take what you want," Terry told them, "but I hope you don't shoot me."

"No problem, man," one of them said. "Hey, what's all this stuff, radio equipment?"

"I'm a broadcaster for the San Antonio Spurs," Terry told them.

"Hey, neat, man! I'm a pro basketball fan! Maybe we'll see you at the game."

They robbed Terry but to his utter relief left. "I started to ask them if I could leave them free tickets at the will-call window," Terry said, grinning.

— ❏ —

One of the most exciting interviews I ever had was with Bibb Falk, the old Texas Longhorn baseball coach. I'd heard he was tough so naturally when I was in Austin sports editor Lou Maysel sent me to talk to him. I never realized if Lou was just breaking me in or what. But Bibb had this bat in his hand, taking practice swings in his office. As we talked he'd take a swing, coming closer and closer to my head. I agreed with everything he said and left early.

When John Anders was a student at Texas and assigned by the *Daily Texan* to interview Bibb, he was understandably nervous. But he took a businesslike approach and properly introduced himself.

"Mr. Falk, I'm John Anders with the *Daily Texan.*"

"So you work for that s--- rag," Bibb said. It's extremely difficult to have a comeback when an interview begins that way.

At least my time as a sportswriter prepared me for just about anything that might happen during an interview. Well, not everything. I went to talk to this older gentleman after I started writing a Metro column. He was very nice but a little nervous. So I decided to tell him a few humorous stories to loosen him up a bit. Then I heard him snoring. He'd fallen asleep.

11 The Prince of San Antonio

"I guess we were all crazy back then. We aren't now. We don't do that stuff anymore. Maybe in middle age we got some sense. But really, I guess we just got old."

—Dan Cook

On a hot, late morning in summer, John Anders went with me to the Alamo City to see Dan Cook, the legendary star of newspaper, television, occasionally radio, and frequently extracurricular activities. We were bearded and dressed comfortably in summer attire of out-of-style castaways. I was going to interview Dan because he was at the heartbeat of sportswriting during those madcap, unhinged days. Anders wanted to come along because he didn't want to miss seeing Dan Cook, who can certainly be funny and very entertaining.

We visited in the upstairs office of his home in a nice, sprawling walled-in neighborhood in north central San Antonio. We made it through the guard gate into the section, but neither Anders nor I take directions very well. So we couldn't find his house until he stood in the driveway and yelled at us as we passed for the second or third time, depending on who tells the story. He had finished his usual tennis match earlier in the day and also had just completed his column for the *San Antonio Express-News*. Like some of the older guys, he still used the old two-finger method of typing and enlisted his daughter, Alice Anne Ashton, who lives next door, to send it by dreaded computer to the newspaper. If she's not around then his son, Dan III, gets the job. Progress is dark out there, to be avoided whenever possible.

After we visited for a while, Dan, his usual generous self, offered to take us to lunch, and had we sincerely asked, I'm sure he would have loaned money to each of us. He tends to do that with people he knows and occasional strangers. Seizing the moment and without insincerity, we each mentioned being a little short of cash at the time. Dan was reaching for a roll of bills when he realized we were putting him on. Unfortunately, he still took us downtown to the Petroleum Club, a somewhat elite spot where the well dressed dine. We tried to beg

off, considering the way we looked, and suggested a less elaborate place because otherwise at the Petroleum Club we'd probably be stopped at the door. But he insisted, saying it was no big deal and that we looked fine. Sure.

We entered the elegant, private establishment and people kept greeting Dan because he might be, with the exception of Spurs' stars such as seven-footers Ned Duncan and David Robinson, the most recognizable personality in San Antonio. He's been writing for the *Express-News* since 1952, and his column picture has been staring at generations of residents. And he was seen doing sportscasts on KENS-Channel 5 since 1957. Even after we were seated and had begun to eat, I kept noticing diners looking in the direction of our table and realized it wasn't just because of Dan but also his unlikely-looking guests. We had an excellent meal, a nice visit, and returned to his home to talk more.

A week or so later I phoned Dan, who explained, "I went back to lunch at the Petroleum Club, and a waitress came up to me and said, 'Mr. Cook, I think it was wonderful that you'd bring those street people in here and feed them a meal.' "

— ☐ —

Dan, seventy-four, might well be classified not only as the dean of South and Central Texas sportswriters but also the most venerable of the real characters still working in the profession. If he'd be still long enough, the city of San Antonio might hang a historical marker around his neck. Whenever older sportswriters, old geezers as it were, get together and tell stories, many of the yarns concern Dan Cook. He doesn't mind telling them on himself. Dan is as at ease making himself the butt of his stories as he is others.

Here's Dan Cook caught in a rare moment wearing a tie. He denies it's a clip-on.

In his younger days he boxed a bit, played some football and baseball, and ran track and even thought about becoming a coach until bitten by the poisonous journalism bug. And he's a charter member of the group of us who have difficulty giving up our sports activities in spite of our bodies urging that we do so.

Dan has a flair for dramatics, often unwelcome. He's a proud, straight-talking, macho type guy with a reputation as someone who might throw a punch when provoked. He doesn't back down from a challenge whether it concerns tossing peanuts into a glass or more physical activities. And so years ago when he was being dragged feet first towards middle age, he received a telephone call from a young disc jockey inquiring about a possible touch football game between the broadcast and newspaper types for charity. Dan told him the "Press Packers" didn't have a touch football team but played the real game, tackle. Then he hung up. Furthermore, he wrote a column about his exchange with the radio guy, which irked the broadcasters to the extent that they accepted the challenge to play full dress tackle football.

Now in those days Dan was having prostate trouble and had no business playing tackle but recalled, "I had to play. There was no way I was going to chicken out against those jerks." Also, the newspaper had no football team. So he quickly organized one, the teams borrowed uniforms from local schools, and the game was on in Mission Stadium. Some 6,000 fans showed up to see the media celebrities bang away at each other. Dan, 6'2", some 200 pounds, was a rugged guy so he had to play fullback and defensive end. He was in a lot of action and got hit a lot, which wasn't good for his prostate, but more importantly the newspaper guys won, 37-0.

The following morning Dan was in excruciating pain. He was covering an afternoon game

between TCU and Texas in Austin but wasn't sure he was going to make it. Finally, he curled up in pain in the backseat of a friend's car and was driven to Austin. It was an important game with heavy media coverage from both in- and out-of-state writers.

Naturally, Dan's old adversary at the rival *San Antonio Light*, sports editor Harold Scherwitz, was there. Typical of their rivalry was when Scherwitz wrote a letter on country club stationery to the *Express-News* publisher saying, "My father would roll over in his grave if he knew you were paying this guy Dan Cook a decent salary because he's a terrible writer and person . . . ." It was signed B. Bart. The letter caused Dan problems before he proved it was from Harold. So during a summer heat wave Dan took out an ad in the *Light*, selling a four-ton air conditioner for only $200. He listed Harold's phone number as the place to call. Later, Harold estimated he'd received 1,000 calls.

In the press box Dan was obviously in pain. It is doubtful Scherwitz was overly concerned or even noticed Dan's pain as he took his seat in the press box. Dan's old friend Bill Van Fleet of the *Fort Worth Star-Telegram* was worried about him.

"Dan, you look like you're in great agony," said Bill.

Dan explained the problem and said, "Bill, I don't think I'm going to make it. It's just a question of whether to go to the emergency room here or hurry back to a hospital in San Antonio." Bill indicated something had to be done.

A few minutes later this man in a green checkered sports coat came over to Dan and introduced himself as a doctor. "Mr. Van Fleet told me you needed help. What's the problem?" Dan told him and quickly took the doctor up on his suggestion that they go into the restroom where he could examine the patient.

There was Dan leaning against the wall inside the restroom, his eyes closed and face contorted in pain as the doctor was down on one knee examining him. None other than Harold Scherwitz walked into the restroom, stopped cold in his tracks as if bumping into an invisible barrier, and said,

"Oh...excuse me." Then he hurried out.

"It was awful," recalled Dan. "I mean I couldn't go up to Harold and try to convince him it wasn't what he thought. There were a lot of out-of-town writers in the press box, and I had no idea what he might be telling them. I knew I had to write a column explaining. It was the hardest column I've ever had to write."

— ◻ —

Scherwitz thoroughly enjoyed Dan's situation. Dan didn't especially care for Harold but did relate another coup by his rival, who was a character in his own right. The city of San Antonio was having trouble with the surfaces of its tennis courts cracking in the hot sun. So Harold got a letterhead from a chemical company and used it to write a letter to the editor of the *Express-News*. He explained there was a new product developed for tennis courts that was having great success in the torrid heat of the Panama Canal. The product was "Tihsgip." Soon an editorial appeared in the *Express-News* suggesting city officials must do something about the cracking tennis courts and should take a serious look at "Tihsgip." To understand the magnitude, spell the product backwards.

— ❑ —

Dan has been a one-man conglomerate. Besides his newspaper and television work, at one time he did sports reports on KONO radio, was the source of a tout sheet that sounds like something out of Damon Runyon, and co-owned his club, Dan Cook's Time Out, with friend and fellow sportswriter Bob Ostrum. For a while he was doing five columns a week and three daily television sportscasts on Channel 5. Finally, he did cut down to two evening sports segments before retiring from the station in 2000. Then the station, hating to lose his popularity, talked him into doing two ninety-second sports commentaries a week with some flexibility to do one or even none. He's also only doing two columns a week and, considering his old schedule, he feels completely retired.

In the old days he'd go to the office at 10:30 A.M., do his column, then head for the television station for his sports shows and then drop by his nightclub where, at any given time, he might host Willie Nelson, Darrell Royal, and Mo Bandy or prominent city officials who liked to rub noses with Dan and other celebrities.

Back then he was certainly drinking with the best, or if you will, the worst of them, but his family was still very important to him. He even spent $1,500 in the 1960s to turn the garage into a glassed-in playroom at his house. Shortly thereafter Dan headed home in the early morning hours after a night of drinking and telling stories. He forgot the garage was a playroom and drove right into it as shattering glass sounded like a cannon going off.

The noise woke up his wife, Katy, not to mention kids and neighbors, and she yelled, "What in the world are you doing!"

"Nothing, honey, I just forgot my keys."

— ❑ —

When we returned to Dan's house that day after he'd fed the street people, he was asked how in the world he stayed married during his hellion days. "It got to where Katy had trouble seeing and I was having problems hearing so we couldn't get a divorce because we needed each other," remarked Dan, as Katy, his wife of forty-eight years and counting, laughed in the background. "Now she's had cataracts removed and doesn't need me. So I got to be more careful."

For better or worse she understands Dan, and he is quick to point out, "She deserves a medal." He likes to illustrate Katy's devotion by her reaction during one of those crazy nights of yore.

Dan used to get off late and meet his buddies at a favorite bar and tell tall tales and make bets on important things concerning our country, such as how long it would take the waitress to bring their drinks, or the great athletic feats they could perform. Dan claimed he could throw a golf ball into the cup on a par 4 hole at Breckenridge Park in four tosses. A pot was

started and the group left in the early morning hours for the park, where Dan would put up or shut up. Unlike the others, Dan was unaware there was a sudden rainstorm. Pride and confidence would not let him settle for a rainout. He tried, but it took him six shots. A friend was upset, saying Dan cost him twenty bucks.

"When I got home at that ungodly hour, Katy woke up and saw me in the kitchen taking off my wet clothes," said Dan. "She was obviously curious why I'd show up at that hour soaking wet. So I told her what happened and she said, 'Seems reasonable to me.' Then she went back to bed." Had it happened to many others in the profession, they would have found their clothes in a nearby tree the next morning. Incidentally, another time he actually won a bet with his buddies as to which one could get on a swing at Breckenridge, get it going, then leap the farthest distance.

— ❑ —

Dan's popularity as a sportswriter and columnist was

equaled by his work on television. He was the antithesis of the well-groomed guys doing sports, often showing up tieless in a sports shirt. He just did what came naturally to him, avoided primping, and was anything but phony. Plus, you never knew what was going to happen. There was the episode when wrestling superstar Fritz Von Erich came to San Antonio for a professional wrestling extravaganza, which would be watched by a SRO crowd. Fritz's real name was Jack Adkisson, and he was a former SMU football player, but he'd gained fame in pro wrestling by pretending to be German and using his notorious "Iron Claw." That was the hold where he'd grip an opponent's head with his huge right hand and then squeeze the arteries in the temples until the guy allegedly passed out.

When Fritz called and asked to be on television, Dan agreed. But Dan wanted a serious interview, not all the usual yelling into microphones, prancing around for the cameras, and screaming terrible threats about what they were going to do to an opponent and all the playacting.

Fritz showed up in a tux, wearing an Iron Cross and a monocle, and speaking with a German accent. Dan explained to Fritz that he wanted to do an intelligent, legitimate interview. Lights, camera, action. "I knew I was in trouble when I introduced Fritz and began asking questions.

"This gentleman sitting next to me is drawing capacity crowds everywhere he goes. Fritz Von Erich, are you ready to wrestle!?"

"Ya, I am ready!"

Trying to ignore the German accent, Dan asked Fritz if he owed his success and great popularity to the Iron Claw. Fritz was sitting behind a table with Dan and stood up and put the Iron Claw on him. "Here's this huge guy squeezing the hell out of my head, and I was about to go under," said Dan. "So I did the only thing I could think of and reached under the table and grabbed his ying-yang. He was squeezing my head, which the television audience could see, and I was squeezing down there, which couldn't be seen behind the table. It was live on the air. I had one squeeze left and used all my strength. He made this noise then got up and walked off the set."

Dan, trooper that he was, had only been on the air about twenty seconds but said, "Uh, we'll take a break and I'll be right back."

In another show he made television sports history when he interviewed African boxer Kame de Abrajar, who was fighting Texas heavyweight champion Terry Krueger in San Antonio.

"I was told he didn't speak a lot of English and hated to give interviews," recalled Dan. "I had it set up with his people that I'd ask something real simple. If I got into trouble, I'd ask him what was his best punch then he'd show me and that would signal the end of the interview."

Dan introduced him, "Next to me here tonight is noted African heavyweight Kame de Abrajar. Tomorrow night he'll be taking on Terry Krueger. Have you ever seen Krueger fight on television?"

Thoughtfully, the fighter said, "Krueger s---!"

Dan had a momentary blank look on his face and then said, "Ladies and gentleman, in African dialect that word means something entirely different."

"Krueger s---!"

Dan quickly asked, "What's your best punch?"

"Left hook!" said Kame and immediately clipped Dan on the face with a left hook and walked off the set. Dan later said if the blow had been hard, he'd have gone after the guy then and there. However, he showed great restraint and finished the show.

"The next day I found out the slob was from Oklahoma City. I'd been closer to Africa than he had," said Dan.

If you get the impression that people were taking shots at Dan, then you are correct, although

> "Here's this huge guy squeezing the hell out of my head, and I was about to go under," said Dan. "So I did the only thing I could think of and reached under the table and grabbed his ying-yang."

retaliation was just a heartbeat away. And sometimes winning is harder on your body than, well, just walking away.

Dan and Bob Ostrum opened their club in 1975. It closed in 1978 because even Dan realized he was spreading himself too thin, considering his newspaper and television obligations. But the memory of Dan Cook's Time Out lingers on. One night he was in the club and a man and woman began fighting. The manager of the club wasn't there at the time, and when Dan saw the guy, a rather large man in town from Green Bay, grab her by the hair, he went over to break it up. He told them they had to leave, and on the way out the woman grabbed his shirt. He was afraid she'd tear it so he actually went outside with them, which was a mistake. She let go of his shirt, and Dan told them to come back another time, that he'd see them later. But the woman protested, saying she'd left her purse inside.

"So I take her back inside to get her purse," recalled Dan. "Then this guy follows us. I don't want him back in there, and he doesn't want to leave so

I just start waltzing him back outside."

When they get outside, the guy puts his foot behind Dan and trips him. As Dan is going down hard he grabs the big guy, who falls on him, and they go crashing to the concrete. Dan's arm is broken from the fall, and the situation becomes even more serious when the guy gets up and steps on his stomach. Realizing the situation was grim, Dan struggled to his feet and grabbed the guy by the tie to protect himself. It was a clip-on tie. Dan uttered something unprintable and then drew back his good arm and hit the guy in the mouth as hard as he could.

"His front teeth come out and lodged in my hand," said Dan, shaking his head at his memory of his ill luck. But the guy holds his mouth, staggers, and Dan is ready to hit him again when Ostrum, a peace-loving gentleman who'd come outside, said, "Dan, he's had enough. Let it go."

Dan went to the emergency room to have his arm checked and get the teeth out of his fist. The doctor looked at his hand and said, "I might do a transplant." When Dan asked him what he was talking about, the doctor told him, "Follow me." They walked to another section and looked in where this big guy was sitting there with his front teeth out.

"Don't tell him I'm here," said Dan. "I don't want a rematch."

While the bulk of his audience agrees with Dan and his entertaining but blunt way of stating opinions, there are always others who do not appreciate his humor.

During the Iran hostage crises Dan happened to remark on his sports show, "...the Iranian students protesting in the park probably wouldn't feed the pigeons there without expecting two feathers in return."

Dan's daughter Alice, then sixteen, asked him to take her to a local disco. After a while Dan decided the place was a little rowdy and they should leave. As they walked to the car they heard somebody uttering what appeared to be obscenities and turned to see a rather large guy staggering toward them. Dan hurriedly took his daughter to the car, locked the door, and

turned to face the approaching man.

"I don't know you, pal, but you're the luckiest guy in the world. If I didn't have my daughter with me I'd knock out your teeth," Dan said in his usual subtle way.

The drunk kept coming but then stopped and started backing up as Dan moved toward him. Then he fell backward. Dan shrugged, got in the car, and drove off as the man continued to reel in the parking lot.

Dan got a letter a couple of days later from what turned out to be the guy in the parking lot. He apologized to Dan and his daughter for his behavior. Then he pointed out that he was just offended by Dan's racist slurs about Iranians. In a P.S., the man added that Dan should try to cool his temper because it could be dangerous for him and his job.

— ❑ —

A more serious gambling experience took place in the 1960s, starring none other than Dan Cook. He had been picking football games in the paper and doing pretty well. A friend who owned a print shop told him he was doing better than the tout sheets available.

"Let's you and I put out a tout sheet and sell it," his friend suggested. "You type it up, I'll get it printed, circulate it, and do all the rest."

"What's the top price for a tout sheet?" asked Dan. Told it was $1.25, he said, "Okay, we'll sell ours for $2.00."

They called it "The Huddle" as "In the Huddle with Jim Tuttle." They registered with the FBI under the fictitious names act, and Tuttle, of course, was Dan. He falsely claimed to have four agents from around the country who fed him up-to-date information on the teams in their area, such as injuries, etc. He gave the representatives names such as the ever popular Foots Johnson in Los Angeles. Dan hit big at the beginning, picking decisive underdog Baylor over Syracuse. The Bears won 35-12, and for a while Jim Tuttle became a folk hero among bettors. But the business did not always run smoothly. Once when they failed to get the tout sheet out there was a big protest from their clients. Dan

wrote that the problem was the great Foots Johnson had been ill. Another time when Dan had a bad week making picks, a guy wrote, "I wouldn't be surprised if this whole thing is just one fat SOB sitting in his garage putting out that crappy sheet." Dan laughed, noting the guy must be psychic.

"We each had a key to a post office box where the money was sent," said Dan. "We agreed that the box wouldn't be opened until we were both there. So naturally we always tried to beat each other to the scene. One day I showed up and he was standing in the corner and I didn't see him. I glanced in the box and it was full of envelopes with money. I paused for a few seconds and heard him say, "Don't do it."

Dan and his partner decided to fold. "In the final edition I wrote something like 'Dear readers and all our loyal customers, we've decided to stop printing because the great Foots Johnson is dead. He died last Sunday night. He was courageous until the end. He found this man mugging Maggie O'Neal on the streets of Los

Angeles and got stabbed. Then Maggie rolled him... He was only doing his job.'" They received all sorts of condolences from readers. If they decided to bring back the tout sheet, Foots Johnson Jr. would take his beloved dad's place.

— ❑ —

Dan certainly had some close calls during his heyday of boozing and shenanigans and in fact was once believed to be dead, along with four of his compadres. He was in Lubbock taking time out to cover the College Coaches All-Star game while partying and boozing and such. There was a noted Lubbock gentleman named Bob Walker, who always did his best to make the media happy and thus have good feelings about coming to Lubbock and the local school, Texas Tech. He would furnish transportation, booze, etc., and was lovingly given the name "Daddy Warbucks" by the media.

Dan was a little late arriving at Lubbock, but as he put the key in the door of his hotel room, Gaylen Wilkins of the *Fort Worth Star-Telegram*, another

noted after-hours player, hurried up to him.

"Put your bags and typewriter down, we're going to Mexico!" said Gaylen, all excited. Cook questioned his sanity, and Gaylen explained that Daddy Warbucks had asked members of the media where they wanted to go and an unidentified member yelled, "Mexico!" The wish was granted and Daddy Warbucks supplied a plane for them to fly to Juarez. The group, which became known as the "Juarez Five" included Associated Press scribes Deane Freeman and Mike Cochran, TCU public relations director Jim Garner, Gaylen, and Dan.

"It was late, I was tired and told him there was no way I was going to Mexico," said Cook. "So the next thing I know I was on the private plane going to Mexico."

The pilot didn't file a flight plan but they made it safely. An identical plane, with a Texas Tech professor aboard, had filed a flight plan and sadly had gone down in the area. But as Mark Twain is quoted as saying, "The reports of my death have been greatly exaggerated."

"We got drunk and had a good time in Juarez but almost got thrown in jail because Cochran not only began acting like the Godfather but thought he was," recalled Dan.

Meanwhile there were reports that the same type of plane had crashed, killing all aboard. Sportswriter Bob Galt's wife heard the report and ran into the pressroom screaming that Dan and the guys had been killed in a crash. Things got pretty gloomy. There was shock. Sadness. Some tears.

Then the Juarez Five later showed up at a party for the press. Their buddies were stunned, then angry with the Juarez Five for scaring them, which of course wasn't their fault. "Hell, it was like they were disappointed," said Dan. Lubbock sportswriter Burle Pettit was really looking bad after those hours of worry and stress. Then he remarked, "Dan, you really had us worried. Why, you could have gotten Daddy Warbucks in a lot of trouble."

— ❑ —

Sure, Dan Cook has certainly slowed down, but a phrase he made famous is still being used in the sports world when one team is trying to come back. "The opera ain't over 'til the fat lady sings."

"I can't remember where it came from," he said. "I think I might have seen it in a quote book. I used it in a column, which ran through the first edition and then was taken out. Then I mentioned it on my television show."

Longtime NBA coach Dick Motta heard Dan use the phrase on television and adopted it for himself, while giving Dan credit. Now it's universal. When Dan heard Motta give him credit for the phrase he wrote Dick, "Take anything I say or write and use it. But get it right. You said, 'The opera isn't over until the fat lady sings.' 'Ain't over' is correct."

He retired from television in 2001 and one of these days will leave the newspaper business, but the stories about Dan Cook will be like that phrase long after he fades away from sportswriting. They "ain't over."

12

The SWC, Above and Beyond

"Instead of partaking of the night life, drinking beer, and playing poker, the sportswriters now favor diet soda pop, torrid games of miniature golf, or Trivial Pursuit."

—Dan Cook on leaving the SWC press tour

The trip from Dallas to Fayetteville has never been the same since the old DC-3s, those proud birds with the bushy tails, were laid to rest by airlines. Old-timers might remember that the DC-3 was a great plane, which gained fame for its toughness during the Burma Run in World War II. In the early 1960s they were still taking passengers on short jaunts.

Once that happy, loose group of sportswriters and photographers on the Southwest Conference press tour were just aground in Fayetteville when the starboard engine began spitting fire...more than usual.

A poker game was coming to a close when Al Panzera, the *Fort Worth Star-Telegram* photographer, happened to glance out the window. "The plane is on fire! The plane is on fire!" he shouted. "Everybody be cool! Be cool!" After this word of advice Panzera leaped to his feet and went tearing down the aisle for the rear exit. Blackie Sherrod had just gotten up from a nap and struggled into the aisle, facing the rear of the plane, when he was blindsided by Panzera, knocking him back into his seat.

Not to be shaken and being "cool," Blackie got up, straightened his clothes and his dark glasses, and got back into the aisle. Meanwhile, Panzera had discovered the back door was jammed so he yelled, "Be cool!" and rushed back up the aisle. He flattened Blackie again, sending him tumbling over the nearest seat, feet sticking up in the air, heart in feet. The fire was extinguished and everybody lived for another day, although Blackie heard footsteps for some time to come. When the writers voted on the hardest runner in the Southwest Conference, Blackie picked Al Panzera.

— ❏ —

The two guys were unshaven, weather-beaten, and certainly looked like thugs as they walked into the bank on the outskirts of Fort Worth. They were carrying leather suitcases, the kind in which you might store an automatic weapon. The tellers stopped working. Customers turned to look. Fortunately, the two bank guards were nobody's fools. They started toward the two guys, who had realized what was happening and knew they had to get out of there fast, jump in the car, and take off. But they froze for seconds, which seemed like minutes.

"Hey, officers, we screwed up," said Deane Freeman. "We're looking for the Ramada Inn."

The guards stopped. And Deane of the Associated Press and Dave Campbell of the *Waco News-Tribune* got in their car and took off. These are some of the dangers of the Southwest Conference tour, where writers bused, flew, and/or drove to cities to do previews on the teams. Dave and Deane had driven from Dallas, where they got information on SMU, and were going to clean up and go to TCU. They got lost in Fort Worth while looking for the Ramada Inn and then confused it with a bank.

Members of the SWC press tour take a time-out. Front row, left to right: Bill Rives, Dick Freeman, Dave Campbell, Lou Maysel, Jerry Wizig, Jack Gallagher, and Bill Van Fleet. Back row, left to right: Blackie Sherrod, Gene Gregson, Abe Curtis, and Bob Rule.

"I don't see the big deal," said Deane. "It could happen to anybody."

Deane was much quicker in those days, which was fortunate. On the same tour in which he inadvertently posed as a bank robber, the group went to Houston to cover the prospects of the Rice Owls. In Houston the writers stayed at the Tides I or Tides II, owned by former Rice Owls star Dick Maegle. Deane, who never lost sight of his job, gathered information on the Owls and headed back to the motel to go over his notes. The door to Room 101 was open because no doubt the maids were cleaning up. They're really slow today, he thought. So he walked in but the maids weren't there. The room was clean. That's dumb, he thought, leaving my dadgum door open.

A huge gentleman walked into the room five minutes later. "What the hell you doing in my room?" he said.

"What do you mean, fellow?" said Deane. "This is 101, my room!"

They went back and forth but Deane was determined and wouldn't budge. Finally, it came to light that Deane's room was in Tides I. He was in Tides II. He apologized and quietly left the room. Deane couldn't keep what happened secret. Soon everybody on the tour knew. No shame among sportswriters went unnoticed in those days.

— ❏ —

Catching the bus was simple. You got on, then got off at a hotel or motel. One, two, three. So there was Jerry Wizig of the *Houston Post,* waking up at the Lubbock Inn after a very important, soon forgotten discussion which lasted until 2 A.M. His head hurt, a common morning state for those on the SWC tour,

but Jerry, ever the trooper, knew he had to catch the press bus at 8:30 A.M. to go to Texas Tech for an early press conference with Red Raiders' players and coaches. Now Jerry had a new digital watch, which was just becoming popular, and checked the time and jumped out of bed when it read an unforgiving 8:15.

The race was on. He threw things into his bags and ran to the front of the hotel. No bus. It was gone. He went into the coffee shop to plan his next move and saw SWC public relations guy Bill Morgan having a cup of coffee. Then Jerry looked outside and realized it was still dark. He punched his digital watch again and it read 7 A.M. Earlier it was registering the date, not the time.

— ❏ —

Bus drivers on the tour deserved battle pay. For instance, one night some of the writers somehow got the keys to the bus and, with Mike Jones driving, headed out to a nearby C&W club. They made friends easily because of the sign on the side, "SWC Press Tour." Against all odds they made it back before the tour continued that morning.

At least they brought the bus back. In the mid-1980s the tour once again was at the Tides Motel. The conscientious bus driver was up and at 'em early to warm up the engine and be waiting for the stumbling, staggering writers. But the bus was gone. It had been stolen. So he sat there with this hangdog look to greet the entourage and explain what had happened. It was later found in a vacant field. One rumor was that a television guy, who once had driven semis, had taken it as a practical joke. There was never enough evidence to prove this.

Bus drivers were part of the group and tried to blend in with the writers. Once a driver was sitting in the hospitality room in College Station when an officer from the Department of Public Safety came in and arrested him. The DPS mistakenly thought his commercial license had expired. Actually it had but had been reinstated a week earlier.

Another driver liked to sit around with the writers and tell them how he'd shot a guy he'd found in bed with his wife. He'd done a little time on probation but that was about it. Big 12 media relations guy Bo Carter, then with the SWC, observed, "Nobody ever said a cross word to that driver."

Then there was the driver who decided to attend a press conference with Aggie coach R. J. Slocum. Coach Slocum was in the middle of a discussion, which was interrupted by loud snoring. The driver had fallen asleep. The following year, R. J. asked Bo, "Where is that damn driver? I want to make sure he's on the front row and stays awake."

— ❑ —

Perhaps the most famous game in Southwest Conference history was in 1969 when Texas and Arkansas, ranked No. 1 and No. 2 in the nation, played for the national championship in what became the "Big Shoot-out." Darrell Royal's Longhorns won in a storybook finish over Frank Broyles' Razorbacks on a fourth down touchdown pass from James Street to Randy Peschel. Everybody who was anybody was there to cover the game. Even President Richard

Nixon attended and picked the Razorbacks to win. Figures. It was also one of the most hectic experiences for writers when it was over.

Terrible weather swept down from the mountains and engulfed Fayetteville, and writers lugging suitcases, typewriters, and various sundries hustled rides to the airport, figuring it might be shut down at any time. It had been.

They'd already given up their rooms in the hotels, and some had commitments the next day. For instance, Blackie Sherrod was supposed to be in Pittsburgh for the Steelers-Dallas Cowboys game. Blackie, Texas PR guy Jones Ramsey, noted Houston writer and columnist Mickey Herskowitz, and Sherrod's staffer Bob "Chickenfry" Galt, who had been given his nickname by Blackie because of the guy's love of the Texas delicacy, had put their heads together and decided to rent a car. They would drive to Fort Smith, catch a plane, and live happily ever after.

Indeed they rented a General Motors car at the Fayetteville airport, and Herskowitz, a take-charge guy, said he would drive the group to Fort Smith. The trunk was packed with all their belongings, and just before leaving, Herskowitz realized he didn't need his overcoat and put it in the truck. Only thing, the keys to the rental car were in his overcoat pocket. No big deal. A rent car guy said he'd drive into town, get a duplicate key from a car dealer, and be right back. But time was running out. If they didn't rush they'd miss the last flight from Fort Smith, which would take them to Little Rock and other connections.

They got a little lost en route but finally arrived at the airport just in time to make a flight. Blackie was tired of the nonsense so he left his buddies behind, leaping out of the car, grabbing his bags, and sprinting through the terminal, sidestepping, stiff-arming, and dodging people in his way. He got to the gate, huffing and puffing, only to find the flight was just taking off. Then he raced back to the ticket counter and asked for a ticket to Fort Smith on the next flight. The last tickets had just been sold to his pals. He looked at them. They grinned. Later he was able to get a flight to Dallas, make a connection to Pittsburgh, and actually made the game. Blackie wrote a column about the experience. I believe the moral was that sportswriters don't have it as easy as people think. Had this happened to Cartwright or Shrake they'd probably have hijacked the earlier plane.

— ❏ —

Dan Cook, Blackie, and some of their buddies went to the races at Hialeah during a Super Bowl week. It was required that you wear a coat and tie to get into the Jockey Club. However, management kept a reserve of sports coats, not all of which were in the best of shape, for gentlemen who might have forgotten their jackets. Of course when they left they had to turn in the coats. That was no problem for Blackie. He'd just bought a new, very expensive sports coat and proudly wore it to the track.

Blackie was just standing there when a little guy, maybe 5'1" and certainly the worse for wear, came up to him, looked at his sports coat, and said, "Hey,

my man, where do we turn in your coats?"

"I swore Cook to secrecy," said Blackie. "That lasted about fifteen minutes before all the media at the Super Bowl knew about it."

— ❏ —

The most unusual play I saw was on a sunny afternoon in the mid-1960s when a good, solid, gutsy player named Mac White was quarterbacking the SMU Mustangs against the Baylor Bears in Waco. During a crucial time in the game, the Ponies broke the huddle and Mac lined up behind the guard instead of the center, causing an unusual feeling for the former and confusion for the latter. But the center only wanted to do his job and went ahead and snapped the ball into empty space. It popped into the air and fell harmlessly to earth. SMU running backs, Baylor defenders, and Mac White were dumbfounded. However, the Ponies recovered.

Word reached us later that Mac had been knocked groggy on the previous play and in a haze had mistaken the guard for the center. He was close but no cigar.

— ❏ —

Fred Sanner, who worked for Lou Maysel at the *Austin American-Statesman* and later was sports editor of the *Abilene Reporter-News*, loved track more than anything. He could be very stubborn and had more respect for himself than judges at a track meet. He was covering a meet where a contestant was disqualified after winning. Fred didn't agree with the decision so he wrote his story as if the disqualified guy won.

Fred was a slow but hard worker who liked to talk. He was alone in the newspaper office in Abilene at 2 A.M. when a guy walked in with a big box. Fred started a friendly conversation with the guy, who finally told him he was looking for the photography department.

"Oh, sure it's right over there," Fred said, pointing the direction.

Fred went back to writing his column, and the guy reappeared with the box. They wished each other well, and the guy left. The next morning there was a fire in the newspaper building and the photographers rushed into their department to save their cameras. They were gone.

— ❏ —

I won't mention the name of the sportswriter for a small-town paper because I like him and he threatened me if I did. Well, he got quite drunk one night and drove home after the bar closed. In those early morning hours when a small town is fast asleep there was no traffic. He was within a few blocks of his place when the cops stopped him and told him to get out of the car.

He pleaded with the officers, saying he just lived nearby and asking them to give him another chance and that he'd never do it again, for sure, for sure. One of the officers said, "Okay, if you're sure you can make it. But don't let us see you again."

"Oh thank you, thank you," the guy said, then opened his car door and got into the backseat.

— ❏ —

On occasion there were writers who might even sip a bit

during a game. However, the brotherhood would help out and even do their stories for them. The guy from Houston was zonked in the press box as he covered, so to speak, a Rice and Arkansas game.

He was snoring away when just before the half the public address announcer said, "That's a penalty of fifteen yards for piling on."

Snapping awake briefly the writer said, "You damn right it is!" The he slumped back over into never-never land. Several writers wanted to help him out although the effort wasn't coordinated. In those days you gave your copy to Western Union operators in the press box and they'd send it to the newspapers. So three of them handed in leads for the guy. Soon his editor wired back a note, "Stop. I liked the first lead just fine."

— ❑ —

I never went on the SWC bus tour, which added a few years to my life, but was greatly saddened when the conference folded in 1995. It felt like the death of an old friend, one you hadn't been around much in years but certainly didn't want to lose.

Watching the SWC hobble off into reality's sunset rekindled memories for those of us who grew up with it. Perhaps it served, as a song or a book or a movie might do, as a backdrop for periods of our lives.

Sportscaster Brent Musburger recalled during an ABC broadcast of the Texas-Texas A&M rivalry how as a kid he'd written to Doak Walker at SMU. He said it was such a thrill when the Doaker sent him a signed picture. I've always been a little slow so I got my signed picture of Doak forty-five years after Brent got his. This happened in 1991 when Doak was so helpful in a biography I was writing on Bobby Layne. I have talked to presidents to be and met renowned celebrities of all kinds and wasn't nervous. Yet the first time I talked to Doak, one of my boyhood idols, I acted like a fool, spilling coffee and speaking nonsense in a higher than usual voice.

Some of the greatest SWC games I ever saw were in my imagination as a kid when I listened to Kern Tips on the radio.

He could take you off a screened-in porch or living room floor in Paris, Texas, to magical places such as the Cotton Bowl. His description of the exploits of The Doaker, the Blond Bomber Bobby Layne, and rugged fullback and defensive specialist Tommy Landry were better than real because you could add your own special touches, such as imagining you were playing beside the SWC greats. Imagination has no limits so it did not matter if you were 5'0" and 85 pounds.

I might have started a lifetime of biting my fingernails while listening to SMU's dramatic 14-13 victory over the Longhorns in 1947. I wanted both The Doaker and The Blond Bomber to win. It can do weird things to your nervous system to pull for both teams at once.

I would buy all the preseason magazines and, like others in Paris, was thrilled to find that a picture of my distant cousin and hometown hero, Bobby Jack Floyd, was in one of them. The first SWC game I ever saw was when Bobby Jack's TCU Horned Frogs played Kentucky in the Cotton Bowl. My family had moved to Dallas by that time, and my brother took me to the game, unfortunately won by Kentucky, 20-7. But Bobby Jack ran forty-three yards for TCU's only touchdown. His college career was cut short when he did things like throw a Coke machine down the stairs in the girls' dorm. In my perspective at that time, I missed the finer points and only thought, wow, he must be strong.

The Southwest Conference was on the decline with scandals and the fact that the good high school players went to schools out of state. The last decade before the conference folded, my interest had certainly waned. But the memories of those radio days as a kid had not.

13

Out of the Past

"You think you guys are wild, then you should have been around some of the old-timers."

—Blackie Sherrod

In late December of 1956 *Look* magazine invited committee members of the football writers who picked its collegiate All-American team to New York. They dined at the top restaurants and were offered complimentary tickets to Broadway shows or whatever they wanted to see. But football fever was high in the city at that time because the Giants were hosting Chicago for the NFL championship, and most of the writers accepted tickets to the game, which turned out to be a victory for the home team, 47-7.

"Instead of going to the game, a group of us sat around on the mezzanine of the hotel all day, telling George Rayborn stories," recalled Dave Campbell. Dave was the longtime sports editor of the *Waco News-Tribune*, which later became the *Tribune-Herald,* founder of the ever-popular *Texas Football* magazine in 1960, and on the selection committee for the Texas Sports Hall of Fame. And he was a close friend of George Rayborn.

"George was the most colorful sportswriter I've ever

---

known," said Dave. "You could
tell stories on him all day."

"The profession will never be
the same without him," wrote
then *Waco News-Tribune* columnist Al Ward, Tex Schramm's
former assistant, who was later
general manager of the New
York Jets.

— ❏ —

George Rayborn was built like
a wrestler and had this prodi-
gious appetite for food and beer,
which didn't exactly set him
apart from others in the profession. But he also was an avid
moviegoer, sometimes taking in
two or three flicks a day, and a
track buff who always carried his
trusty stopwatch. He didn't limit
use of the watch to sports but
timed people in everything from
walking up stairs to unmention-
ables. And he devised rankings
for all aspects of movies, such as
the best kiss, the best fight, and
the most fearsome scene, and
even sportswriters, never picking himself as No. 1. The thing
about George was that he never
drank during office hours, which
doesn't mean he didn't down
some beers afterwards.

"We'd all go home late at
night, but he'd stay in the office
and write his column for the
next day," said Dave. "We sus-
pected he might be enjoying his
beloved beer, but there were
never any empties around."

Next to the newspaper was a
one-story building that had a
roof that was almost level with
the newsroom. One day the
owner of the company in the
building stormed into the newspaper office, all angry and
red-faced. He confronted the
managing editor, who immediately took him over to the
sports department, located near
a window. The managing editor
walked over to the frosted window, opened it, and beheld a
shocking sight on the roof of the
adjoining building. It was covered with what appeared to be a
ton of empty beer cans. What
George had done for years was
finish a beer, then toss it out the
window onto the roof.

"You ought to hear it when
the wind blows," said the owner.
"It sounds like a buffalo herd."

George took pride in his eating ability and formed a one-man
assembly line to make himself
sandwiches at the office. He'd

tote bread, mayonnaise, lunchmeat, and all the trimmings. Then he'd line everything up in order on his desk, slices of bread, then lunchmeat, etc., and make six to eight sandwiches. Tragedy struck when George left briefly for the composing room and Dave and another guy lifted his desk and took it to the elevator and sent it downstairs. George was puzzled then devastated by the dastardly trick. But he had a nose for food and soon located the sandwiches. And he once was heavily favored to win a strawberry-eating contest but finished a very disappointing third. Afterwards he lamented, "I was beaten by a human hog and a man eating over his head."

Another time George, an excellent swimmer, bet he could make it across Lake Waco and did it. He obviously enjoyed betting about such things and even claimed he could stand up, grab the telephone, and say, "Sports

> **George left briefly for the composing room and Dave and another guy lifted his desk and took it to the elevator and sent it downstairs.**

Department" then drop the receiver and catch it before it hit the ground. He was mostly able to do this.

Movies were his passion and he became an expert in all phases of the craft. Among his ratings Lana Turner was the tops among actresses and *King Kong* his all-time No. 1 film, which he'd seen dozens of times. He even wrote a book on his movie ratings.

Actually, George had been an outstanding shot putter at the University of Texas. At the same time he covered track for UT's *Daily Texan*. He'd show up in the press box in sweats to cover a meet. When it came time for him to toss the shot, he'd excuse himself to go down on the field to compete. Then he'd come back and write, "George Rayborn wins the shot put with a toss of...."

He loved all sports but had a special interest in track. Before rating high school tracks in

Central Texas he ran around each one to get a better perspective. George was certainly one of if not the foremost authority on high school sports. He was the first to select an all-state high school basketball team. Before, only players who went to the state tournament could make all-state.

There was no way the newspaper would give him expenses to go to the Olympics in those days so he paid his own way. He became intrigued with Russian weightlifters at the Olympics in Helsinki, Finland, in 1952 and returned to Waco to give his impersonation of them with or without being coaxed in the least.

Al Ward recalled George had great concentration when he wrote and was always grammatically correct. But George did talk to himself when a story he was writing frustrated him. "All right, fat boy, settle down. Settle down," he'd say. And he drove fast and got a lot of traffic tickets. But when he believed he'd gotten an unfair citation in North Texas, he wrote the justice of the peace a long letter explaining the officer's mistake. The JP wrote back, thanking him for his letter but telling him to just send in $17 anyway. Al said George wasn't really upset about paying for the ticket but had a fit about the JP's bad grammar.

Dave Campbell and his wife, Reba, drove to Orange when George was visiting his mother, who lived there. "He didn't drink around his mother because she really didn't like it," said Dave. "We got there Friday and were going to leave on Saturday night. But it was raining that night, and his mother begged him not to drive in the storm."

"Then I guess I'll have to drive across the state line (Orange is near the Louisiana border) and get a case of beer," George told her.

"Oh no, George, you can't do that," said his mother.

"But I can't sleep without it."

His mother was upset and pleaded with him not to go. "I'll tell you what I'll do and you'll be able to sleep," she told him. "You go up to bed and I'll bring you some warm milk. That'll put you to sleep."

George told her there was no way that would happen but went up to bed to humor her. When she took him the milk he was sound asleep.

He was a little different even as a youngster. He was fascinated with spiders and had this theory that a spider would grow to an enormous size if fed well. So he captured a tiny spider and set up house for it near the ceiling. The spider spun its web and George would kill flies and feed it. Sure enough the spider grew and grew. Finally, it got so big George became frightened he had created some kind of man-eating creature. The spider had to go. He tried to smash it with a broom but it was no dumb spider and eluded the attack. Frustrated, George got his dad's rifle and shot it. Naturally, he also blew a hole in the ceiling.

George Rayborn left Waco to work for a suburban newspaper near Los Angeles. He wrote sports but was also the movie critic and got to attend the Academy Awards. After he was diagnosed with throat cancer, he refused to be treated and in the early 1970s moved back to Austin, where he had relatives. He told his friends the thing he most wanted to do was attend a big, international track meet and

then he'd ask for nothing else. He did, then died shortly thereafter in June of 1974. He was buried in Austin, and his friends gathered at Scholtz Beer Garten after the funeral and drank beer and told George Rayborn stories. It was appropriate because that's what George loved to do, drink beer and tell stories.

— ❏ —

Henry Harrison "Jinx" Tucker, the scourge of Central Texas in the 1930s, was probably the last sportswriter to compose his stories directly on the linotype. And they were some stories, with long, winding leads and page after page of copy. In his heyday at the *Waco News-Tribune*, Jinx not only covered events but also wrote thirteen columns a week for the morning, afternoon, and Sunday editions. Considering his work had such long leads and so many pages of copy, his yearly total would have filled more than a volume of *War and Peace*. Like all of us he had his detractors.

Now Jinx had played a lot of baseball while growing up in Brennan and actually got his nickname due to his efforts on the diamond. His neighborhood team was winning a particular game handily when Jinx, who showed up late, entered the game. The team then lost and a teammate remarked, "You're nothing but a jinx."

Art Shires, a star for the Waco team in the Texas League, was one of those who sometimes took offense to Jinx's baseball coverage and besides, you couldn't get rid of the guy. Jinx would even go out to the ball games early and shag fly balls during batting practice. One fateful day he showed up in a new pair of black and white shoes. He obviously didn't want to mess up the shoes so he took them off and shagged flies in his socks.

When Art finished batting practice and returned to the dugout, he noticed the shoes and told a batboy to get him some nails. Then he took a bat and nailed Jinx's shoes to the wooden bench in the dugout. Jinx returned to the dugout to prepare to cover the game. As he tried to put on his shoes they wouldn't move. He cussed up a storm and was furious. No doubt he later took it out on Art in print. Art figured it was worth it.

Predictions do go awry. The 1941 Texas Longhorns were living up to predictions that they would contend for the national championship. The team was even on the cover of *Look* magazine and had clobbered six straight opponents when they came to Waco to play the Baylor Bears. Jinx wrote Texas would win, 50-0. Baylor tied the Longhorns, 7-7, but Jinx shrugged it off. Like Texas, he couldn't win 'em all.

After SMU beat Texas, 7-6, in 1949 in Austin, he wrote something to the effect that, "God is still a Methodist, and from what I hear the officials for SMU's games in the Cotton Bowl must have been Methodists too."

Jinx had a buddy, Oscar Lawrence, who went around with him. Jinx did the driving, although later he would have his own chauffeur so, among other things, he could sip a bit to and from whatever he was covering. Among other tools of the trade Jinx and Oscar brought two fifths of whiskey to a Cotton Bowl game. The day was cold and miserable, and Jinx suggested Oscar carry everything but the whiskey. As they got out of the car Jinx dropped one of the bottles. Time stopped and then Jinx remarked, "Oscar, I just dropped your whiskey."

— ❑ —

In 1954 Blondy Cross of the *San Angelo Standard-Times* and Putt Powell of the *Amarillo Globe-News* were shooting dice in a hotel room in Abilene during the annual Texas High School Coaching School, an event widely covered by the state media. They were killing time until they were scheduled to play for the championship of a golf tournament for sportswriters. Putt admitted he was the "world's worst golfer" and to prove it had an astonishing 36 handicap. Blondy didn't exactly light up the course himself.

Once after Putt holed out in two shots on a par three hole, Amarillo golf pro George Aulbach remarked, "He's the only golfer in the world to make a hole-in-nothing."

So Putt and Blondy were feeling a little lazy and decided it was just too hot to go out and play golf, which obviously took them forever. So they decided to settle the championship by throwing dice. Blondy won but they adapted the score to golf and the wire services picked it up. They were elusive at times.

— ❑ —

Putt started working for the *Globe-News* in 1930. He delivered newspapers, worked the switchboard, and ended up with a column, which he called "Putting Around." He loved the Amarillo High School Sandies, and during the war when times were tough, he rode with fans to games that were out of town because he had no automobile. Like all sportswriters he also had his detractors.

One angry reader called Putt and told him he was going to come down to the newspaper and whip his tail "good." So Putt answered, "Well, come on down but you'll have to stand in line."

It so happened that Putt was buddies with a huge wrestler, Dory Funk Sr., who had come by the office to visit. Putt told Dory about the threatening call just before this guy showed up, breathing fire. Dory strolled over to the guy and asked, "Can I help you?"

"You sure can. I'm after that fool Putt Powell. I've come to whip his tail."

"You're looking at him," said Dory.

The guy did a double take, turned pale, and muttered it was nice to meet him as he started to leave. Dory followed him and kept saying, "Let's get it on, here and now! Whip my tail if you think you can." The guy's health was getting worse by the second so Dory and Putt started laughing. So did the visitor. I mean, what else could he do?

Once when Putt's kids were asked in school what their father did for a living, one of them replied, "He types."

— ❑ —

When I got out of college in 1960 and went to work for the *San Angelo Standard-Times*, this older gentleman, wearing a high school letter jacket over a schoolboy letter sweater, slowly walked into the office, went to a binder holding back issues of the paper, and quietly searched for something or other. When I asked who he was, one guy

replied, "That used to be Blondy Cross." Another said, "He still is."

High schools in the old days would sometimes give letter jackets to sportswriters who covered them. Blondy, who had given the nicknames to numerous schools in the area, had many letter jackets and letter sweaters and would wear two or three at a time. He reported games by walking the sidelines, and when his favorite schools, Ballinger and Sonora, played, he alternated wearing each school's letter jacket.

Blondy lived near the newspaper, at the Lowake Inn and the Red Rooster, the beer drinking spot of choice for the *Avalanche-Journal*. Houston Harte, publisher of the paper, once told him he'd give him $100 if he'd stop drinking for three months. One sportswriter recalled it was $500 for six months, but sportswriters sometimes get things wrong and the ending is the same anyway. To the surprise of everybody, Blondy made it then immediately spent the money on booze.

The Lowake Inn was a famous place in a tiny

community of the same name. You picked out your own huge, lean steak at a meat counter for cooking and were served bigger than life potatoes and salads and so forth, and the beer was forever flowing. It was located a short drive from San Angelo and about nine miles from Rowena, Bonnie Parker's hometown. Customers would drive or fly small planes to Lowake, landing in a vacant lot across the road. Among those who would fly in for a meal was Preston Smith when he was governor of Texas and goodness knows who else.

> Some said the donkey only turned purple when it drank beer, giving it something in common with various sportswriters.

The *Standard-Times* always ran a Red Rooster on the front page if it rained. Blondy, who sometimes wrote his stories from the Lowake Inn, always called in the rain report from there. "This is Blondy Cross. Got a fourth inch of rain at Lowake." Connection broken.

Characters at Lowake weren't always people. There was a goat that thought it was a dog and would sleep on the front porch and nod when patted on the head. Some said the goat would shake hands although as nearly as I can determine that was never proven.

And Blondy repeatedly mentioned the "Purple Donkey" in his column. The Purple Donkey was supposed to do tricks, although the only one ever substantiated was that he brayed when the school bus passed. Some said the donkey only turned purple when it drank beer, giving it something in common with various sportswriters.

— ▢ —

There were a number of noted writers passing through the *News* sports department before Walt put together the circus which was our staff. Before Prieleaux "Tex" Maule made a name for himself with *Sports Illustrated* as the leading authority on professional football, he too wrote sports for *The Dallas Morning News*. However, Bill Rives, then sports editor, also assigned him a great deal of rim duty in spite of Tex declaring accurately that he was the best writer on the paper.

Tex also figured he should have been the sports editor instead of Rives. So he was very frustrated with his career when he got a call from Sid James, publisher of a new magazine called *Sports Illustrated*, offering him a job. Tex was ecstatic and enthusiastically announced he was departing the News.

Tex invited all the staff to the cafeteria for coffee. They included Rives, Walt, Harry Gage, Merle, Ray McMurray, and Tony Zoppi, who would go on to become a nationally famous nightlife columnist with pals such as Frank Sinatra and Tony Bennett and later an executive with the Riviera Hotel in Las Vegas. He might have had an acting career.

"In the cafeteria Tex insisted on picking up the tab for coffee," Zoppi recalled. "That in itself was historic. Tex had a gift for dodging checks, and his insistence on paying for all that coffee threatened his amateur standing.

"He announced that he had just accepted a lucrative position with *Sports Illustrated* and was leaving for New York in two weeks. Then he looked at Rives."

"Bill," Tex continued, "don't think it hasn't been fun working with you guys because it hasn't."

The sportswriters were making in the $90 a week range, but Tex said, proudly, "I'll be getting $15,000 a year." And he continued to brag about his good fortune and later even jumped managing editor Felix McKnight. Talk about burning your bridges.

When they returned to the sports department, Zoppi slipped over to the society department and talked one of the women into dialing Maule's extension and pretending she was a long-distance operator. She informed Tex that Sid James was calling.

In his best New York accent Zoppi got on the phone and said, "Hi Tex, this is Sid James."

"Good to hear from you, Sid," Maule replied. "What's up?"

"I'm just calling to tell you we won't be needing you for another six months."

There was a deafening silence on the line, and finally Tex replied in a shaking voice, "Jeez, I wish you'd called me about an hour ago. I just resigned my job here."

"Hell, just tell 'em you want to stay on another six months. You and Rives are buddies, aren't you?"

Maule said weakly, "Oh yeah."

"So okay, tell Rives you're staying on."

"Uh, can I ask you why you're postponing the job?"

Zoppi couldn't resist and said, "Yeah. We want to try a very talented guy named Zoppi."

"Before I could finish, Tex was on his feet and spotted me laughing in the society office," said Tony. "He was foaming at the mouth, knocking over chairs in an effort to get at me. I ran for the elevator, got in my car, and sped away home."

That Christmas the Zoppis received a beautifully wrapped gift from Neiman-Marcus. "I opened it immediately and told my wife we'd received a fine fruit cake," said Tony. "Then it fell completely apart when I tried to cut it. My wife, who was raised on a farm in East Texas, doubled over with laughter. Tex had sent me a big buffalo chip."

Tex Maule had an extremely interesting background as an insurance investigator, gym teacher, and flying trapeze artist with a circus in the 1940s. He also worked on the *Austin American-Statesman* with Tex Schramm.

— ❑ —

During the 1940s the *Austin American-Statesman* had a publisher and editor who were old school and then some. But they were colorful, whether they meant to be or not. Managing editor Buck Hood tended to drink more than a bit, and publisher Charley Green was prone to outbursts about things he didn't appreciate or thought he didn't appreciate. Wilbur Evans, later public relations director of the SWC, was sports editor and had an excellent staff of youngsters, including Schramm, Maule, Jack Gallagher, Weldon Hart, and Jimmy Banks.

Tex, a Southern Californian, had gotten out of the service and returned to school at the University of Texas, a school his father had also attended. He'd worked for the *Los Angeles Times* one summer and remembered how the newspaper used a vast network of correspondents to call in scores and data on high schools around the state. He developed the same process in Central Texas and also inaugurated awards for outstanding schoolboy players, sponsored by what he called the Austin American-Statesman Foundation. For his work Wilbur presented him with $100. Green, who counted pennies like bricks, had a fit and chewed out Wilbur, who took the blame and spared Tex the publisher's wrath. That wouldn't last long.

Tex also had an interest in betting on the horses, at that time considered a sinful pursuit in Texas. So Tex wrote a column advocating legalized betting on the horses. He recalled a one-sided conversation with Green, which went something like this:

"In case you are blind and can't hear, read, or see, perhaps we should get something straight, young man. This newspaper, as are most all Texans, is diametrically opposed to pari-mutuel betting. This state is against it. And so here, on my very own newspaper in the capital of Texas, you have the gall to write that we should legalize horse racing. I can't believe this! I simply can't believe this!" Okay, so Tex didn't write about horse racing and pari-mutuel betting any more.

Jimmy Banks once recalled how Buck Hood, who had been drinking, liked to lecture the young staffers. "The worst thing about that was that he'd get you just about the time you were getting off. He would drive you crazy. He'd be about half-coherent and then say, 'Get what I mean?' You always said you did because you wanted to go on home."

Gallagher and Banks were also participants in a popular ploy by sportswriters to confuse angry readers about their identity because it was prudent and safer to do so. Gallagher had been greatly critical of the local boxing and wrestling scene so naturally one of those involved was after him. The angry slugger called the newspaper, got Banks on the phone, and asked, "What does Gallagher look like?

I'm coming up there to get him." Banks described Gallagher as big and mean. When Gallagher heard what had happened he substituted a picture of giant boxer Primo Canera for his column photo. The boxer never showed up.

— ❑ —

Like many of us, Tex had some unusual experiences on the rim. He was working alone, making up the paper, editing copy, writing headlines, and whatever else needed to be done. The big story that night was Joe Louis defending his world heavyweight championship. The fight would be late so Tex left a space for a story and pictures. There were three wire services in those days, the AP, UPI, and INS. Tex figured he'd read all three and use the best story.

The fight ended much sooner than expected, and all hell broke loose with leads and first, second, and third adds moving on all the wires. "I'd start to do something and then something else would come on the wires," he recalled. "I had wire copy on the floor, the desk, around my neck, and in my pockets, trying to sort it out. It was a nightmare, but somehow I got something in the paper, even if it turned out to be the AP lead, an INS first take, and a UPI second take." Fortunately the story made enough sense, but I was thinking what a shame that Anders and I weren't around then working the rim for him.

— ❑ —

The defunct New York Yanks became the mess that begot an even bigger mess called the Dallas Texans when Big D got its first NFL franchise in 1952. Attendance in the Cotton Bowl was so bad that by midseason the franchise was sold back to the NFL, played all the remaining games on the road, and became the Baltimore Colts the following year. Nobody cared about pro football then in Texas, but Tex Maule had become the Texans' public relations guy and tried his best to get coverage.

When Bud Shrake, then of the *Fort Worth Press,* was sent to cover a game, he had trouble finding a parking spot in the press area because spots were taken by wives and friends of club officials and players. After Bud complained, Maule apologized and sent fifty press box tickets and parking passes to the *Press.*

During those days there was a large barn-like drinking spot on the State Fair grounds near the Cotton Bowl. It being a private club, you had to have chits to purchase drinks. Bud and Dan Jenkins decided to stop by for a couple of drinks before the game. Somehow they were able to use parking and press box passes as chits. They had a great time, made many new friends, and didn't even make the game. However, waitresses, bartenders, short-order cooks, and all matter of life did, filling the media parking area and showing up in the press box with proper credentials. Maule failed to see the humor and was a little testy about the situation even after the Texans folded and he went to work for *The Dallas Morning News.*

And oh yes, there was a photographer working for the AP in those days who bears mentioning because he certainly would have received support for the Distinguished Soup Nose Award.

And besides, it was named for another photographer.

— ❏ —

The year was 1940 and Texas A&M had a big, muscular fullback named John Kimbrough, who made All-American by crashing through opposing tacklers with his famed straight-up running style. And the Associated Press had a photographer named Jim Laughead, a mad-hatter, who was not yet the most renowned photographer of sports in the country.

Laughead didn't like the generally accepted idea of shooting pictures of players just standing there with or without a grin on their faces. Instead he came up with the idea of posing them as they pretended to be in action, such as fading back to pass, stiff-arming a tackler, and diving through the air as if blocking or making a tackle. He was just about out of ideas when he got to College Station to photograph the Aggies and their superstar, John Kimbrough. Then he noticed a picket fence that surrounded the Aggie practice field. Why, he would have Kimbrough

run through that fence, demonstrating his power.

Naturally Laughead would
have to tamper with the fence so
it would break apart at the
slightest touch. He found a brick
and broke up a section, then
pieced it back together so it
would fall apart at the slightest
touch. Great, his shot would
show the fence breaking apart in
all directions as Kimbrough ran
through it. Then he marked the
spot. Unfortunately, A&M had a
very conscientious caretaker in
those days, and he came out to
the practice field just after
Laughead had retired for the
morning. The caretaker spotted
the break in the fenced and
repaired it as good as new.

At picture time Laughead,
whistling a happy tune, talked to
Kimbrough. "John didn't want to
do it," Laughead said. "But I
kept after him. I told him it
would be easy. Just run through
the fence at the spot I showed
him. Finally he consented, probably just to shut me up."

And so the Aggies' biggest
star, Kimbrough, prodded by
Laughead, finally got back about
twenty yards and came roaring
like a steam engine full speed

ahead and hit the fence at full
gallop. Obviously the fence
didn't cooperate, and Kimbrough
fell backwards to the ground,
gasping for breath, seeing stars
and flashes of fire. When he
finally cleared his head, perhaps
he saw Laughead, growing
smaller and smaller as he disappeared with his cameras over
the horizon.

Laughead was with the AP for
sixteen years before forming his
own business in 1945 with his
son-in-law, Jim Bradley. They
were known as "Ol' Huck and
Buck" because before snapping
a shot Jim would yell, "Now let's
huck and buck!"

Laughead dressed for action
as if he was the last guy in line
for discarded clothes. Typically
his working attire included a
bright red vest with emblems of
the college teams he photo-
graphed on one side and the
pros on the other and old baggy
blue jeans. On certain occasions
he would sport a pinkish Hawai-
ian shirt under the red vest. And
he always wore The Hat. The
Hat had been made famous in
legend and song around the
nation's campuses. He bought it
around 1940 for a couple of

dollars and it became his trademark.

He was an avid SMU fan and his most famous subject was Doak Walker. Walker was a nice, clean-cut fellow who came to SMU in 1945 and then returned for the 1947-48-49 seasons after a stint in the army. He came by Laughead's office during that first season and said he had five letters from kids, asking for autographed pictures. Doak offered to pay for the pictures, but Laughead realized he was in school and didn't have much money.

"I told him anytime anybody wanted a picture of him to just come by the office and I'd furnish one for nothing," said Laughead. Before Doak left SMU Laughead had given him 39,500 free pictures. In those days even if you figure $1 a picture, it didn't turn out to be the best of financial moves.

In the 1930s he snapped a famous pose for the Associated Press of Clyde "Bulldog" Turner, the Chicago Bears' great center, who was playing for Abilene Christian College at the time. Nobody had really heard that much about Turner, but they did after Laughead came up with the idea of posing him with a calf, which must have weighed 400 pounds, on his shoulders. It wasn't a problem for Bulldog, a rugged, strong farm boy who just picked up the calf on cue and grinned. Hardin-Simmons had a clipping service in those days and received over 6,000 clips from newspapers that ran the picture. Turner was no longer an unknown.

Laughead received some unsought publicity when he went with his beloved SMU Mustangs to play Ohio State in 1950. The Ponies rallied from a 20-0 deficit to beat the Buckeyes, 32-27, on a pass from Fred Benners to Ben White just before the final gun. Laughead snapped White catching the ball and got so excited he rushed into the end zone and leaped on White, slapping him on the back and hugging him as they both tumbled to the ground. He got there so fast it almost looked like he helped Ben catch the ball as 80,000 fans and game officials watched.

"Now if you don't mind," an official told him, "we'd like to try to kick the extra point."

A short subject called "Pete Smith's Football Highlights" was popular in movie theaters around the country at that time and used the Laughead episode with the introduction, "Now watch the Texas photographer who helped catch the pass when SMU beat Ohio State."

— ❏ —

When a young Harless Wade (very difficult to imagine) and Don Oliver were working for the *Abilene News*, they were playing golf with football legend Sammy Baugh, who was then head coach at Hardin-Simmons, and his assistant, John Steber. As they approached No. 9 there was a dreaded water hazard. They all pondered whether to be conservative or try to clear the water. The others had cleared the water when Oliver took his turn.

What the heck, Oliver went for it, too. His ball plopped into the water. He tried again. Splash! Then he calmly put his equipment in a pull cart and went to the edge of the pond. One by one he carefully threw each club into the water. Then one by one he threw each ball, each tee, and finally his golf bag as the others witnessed this most innovative response to the game. They laughed but the game must go on so they left Oliver there. They stopped and looked back and saw him take off his shoes and throw them into the water. Then he tossed the pull cart into the water and finally, as he walked away, sailed his cap into the water.

> One by one he carefully threw each club into the water. Then one by one he threw each ball, each tee, and finally his golf bag as the others witnessed this most innovative response to the game.

"Later we could see him through the trees from another hole," said Harless. "He had his caddy out there trying to fish his equipment out of the water." Golf equipment is expensive so in retrospect sportswriters aren't as dumb as you might think.

Harless is a golf nut who covered all the major and minor and in between tournaments during his career. Looking back he said he'd never witnessed a performance like Oliver's that day. Then I reminded him of the late, great Lefty Stackhouse.

— ❑ —

I was never a golf writer nor ever wanted to be, although I was called upon at times to do columns or sidebars at golfing events. Forget Arnie, Jack, Gary, and the gang, my favorite column subject was none other than the immortal W. A. "Lefty" Stackhouse, which I suppose says something about me. I'd written a column about him but wanted to go to San Marcos to do a long feature, but Walt didn't like the idea.

"There are a lot of other subjects we have in mind for you to do," Walt told me. When I mentioned that not only was Lefty a very amusing character but there would be a moral to the story, he asked what it might be. I fumbled around and said, "Don't play golf."

That probably did in my idea because Walt and about everybody else in the department played golf. They would say it was competitive, relaxing, and a good, safe form of exercise. Sure, I know, doctors often recommend and even urge their patients to play golf to help them relax, combat heart problems, hypertension, and whatever. I had seen how this worked, watching tears come into the eyes of grown men, seen them act like children and/or madmen. I have seen them slam clubs into trees, sling them, and kick holes on the greens, which leads me to the weird behavior of Lefty Stackhouse.

Lefty was an outstanding golfer, a good pro who played with some of the best in the 1950s and '60s. Off the course he was an easy-going, friendly guy who would give you the golf shirt off his back. His dark side was always lurking on the course.

Lefty carried on a constant chatter with himself, his clubs, and his golf balls when he played. If things went wrong, he often not only threatened his equipment but also himself and even doled out punishment.

After he believed his right hand caused him to hook, he calmly walked over to a nearby tree and proceeded to slam his fist against it. Then he stared at his aching hand and said, "Now hook that ball again, you SOB!"

George Plimpton once wrote about watching Lefty miss a gimme shot then hit himself in the head with a putter. Suddenly Lefty dropped the putter, staggered, and fell to his knees as others turned their heads in awe and/or laughter. Another time when his putter let him down during a tournament in Houston, he tied it to the bumper of his car with a rope and dragged it all the way to the next tournament in San Antonio. Take that, putter!

Lefty was having an outstanding round in one tournament. He had coolly and calmly performed to the best of his ability and was an easy leader coming to the 18th green. He faced an easy foot-and-a-half putt to finish with a birdie. He felt young, happy, as if a fresh, cool breeze was in his face. He waved to the gallery. He approached the ball, tapped it and . . . it lipped the cup and stopped a fourth of an inch from the hole. Lefty stepped back, stunned. Then he dropped his putter, staring at the nearby trees, and suddenly lowered his head and charged toward them. He butted the first tree he met with such force that it knocked him over backwards to the ground. He had to be helped to the clubhouse.

He also punished a lot of clubs by bending them on trees or tossing them toward the far horizon. His most innovative time was perhaps when he hit into the water with more definitive results than Don Oliver. He walked to the edge of the small lake and called for his cart. He then threw his club into the lake. He took his bag out of the cart and tossed each club and each ball and each tee into the lake. As those around him watched, mesmerized, he took off his shoes and threw them into the lake.

The silence was broken when his caddy began to laugh. When Lefty inquired as to why he was laughing, the caddy said, "That's the funniest thing I've ever seen, throwing all that stuff into the water. I've never seen anything like it . . . ha-ha-ha-ha."

Lefty smiled then calmly walked over to the caddy, picked him up, walked back to the lake, and tossed the guy into the water. Shrugging, he then jumped in himself. Except for the caddy, who made his way to land, Lefty just left his equipment under water.

Lefty was a good golfer, a little wacky, and drank a lot. It appeared some information about his life was used in the Kevin Costner movie *Tin Cup*. Lefty coached the Texas Lutheran College golf team and was also a pro at a Seguin country club. He died in 1973 while playing golf at the country club. He was sixty-four and it's extremely doubtful another professional like him will ever appear again.

14

Other Forgettable Feats

> "It's not that you're getting older, it's just that the world is going by faster."
>
> —Larry Gardner, physical therapist

It is so difficult for some of us to grow up and put aside the great meager moments of our athletic careers. We hold on and try to revive that old feeling of competition, participation. We do this without rhyme, reason, or the logical pursuit of happiness because the older you get the more susceptible you are to injuries. But sometimes competitive fires run deep, all the way to the seat of your pants, and you must pay the consequences. And if you are a sportswriter, you are around athletes, so perspective becomes ever more elusive.

There are times when friends goad you into doing something that you would have known in your heart not to do had it not been for, say, wicked martinis. A classic example of such a devious friend was (and no doubt still is) Tom Stephenson, a former journalist who left the profession to make money at various other business ventures. But he could never completely forsake writing and continued to free-lance at his own discretion. He was working on a magazine article concerning "The Perfect Martini." He enlisted the help of

John Anders, who has been to war and obviously knows a thing or two about good martinis. They checked out the martinis around town and finally established a beachhead at a local pub.

Soon they were talking about their old days as athletes. Tom was a former football player at Missouri, and Anders was a champion high jumper in high school. It did not matter to John that his accomplishments had happened forty pounds and no telling how many years ago. Tom encouraged him and mentioned, whereas he could still accomplish many athletic feats, John probably could not.

Anders immediately picked up the gauntlet, which in this case was a martini, swigged, and then claimed he could still high jump at least 5'6" even at his age and condition. Tom said, "Prove it." They went outside to the parking lot. Then Stephenson got a "No Parking" sign and enlisted a curious parking attendant into helping him hold up the sign to what appeared to be 5'6", and the scene was set. Anders stretched, slightly pulling his bad back, then backed off to get a running start as Stephenson laughed and joked. Then like Brick in *Cat on a Hot Tin Roof* Anders paused, hearing cheers nobody else heard, threw his ears back, and charged toward his rendezvous with ill fortune. He actually cleared the barrier, which Stephenson and his helper kept pushing a little higher and higher as he got closer. He cleared the barrier! Yes! Yes! Only thing is he landed on his elbows.

"Why," said John, "I believe I've fractured both my elbows." No way, said Stephenson. He was wrong. Casts were placed over John's elbows. He had to write hurt for a month and cradle the telephone receiver in his arms and bend his head to his chest in order to talk. There were times when he also found out who his friends weren't.

John should have known to stay away from Tom Stephenson and/or I should have warned him. When I was a thirty-eight-year old teenager, I journeyed with playwright Preston Jones from one place to the NFL Pub just off busy Oak Lawn Avenue in Dallas. Okay it was one of those stupid nights. Two hours later a young woman started talking to us and claimed she could roll her eyes in opposite directions. Darned if she didn't do it as well as I can remember. One eye went one way while the other went in the opposite direction. Preston was my witness as she did it five more times. For the record, I also saw a young woman play a medley of tunes on her teeth at Joe Miller's.

So it was one of the crazy nights, becoming worse because Stephenson was lurking in the shadows. He talked about his success at Missouri as an undersized offensive lineman. He did it because he was quick and fast. I happened to mention that I once had some speed. Actually, at North Dallas High School I played summer baseball with Charley Allen, who had won the city 100-yard dash championship. We'd race in our baseball uniforms, and I ran nose-to-nose with him. Of course, he mentioned that my nose was longer than his and that actually he had beaten me by inches.

Naturally, Stephenson, maybe fifteen years my junior, challenged me to a race. It did not occur to me that obviously he was much younger, likely in better shape, and was handling his liquor better than I was martinis. But hey, once you have it you never lose it! In the early morning hours we ventured into the parking lot. There was one false start when I ran into the adjoining building after takeoff. Then we both took off, running parallel to the street, he in a straight pattern and I in a kind of semicircle. Stephenson had the lead but I tried to accelerate, and the next thing I knew my body was being propelled forward, four, five, six feet. I skidded another three, four feet. I had no idea what had happened unless I'd become so fast I'd run out of my body. Not so. I'd been hit by a passing car, skinning both elbows and knees, ruining my shirt, pants, and shoes, breaking my watch, and losing my billfold.

Stephenson finished the race, yelling that he had won. Then he came back, looked down at me, and as he helped me up, asked, "Are you hurt?" Funny, the driver never stopped. The only consolation I had was that to this day he might wonder if he killed somebody that night.

— ❑ —

Among other ventures when I was young and foolish, as opposed to old and foolish, was when I boxed an exhibition in the late 1960s with Curtis Cokes, then the welterweight champion of the world. I'll save you the suspense. He won.

Among other things I also wrote about pro boxing, which in Dallas meant Curtis Cokes, who had become welterweight champion of the world. Curtis and I became friends during the times I considered myself another Paul Gallico or George Plimpton, those foolish people who would compete with the pros in order to write about the experience. It seemed like the normal, unnatural thing for me to get into the ring with Curtis for, say, three rounds. Curtis and his manager Doug Lord, another old friend, agreed it might be funny. Curtis let me know he planned to go out of his way not to hurt me, which certainly gave me more courage.

The pre-boxing exhibition didn't start well. I hadn't boxed in years and went to the gym early and figured I'd punch the heavy bag, dance around, and try my best not to look like the fool

During a sparring session in 1969 with world welterweight champion Curtis Cokes, Bob St. John shows his boxing prowess in this sequence of pictures. (Photos by Jim Work)

I was. So I turned my hand wrong while hitting the heavy bag and heard a snap, kind of a popping sound. After jumping up and down in pain, I quickly noticed people were watching and pretended I had suddenly started dancing around and shadow boxing. I can't confirm what they thought I was doing. My hand was swelling, and it was later determined I'd cracked a bone, and as usual wrote hurt for a while. My hand was injured as I got into the ring, although there was little danger of injuring it anymore because I wasn't apt to land a punch.

In the first round I was dancing around, throwing a left jab, and he was staying under control. I can't be sure exactly what happened. I believe I might have landed a jab and Curtis, a great counterpuncher, accidentally retaliated and hit me. Or maybe I just hit myself. Time clouds memory. But a sequence of pictures in the newspaper showed the result better than a thousand words. I suddenly hit the deck on my seat, rocked backwards, and crawled back to the corner, sitting there with a whimsical expression on my face. The next morning I had a headache either because he hit me with a soft right or I hit myself with the hardest punch I'd ever thrown.

— ❑ —

I could rationalize the loss to Stephenson as only a temporary setback to my ego. Anybody could have been hit by a car and lost a race. Who's to say, if he'd been hit by the car I might have won.

But it took a while to get over being humiliated during training camp by Danny Reeves, a friend of mine for goodness sakes. I'm not sure what went wrong in our death-defying foot race because I really prepared, such as not even going out with the guys for dinner and drinks the night before.

Reeves had watched me jog and commented he couldn't tell whether I was going backwards or forwards. Very funny. I was aware that Danny had bad knees, injured during his playing days, so I quickly accepted his challenge to race. The good sport that I was I'd try not to embarrass him. So after practice one day we decided to race for 30 yards. Assistant coach Mike Ditka would be the judge at the finish line. I have a hard time believing he could outrun me, even though he once was a real, live NFL running back. Perhaps I choked. Whatever. He easily beat me by a couple of yards. I challenged him to a 20-yard race. He easily beat me by a yard. He laughed when, as a mathematician, I figured the odds were getting better and challenged him to race ten yards. No deal.

Ditka summarized the race by saying, "That was the most pathetic, ridiculous thing I've

Dan Reeves and Mike Ditka were always game for competition during training camp, although they had their ups and downs. (Dallas Cowboys photo)

ever seen. You both looked ridiculous."

Hey, Ditka had his moments too. Landry used to play tennis with his assistants and assistant general manager Joe Bailey and other recruits. The matches usually drew a crowd of college students and visitors. One particular day Ditka, known for his explosive temper, just couldn't seem to get his game together and could be heard uttering unpleasantries. After he missed a shot, Mike looked up at the sky, yelled, and then slammed down his racket, cracking the frame in several places. That wasn't enough. To further express himself he picked it up again and threw it at the net. It went under the net and smashed into Landry's ankles. Landry didn't yell but was hopping around in pain as Ditka, a tough guy intimidated by Landry's aura, turned pale in the hot sun.

There was silence as Landry recovered and looked at his partner, Reeves, and said, "Boy, you can get hurt playing this game." Others joined Ditka in laughing nervously.

— ❏ —

I was able to get Roger Kaye of the *Fort Worth Star-Telegram* involved in our basketball games and also get even with Reeves for beating me in a foot race in an earlier camp. Revenge has no time limit.

During a discussion about our basketball games Danny mentioned that he had played a little hoops himself. As usual a challenge was answered and it was decided that I could take defensive backfield coach Gene "Bebes" Stallings and then try to find Danny someone to be on his team—maybe another media type like me who was a fair to middling basketball player.

I agreed and when he asked me who it was, I mentioned Roger Kaye. Danny said Roger, thin and pale, seemed like a good guy and all that but didn't look much like any kind of athlete, much less a basketball player.

"That's what we thought until he started playing with us," I said, then laughed. "We chuckled and then he started dribbling behind his back, between his legs, and nobody could keep up with him. We later learned that he made all-state at some Fort Worth high school."

"You got to be kiddin'."

"I'm not. But I'll level with you. He doesn't have this great shot he once had. But, hey, the guy can dribble and pass."

"This sounds crazy," said Danny, looking at me suspiciously. "I guess you can't always tell." I shrugged, remained serious. Suspense was building for the game.

— ❑ —

Gene and I go way back, and I was aware that, besides being a football star at Paris High School and Texas A&M, he'd also played some basketball. I played ball against Gene in elementary school in Paris before my family moved to Dallas when I started the eighth grade. Incidentally, he had a great influence on me spiritually.

Gene was a couple of years ahead of me in elementary school and already tall, especially to those of us who were already short. And even though our coach told us that our team, our school, our family, and our country depended on tackling him, it wasn't something I

welcomed. He played tailback in the old single wing and had this big fullback, bigger than anybody on our team, leading the way. So sometimes I'd say a quick prayer that Gene and that big guy would run the opposite way from my defensive position because I knew it would hurt a lot even trying to tackle him, much less actually doing it. My prayers weren't always answered, but at least I was praying.

I had convinced Roger to join our game, telling him he needed some exercise and to come to the gym. It was just a friendly game and, why, he'd be on Danny Reeves' team. Roger said he hadn't played much basketball and wasn't very good. I added that he'd have a chance to get to know the coaches and probably get a human-interest column.

"I havn't played much basketball either but, hey, it's just a game," I told him.

Danny knew he'd been had right away. Roger had no idea what to do with the ball, bless his heart. He dribbled with one hand, both hands, tried to soccer kick the ball, and it got to the point where when we took the ball away from him we'd give it right back.

Reeves, an incredible competitor, was furious. He'd get the ball and try to kill us, specifically me, when he drove to the basketball. I'd get out of the way and let him bang away with Gene, also a tough guy with temper control. They didn't have a chance. Danny wanted a rematch but I used my standard line, "No way. You guys gave it

your all and just came up short. We have other teams to play."

— ❏ —

Carlton Stowers was covering the Dallas Cowboys for the *News* when Jim Dent was on the beat for the *Star-Telegram*. Jim was a former high school athlete, and as happened to some of us who preceded him, the fresh Thousand Oaks air and the surroundings in training camp got to him. He began running, lifting

Bob St. John tries to show off his, uh, receiving abilities during training camp. Nobody noticed. (Photo by Richard Pruitt)

weights, and getting in shape or "playing for a tie" as we phenoms of the California night used to call it. Why, he even believed he was faster than ever! Perhaps he was. We'll never know.

Carlton, ten years Dent's senior, was also jogging, and it probably didn't hurt that much because he wasn't drinking martinis and philosophizing or dozing while Luksa philosophized until the early morning hours. Dent noted Carlton was jogging daily at a slow pace. He had even heard Carlton ran a little track at the University of Texas, but if he couldn't jog any faster than that, he couldn't beat a turtle. So he challenged Carlton to a race.

Carlton didn't take the whole thing very seriously, but Jim did. It got out of hand. Pretty soon everybody was taking bets as to who would win. Jim, smug and confident, was covering most of the bets. The money won might even go into a pot for perhaps a quick weekend trip to Vegas. Rumor had it that Gil Brandt, head of the scouting department, was also involved in the betting process. Gil usually knew

something nobody else knew and wasn't in a habit of making wild bets. Dent figured there was a first time for everything.

They met at the California Lutheran football field. Dent was suited out and even wore football shoes so he wouldn't slip on the turf. Carlton had on his standard soiled tennis shoes. Dent had determined they'd run a 100-yard dash or, in Carlton's case, a 100-yard trot. A capacity crowd of seventeen showed up to watch.

"Listen Jim," said Carlton. "It'll kill both of us to run 100 yards. Let's do 50 or maybe 30."

"No way," said Dent, smiling confidently.

Off they went. The crowd was on its feet. Odd. Carlton kept pulling away. And away and won easily. Dent kept going and nobody saw him for a couple of days. To put things in perspective, Carlton led off for the sprint relay team at the University of Texas, which had one of the most prominent track programs in the country. (Carlton could barely walk for two days and nobody saw Dent for a couple of days so he no doubt was hurting both mentally and physically.) But things were seldom in perspective for the media types as would-be athletes in training camp or otherwise.

— ❑ —

Carlton left sportswriting in the early 1980s to pursue a career as a distinguished, award-winning author of crime books, twice capturing Edgar awards for top books of the year in the category. But after thorough research I could not find any rampageous activities during his time in sports, which is sad in a way because he never did anything that even approached being nominated for the Distinguished Soup Nose Award. I don't think I can speak for Carlton when I say this was the one thing he regretted during his years as a sportswriter.

However, some people are late bloomers. And in midlife some can even go on and try an unfamiliar sport whether they are ready or not. For instance they might take up diving, which requires split-second timing, coordination, form, and certainly athleticism. As you know in the Olympics divers are judged on

the strictest 10-point scale. But let me take you back to that morning in a quiet Cedar Hill neighborhood when all seemed right with the world.

Carlton Stowers, that careful and practical man, was simply mowing the yard like millions of others in Norman Rockwell America. He was puffing his ever-present pipe, taking pride in the performance of his prized lawn mower and totally unaware that he was soon to join us in ... THE TWILIGHT ZONE.

He was thinking what a great machine he had. By gosh it can turn on a nickel and clip grass right to the edge of, say, the swimming pool. So he figured he could zip right through a strip of grass by the ol' pool. Get ready, grass! He backed up to get momentum for the charge! SUDDENLY HE WAS AIRBORNE, FALLING BACKWARDS THROUGH SPACE, SPLASHING AND FLAPPING BEFORE SINKING AS HIS PIPE, STILL IN HIS MOUTH, SANK LIKE THE PERISCOPE OF A TINY SUBMARINE.

Yes, he fell backwards into the swimming pool, dragging the

lawn mower with him. His wife later described the dive to this writer as a kind of reverse, disjointed plunge. She immediately gave him an 8.3 on the dive and a perfect 10 and a gold medal for "unique people who fall backwards with their lawn mowers into swimming pools while puffing on pipes." But how could Pat be objective? The DSNA executive panel has long ago disbanded, but I was able to consult old-timer Frank Luksa. Giving Carlton the benefit of the doubt because he is our friend, we determined he scored a –27.

This would have qualified him for the DSNA, but of course the days of the award have passed into history and like so many he is sadly only left with "what might have been."

— ❑ —

Well, there always comes a time when you have to hang 'em up, admit your career is over, and move on to other things. I'd continually suffered injuries running, lifting weights, playing pickup basketball games, tripping and falling off curbs, missing chairs when I tried to sit down, and the old bod just

wasn't what it used to be. There was not much hope as I passed the big Four-Oh that my childhood dreams of playing third base for the Cleveland Indians would ever be realized. But I was experienced and mature and maybe, just maybe, I could go on.

As happens with other athletes, such as Roger Staubach and Troy Aikman, you begin to come to grips that your career is over during the off-season. It happened to me when I was jogging around a high school track near my home in Richardson. I was making good time when this guy passed me. He was wearing black silk socks with his tennis shoes, cutoff slacks, and a tight T-shirt showing the muscles he didn't have. His gait was like a bicycle with a bent wheel. But I couldn't catch him.

Then during training camp conditioning coach Bob Ward watched me work out with weights and remarked, "St. John, you continue to live up to the low standards you set for yourself." Was that a subtle hint, a hidden message?

Then I realized it was over and there was no going back. I

would miss the camaraderie of the guys, the competition, the little kid who laughed watching me work out, the silent cheers. I didn't want a press conference or anything like that, but I felt Tom Landry should be the first to know. I saw him in the lunchroom and sat beside him. He stared at his plate, then off in the distance as if to say, "Now what?"

"Tom, I wanted you to be the first to know I'm giving it up," I said, trying my best to be serious. "It's time to quit. When you reach a certain age you lose your quickness and speed. I've reached that age, Tom."

Landry, never looking at me, mumbled, "It goes a lot faster when you've never had it."

It turned out my retirement was premature. As Blaine Nye, who kept announcing his retirement, then showing up to play another year, said, "Never carve what I say in stone." So I got on a bull.

— ❏ —

My infamous bull ride has been written about in newspaper columns (mine), mentioned in a couple of books (mine), and unglamourized twice on television. Just when my readers thought it was safe, well, here we go again. Actually it happened in 1982, five years after I had announced my retirement from the athletic world of doing stupid things and had left the sports department. Yet the seeds of destruction were planted while I was indeed a sportswriter in the mid-1970s. I was researching my book *On Down the Road*, a sociological study of the rodeo cowboy culture, while holding down my job at the *News*.

For those who haven't read about the bull ride or seen it on television or been around during one of the 1,000 times I told the story, this time I AM going to keep you in suspense for a while, so have some respect and stop nodding off. Did I stay on the required eight seconds and become a middle-aged bull rider?

— ❏ —

The idea had been in my head the year I worked on the book, but it solidified while I was gathering material at the legendary Cheyenne Frontier Days. I was supposed to be in Thousand Oaks covering the Dallas Cowboys training camp the final few days of the rodeo but went AWOL. Walt was an understanding guy, but skipping days at camp to pursue my career as an author was a bit too much. So I hired my buddy Andy Anderson, who was working for the Cowboys public relations department after the *Fort Worth Press* folded, to cover for me. He'd do training camp stories in my name and ship them to the paper. Nobody would ever know. It went fine at first and then an important story broke, the subject of which slips my mind. Andy's ego got the best of him. He put his own byline on the story! My cover was blown. Fortunately, Walt would overlook this.

After nine days in Cheyenne with the likes of Larry Mahan, who had won more All-Around titles than anybody, I almost had to be shipped to training camp in a box. He was the first of the rodeo cowboys to understand public relations and marketing. He kept winning all-around titles, was handsome, personable, and the perfect ambassador for rodeo. He didn't drive from rodeo to rodeo, like most all the cowboys did then, but had his own plane. Others would pick up on the possibilities later, but he opened the doors to the future and stepped through. He was always on the go, full of energy, and insisted I experience rodeo life out of the arena, which in Cheyenne meant the Mayflower.

The Mayflower Dance Hall was where the cowboys drank, danced, and fought, among other pursuits. Mahan and I went there, me for the first time, and it was like nothing I'd ever seen. The Mayflower was actually café, package liquor store, tavern, and dance hall. The place was not only packed but overflowed into the streets where people leaned against surrounding buildings and rested on pickup fenders. The music inside was loud, punctuated with shouts and screams.

Two cops seemed lost outside, trying to get up the nerve to go in. Mahan walked right in, dragging me with him. He disappeared and I stood there actually minding my own business when I turned my head just in time to see a fist coming at me. I leaned back and the blow glanced off my hat, knocking it to the floor. I kind of nudged the guy, who lost his balance, and then got out of there. It occurred to me Mahan might be behind this, but he denied any involvement.

Larry did save me from further problems with the newspaper. He offered to fly me in his Cessna to Denver, where I could catch a flight to Los Angeles and then go to Thousand Oaks. Actually he had meant to fly directly to Lubbock, rent a car, and drive to Guthrie, where he had a part in *Mackintosh and T. J.,* starring Roy Rogers in his first movie in years. I was thinking how nice he was when suddenly he said he was tired and for me to take over the controls. He pretended to fall asleep so I grabbed the controls. I didn't think it was funny. Neither did he as he quickly started piloting the plane again.

After my book came out I was in a western wear store in Oklahoma City during the National Finals. This beautiful woman came up to me and started telling me she'd read the book and just had to meet me, that I was the most interesting

person, handsome, sexy and all that. I was lapping it up when I heard somebody laughing. It was Mahan, hiding behind the counter. He'd put her up to it. Sometimes I hate reality.

I had mentioned to Mahan that I was going to ride a bull. He snickered. I mentioned the same thing when I got to training camp to Walt Garrison, who as you know was a real cowboy. "Then they ought to bar the women and children from watching," Walt said. But I was determined. Now you might wonder if I made the decision in the mid-1970s why it took me nearly ten years to get on a bull. Well, once I make up my mind about something I don't like to rush into it.

— ❏ —

The impact, the reality didn't really hit me until I stood behind the chutes at the Mesquite rodeo arena and looked back into the pens and saw this huge, white and reddish Brahma crossbreed with horns that seemed to get longer by the second. It snorted, hoofed at the dirt, and I thought the ground must have been shaking around it, although my perspective was blurred because this was the bull I was supposed to try to ride.

I kept thinking, well, now you've done it. You've gotten yourself into a situation over which you have no control, which makes absolutely no sense. And scenes from rodeos, bull rides past, kept flashing through my mind... A 2,000-pound Brahma knocking out Sandy Kirby and then rolling over him... Denny Flynn being tossed and gored by a bull, its horns splitting his liver and tearing out part of his intestines... Don Gay, the best ever, being jerked and pulled around the arena, his hand hung up in the rope.

Okay, sure they rode more fierce bulls, but they also were bull riders. I was not. I'd not only never been on a bull but until fifteen minutes earlier had not even tried to ride one of those mechanical bucking machines, which certainly aren't to be confused with the real thing. The real thing will crush you, step or stomp on you, and try to hook you with its horns.

Don Gay asked me a number of times if I were sure I wanted to go through with it and I told him no, but I would anyway. I'd become intrigued with bull riders and how they conquered fear and a huge, violent animal. But once they stayed on the required eight seconds and escaped unharmed, they seemed to experience a tremendous high. I thought I'd like to experience that high. But the closer I got the less I cared about such feelings. As mentioned, I had planned on doing it for years, but things kept happening to stop me, such as my bad back, bad shoulder, and attacks of common sense. Then I thought, what the heck, just go out and do it. I would be sneaky, without fanfare, have Don and Neil Gay help me. I'd get on, leap off, and it'd be over. But John Painter, who handled publicity for the Gays at the time, was naturally publicity conscious. So he contacted "PM Magazine." Leeza Gibbons was the star of the show and had planned on doing a story on my columnizing and books I had written (some of which I was trying to forget), and I suppose the bull ride would show my crazy side. Whatever.

"I'm scared enough without having a camera on me," I pleaded. "There's no way I'll let you film the bull ride. Forget it." It was then pointed out to me that they'd plug my books, helping sales. "Okay, film it," I said.

Some of my friends, such as songwriter-singer Pat Minter, showed up to watch. I also decided to do a column on the experience so a *Dallas Morning News* photographer was there. It was really getting out of hand.

And so they brought the bull into the chutes and there I was, cameras rolling, looking down at the huge back of the bull and supposedly ready to get on. I'm not believing this, I kept thinking. I'm just not believing this. Then I knew the only way to get out of my self-inflicted mess was after I'd gotten on the bull, the gate had opened, and the animal had exploded into the arena, probably throwing me from Mesquite to somewhere in the vicinity of Fort Worth.

"Just put your foot on his back and climb on," said Don Gay.

"But...but will it make him mad?" I asked.

Don, looking serious, said to just do what he told me. I did, easing astride the bull. The animal's back was so big I almost did the splits. "Good boy," I said as the animal stirred in the chute and I could feel its power under me. "GOOD BOY!"

"This isn't a bad one and should just go out straight," said Don. "It's not a spinner. So just remember what I told you on the mechanical bull. Pull [on the rope with my riding arm] and squeeze [with my legs]."

Strangely I had done all right on the mechanical bull, but when I got on the real bull I kept looking at its horns. And Don continued, "Find a spot on its back and look at that. Don't look at the horns or anything else. Don't listen to anybody but me."

A guy from "PM Magazine" came up and asked if I minded wearing a small microphone during the ride. He said they'd like to get the sounds. "Of me screaming?" I said. Don told the guy to get the microphone out of there. "It might hurt him when he falls," he said. "Get it out of here!"

The bull felt as big as a battleship. But I was in the best of hands with Don, his dad, Neal, a pro rodeo clown, and various other cowboys. Still, I kept thinking I didn't want to do this and I was giddy, nervous, and joked a lot.

I yelled at the TV guy with the camera, "Isn't it time my double steps in and rides this bull?"

"Now you get serious," said Don. "And you listen to me and you listen good. If you do exactly what I tell you, you're likely to get out of this without getting hurt. There's nobody here but you and me. You listen to my voice. Nobody else. Understand? If I tell you to bail out, you bail out immediately. You listen now. You listen good."

I said I would. He told me to move my body up against my right hand, which gripped the rope around the bull's body. My boots were tied on with leather straps because the bull sometimes jerks so hard it'll throw your boots off, and I had on spurs. I mentioned to Don I wasn't about to make the bull mad by spurring him, but he said the spurs would just help me hang on. The bull moved to the left, trapping my leg against the wall. Don and another cowboy pushed it off my leg. I was surprised. My leg was still there.

I kept thinking I was standing nearby, watching myself. It was surreal and I said, "I think maybe I'll just go out and leap off."

"The hell you will!" snapped Neal Gay. "You get aggressive, you hear me! You don't try and that's when you'll get hurt!" I told him, okay I would. I had only been kidding anyway, just making nervous conversation.

"Okay, ready?" asked Don.

"Uh...uh, my hand feels uncomfortable," I said. He told me my hand looked fine.

"Ready?" "Can we talk about this a little mooooooorrrrrreee!"

A cowboy had jerked the gate open, and I felt as if I were being sucked down a funnel, a giant vacuum. Swoosh! It all happened so fast. But strangely, I wasn't afraid anymore. I just remember a constant jarring sensation and worrying about being slightly tilted as I came out of the chutes. I tried to straighten up, to get my balance but couldn't and then I was being smashed to the ground, feeling shock in my lower back and shoulder. The fall also jarred my teeth, ears, eyeballs, and my car in the adjoining parking lot.

I could hear a voice... voices, sounding as if they were from another world, yelling "Get up and run! Get up....!" I got up, thinking the bull might be coming back for me. But the clown had taken it away, and I just walked slowly back to the chutes. I kept thinking that if I hadn't come out of the chutes tilted I'd have stayed on a lot longer. Don had told me to jerk one way as the bull came out of the chutes but I'd forgotten. Pat Minter had watched from the stands and said he timed me in 5.0 seconds (actually it was 4.9) and that I'd hung on for four jumps. Dern, 3.1 more seconds and I'd have had a ride.

Then, fool that I am, as I got back to the chutes, I thought, I can do this. I'll try again. If I only remembered to jerk I could have an official ride.

"I know what I did wrong," I said, looking up at Don as I climbed back up to the top of the chutes. "I want to get back on, try it again."

"No," he said. I asked him again and he said, "No! Look, you did it. You got up the cour-age, you can write about it and say you got on a bull. You didn't get hurt. That's it. You're going to be sore as hell tomorrow."

The Dallas Morning News photographer came over and said, "I got some shots before and after the ride but didn't get any action. You didn't stay on long enough, not even for a couple of minutes so I could get a shot." Some cowboys standing nearby started laughing. I was at a loss for words.

But for some reason I felt calm. It was late afternoon and a sprinkle of rain fell from dark clouds that had covered the sky all afternoon. It felt good on my face as I walked to the parking lot and got into my car, just sitting there for a minute. Suddenly I yelled, "Whooopeee! Yaaaa-whooooo! I did it!"

The next morning I had to get out of bed on my elbows and knees. I was glad Don Gay hadn't let me get back on the bull.

P.S. – My sons love to watch the video of my bullride and show it to their friends. They run it in reverse, showing me bouncing up and jumping back on the bull. They laugh. Their friends laugh.

Nobody thought Bob St. John was crazy enough to try to ride a bull. They were wrong.

The time I stayed on the bull is now up to 7.5 and will be an official ride any day now.

I announced my retirement once again after realizing that I actually could have been badly injured riding the bull and, in fact, was mildly injured anyway. Family and friends complimented me for finally coming to what was left of my senses. I felt good about myself for about a week and then I started playing a little basketball and such, just to keep the competitive fires burning. Then I started playing a lot of basketball and such.

And then after taking early retirement from the *News* in January 2000, I figured I'd have a little time on my hands and could start taking a little batting practice, maybe field some grounders, and who knows, perhaps one day take a shot at playing third base for the Cleveland Indians. Like old sportswriters, old would-be athletes never really fade away.

CPSIA information can be obtained at www.ICGtesting.com
Printed in the USA
LVOW01s1212290615

444276LV00001B/78/P